"Over the plains of Ethiopia the sun rose as I had not seen it in seven years...."

DORIS LESSING'S book, *African Stories,* is perhaps the finest fictional portrait of Africa today, and her monumental novel, *The Golden Notebook,* is an acknowledged masterpiece of modern fiction.

In *Going Home* she has written an astonishingly perceptive and deeply committed book on Africa at a time of change, when possibility hung in the air and there seemed a chance—perhaps the last chance—for an African future in which whites and blacks could live together without hatred and without oppression.

Going Home is a book of conversations—contacts—with administrators and laborers, policemen, agitators, students, politicians. It is a clear-eyed view of the terrible cost of colonialism and a searching look into the face of Africa's future.

This edition—the first publication of *Going Home* in the United States—contains a new final chapter by Miss Lessing, whom the *London Sunday Times* calls "not only the best woman novelist we have but one of the most serious, intelligent and honest writers of the whole postwar generation."

RECENT TITLES FROM
BALLANTINE BOOKS

GOING HOME

BY

DORIS LESSING

DRAWINGS BY
PAUL HOGARTH

BALLANTINE BOOKS　　　●　　　NEW YORK

Acknowledgements and thanks to the Editor of the *African Weekly*, Salisbury, Southern Rhodesia, for permission to quote letters and features from his newspaper; and to Messrs. Jonathan Cape Limited, of London, for permission to quote from the novel *Cry the Beloved Country* by Alan Paton.

First published by Michael Joseph Ltd., London, 1957.
Revised edition by Ballantine Books, Inc., 1968.

First American Printing: February, 1968

Printed in the United States of America

BALLANTINE BOOKS, INC.
101 Fifth Avenue, New York, N.Y. 10003

*My very grateful thanks are due to
those good friends, both here and in
Central Africa, white and black, who
helped me during my trip, and while
I was writing this book, with their
time, their money, their experience and
their advice.*

GOING HOME
is dedicated to them

GOING HOME

I

OVER THE PLAINS of Ethiopia the sun rose as I had not seen it in seven years. A big, cool, empty sky flushed a little above a rim of dark mountains. The landscape 20,-000 feet below gathered itself from the dark and showed a pale gleam of grass, a sheen of water. The red deepened and pulsed, radiating streaks of fire. There hung the sun, like a luminous spider's egg, or a white pearl, just below the rim of the mountains. Suddenly it swelled, turned red, roared over the horizon and drove up the sky like a train engine. I knew how far below in the swelling heat the birds were an orchestra in the trees about the villages of mud huts; how the long grass was straightening while dangling flocks of dewdrops dwindled and dried; how the people were moving out into the fields about the business of herding and hoeing.

Here is where the sun regulates living in a twelve-hour cycle. Here the sun is a creature of the same stuff as oneself; powerful and angry, but at least responsive, and no mere dispenser of pale candlepower.

When I was first in England I was disturbed all the time in my deepest sense of probability because the sun went down at four in the middle of an active afternoon, filling a cold, damp remote sky with false pathos. Or, at eleven in the morning, instead of blazing down direct, a hand's-span from centre, it would appear on a slant and in the wrong place, at eight o'clock position, a swollen, misshapen, watery ghost of a thing peering behind chimney-pots. The sun in England should be feminine, as it is in Germany.

During that first year in England, I had a vision of London I cannot recall now. Recently I found some pages I wrote then: it was a nightmare city that I lived in for a year; endless miles of heavy, damp, dead building on a dead, sour earth, inhabited by pale, misshapen, sunless creatures under a low sky of grey vapour.

Then, one evening, walking across the park, the light welded buildings, trees and scarlet buses into something familiar and beautiful, and I knew myself to be at home. Now London is to me the pleasantest of cities, full of the most friendly and companionable people. But that year of horrible estrangement from everything around me was real enough. It was because, bred in Africa, I needed to be in direct physical touch with what I saw; I needed the cycle of hot, strong light, of full, strong dark.

One does not look at London, but at a pretty house, a glimpse of trees over rooftops, the remains of an old street, a single block of flats. The eye learns to reject the intolerable burden of the repetition of commercialization. It is the variegated light of London which creates it; at night, the mauvish wet illumination of the city sky; or the pattern of black shadow-leaves on a wall; or, when the sun emerges, the instant gaiety of a pavement.

On that morning over Africa I learned that I had turned myself inwards, had become a curtain-drawer, a fire-hugger, the inhabitant of a cocoon. Easy enough to turn outwards again: I felt I had never left at all. This was my air, my landscape, and above all, my sun.

Africa belongs to the Africans; the sooner they take it back the better. But—a country also belongs to those who feel at home in it. Perhaps it may be that the love of

Africa the country will be strong enough to link people who hate each other now. Perhaps.

On this trip home a man with whom I had been arguing bitterly about politics said to me suddenly: Where did I come from? I said Lomagundi. He knew it well, he said. He liked the highveld, he remarked, defensively. For the highveld is reaches of pale, dry grass, studded with small, dry, stunted trees—wide, empty, barren country. I said yes, and the Kalahari, too. Yes, he said; and the Karroo. The Kalahari and the Karroo are stages nearer desert of the highveld, full of bitter shrubs, cacti, lizards and hot stones. They are enormous, with a scarifying, barren beauty. They, too, are almost empty.

For a moment we shared the understanding of people who have been made by the same landscape.

But I am not sure whether this passion for emptiness, for space, only has meaning in relation to Europe. Africa is scattered all over with white men who push out and away from cities and people, to remote farms and outposts, seeking solitude. But perhaps all they need is to leave the seethe and the burden of Europe behind.

I remember an old prospector came to our farm one evening when I was a child. He had spent all his life wandering around Africa. He said he had just gone home to England for a holiday of six months; but left at the end of a week. Too many people, he said; a tame little country, catching trains and keeping to time-tables. He had learned his lesson; he would never leave the highveld again. 'People,' he said, shouting at himself—for he was certainly arguing against his own conscience—'people are mad, wanting to change Africa. Why don't they leave it alone? A man can breathe here, he can be himself. And,' he went on, getting angrier and angrier, 'when we've filled Africa up, what then? The world is only tolerable because of the empty places in it—millions of people all crowded

together, fighting and struggling, but behind them, somewhere, enormous, empty places. I tell you what I think,'
he said, 'when the world's filled up, we'll have to get hold
of a star. Any star. Venus, or Mars. Get hold of it and
leave it empty. Man needs an empty space somewhere for
his spirit to rest in.'

That's what he said. I remember every word, for he
made a great impression on me.

Next morning he went away, and we heard he had gone
up over the Zambezi escarpment into the bush with his
bearer. On the verge of one of the hills overlooking the
river he built a hut and thatched it, and settled to live
there, entirely alone. But he got black-water fever, and the
news travelled back, as news does in these parts, and at
last reached his wife in the city, who—a bush-widow these
many years—got herself a lorry and went off after him
until she reached the end of the road, and then inquired of
some passing Africans who took her to the hill where her
husband was. Between one bout of fever and another, he
sat on a candle-box under a tree, an old man of fifty or so,
looking at the gorges of the river and at the hills. Africans
from a neighbouring village had set water and some meat
by him, and were waiting at a little distance in the shade
of a tree. He was very ill.

'And now,' said she, 'enough of this nonsense: it's time
you came back and let me look after you.'

'Go away,' he said. 'I want to die alone.'

'But there's no need to die. You'll get better in hospital.'

A look of revulsion came over his face, which she
understood too well. 'Oh, all right,' she said. 'I'll look after
you myself.'

He turned his face from her, and looked out and down
to the river. And so she went to examine the inside of the
mud hut which had nothing in it but a case of whisky and

a roll of bedding and some quinine and a rifle; and then went over to the young men, who got to their feet as she approached.

'Now, look after the baas nicely,' she said.

'Yes, Nkosikaas,' they said.

She walked away down along the Kaffir paths several miles to the road, climbed back into the lorry and drove back to town. And when he died, which was several days later, the people of the village buried him and sang their mourning songs over him.

That was the story as we heard it from a group of young men travelling through our farm on their way to find work in the gold mines of the Rand.

It seems to me that this story of the man who preferred to die alone rather than return to the cities of his own people expresses what is best in the older type of white men who have come to Africa. He did not come to take what he could get from the country. This man loved Africa for its own sake, and for what is best in it: its emptiness, its promise. It is still uncreated.

Yet it is only when one flies over Africa that one can see it, as such solitary people do, as the empty continent. The figures are eloquent enough—that is, if one possesses the kind of mind that makes figures live. In Central Africa there are seven million Africans and two hundred thousand white people. It sounds quite a lot of people from one point of view, if one tries to imagine the word *million* in terms of a crowd of people. And if one has lived in a city there, one remembers the pressure of people. Yet it seems seven million people are nothing, not enough—this enormous area could hold hundreds of millions.

But now, steadily flying south for hour after hour, one sees forest, mountain and lake; river and gorge and swamp; and the great reaches of the flat, tree-belted grassland. The yellow flanks of Africa lie beneath the moving insect-like plane, black-maned with forest, twitching in the heat. A magnificent country, with all its riches in the future. Because it is so empty we can dream. We can dream of cities and a civilization more beautiful than anything that has been seen in the world before.

*　　*　　*　　*

It was over Kenya that a subtle change of atmosphere announced we were now in white Africa. Two Africans sitting by themselves had a self-contained and watchful look. Perhaps they were reflecting on the implications of the fact that this being a South African plane the covers on the seats they used would have to be specially sterilized before re-use.

Until now the men making announcements over the loudspeaker had had the anonymous voices of official-dom. Now there was a new voice, unmistakably South African, stubbornly national. Jaunty and facetious, with the defensiveness of the Colonial who considers an attempt at efficiency as nothing but snobbishness, it began: 'Well, ladies and gents, here I am; sorry about it, but I'm not a B.B.C. announcer, but I'll do my best. If you look down on your right now you'll see the Aberdare Forest. You'll understand why it took so long to bash the Mau Mau. See that thick bit over there? That's where we got a whole bunch of them. Starved 'em out. Took six weeks.' This man was not from Kenya, but he was white; and the problems of white Kenya were his, and—so he took for granted—ours too. He went on, swallowing his words, the ends of his sentences, most of the time inaudible. Once he clearly enunciated a whole series of sentences just to show that he could if he chose. 'Down there is Masai country. Of course, I don't know anything about the Masai, but they tell me the Masai are warriors. Or used to be. They like drinking blood and milk. They seem to like it. Or so I'm told. Of course, I don't know anything about these things.' Click, as the machine switched off, and we descended at Nairobi.

Nairobi airport is interesting for two things. One is that it is infested with cats of all shapes, colours and sizes. I have not seen so many cats since one year when my mother got into a mood where she could not bear to see a kitten drowned, so that very soon we had forty cats who almost drove us out of the house before we could bring ourselves to lay violent hands on them.

The other is that the lavatories are marked 'European Type' and 'Non-European Type.' The word *type,* I suppose, is meant to convey to the critical foreign visitor that Non-Europeans prefer their own amenities. It was my first indication of how defensive the colour bar has become. Also, to what irrational extremes it will take itself under pressure. When I left no one thought ill of themselves for defending white civilization in whatever ways were suggested by pure instinct.

The two Africans sat in the restaurant at a table by themselves. The social colour bar is being relaxed here slightly. (The other day I asked an African from Kenya what he thought was the most important result of the war in Kenya; he replied grimly: 'In some hotels they serve us with food and drink now.')

It was at this point that I noticed the old attitudes asserting themselves in me again. If one went to sit at the same table, it would be something of a demonstration. Perhaps they would prefer not to be drawn attention to in the electric atmosphere of Kenya? Or perhaps ... yes, I was certainly back home.

One of the reasons why I wanted to return was because so many people had asked me how it was I had been brought up in a colour-bar country and yet had no feeling about colour. I had decided that a lucky series of psychological chances must have made me immune. But it was surely impossible that I should be entirely unlike other people brought up in the same way. Therefore I was watching my every attitude and response all the time I was in Africa. For a time, the unconsciousness of a person's colour one has in England persisted. Then the miserable business began again. Shaking hands becomes an issue. The natural ebb and flow of feeling between two people is checked because what they do is not the expression of whether they like each other or not, but deliberately and consciously considered to express: 'We are people on different sides of the colour barrier who choose to defy this society.' And, of course, this will go on until the day comes when self-consciousness can wither away naturally. In the meantime, the eyes of people of a different colour can meet over those formal collective hands, in a sort of sardonic appreciation of the comedies of the situation.

But what I did find was that while I am immune to colour feeling as such, I was sensitive to social pressures. Could it be that many people who imagine they have colour prejudice are merely suffering from fear of the Joneses? I dare say this is not an original thought, but it came as a shock to me.

In the Tropical Diseases Hospital in London, where I was last year for a few weeks, a middle-aged white woman was being treated in the same room. When she found there were dark-skinned doctors and patients, she suffered something not far off a nervous collapse. She got no sympathy at all from either nurses or her fellow patients about her dislike of being treated the same way as black people, so she became stiffly but suspiciously silent: bedclothes pulled up to her chin, like a shield, watching everyone around her as if they were enemies. And every bit of china she used, every fork or knife or spoon, was minutely examined for cracks or scratches. The presence of coloured people meant germs: germs live in cracks. Her worry about these utensils became an obsession. Before a meal, after she had sent back cups, plates, cutlery, several times to be changed, she would then wash each piece in the basin in strong disinfectant. Unable to express her dislike of coloured people through the colour bar, she fell back on the china. This is the real colour prejudice; it is a neurosis, and people who suffer from it should be pitied as one pities the mentally ill. But there is a deep gulf between this and being frightened of what the neighbours will say.

In writing this I am conscious of a feeling of fatigue and sterility, which is what I have to fight against as soon as I set foot in white Africa. For a long time I believed this was the result of being in a minority among one's own kind, which means one has to guard against being on the defensive, which means one has to test everything one says and does against general standards of right or wrong that are contradicted all the time, in every way, by what goes on around one.

But I no longer believe this to be true. What I feel is a kind of boredom, an irritation, by all these colour attitudes and prejudices. There is no psychological quirk or justification or rationalisation that is new or even interesting. What is terrible is the boring and repetitive nature of 'white civilisation.'

As soon as one sets foot in a white settler country, one becomes part of a mass disease; everything is seen through the colour bar.

'The patient must get worse before he can get better.' And I know this is a light phrase for human suffering and what the Africans in white-dominated countries suffer in frustration. I do not have to be told or be made to feel what the Africans in white-dominated countries suffer in humiliation and frustration. I know it all.

But in thinking of the future rather than the bitter present, I believe I am one with the Africans themselves, who show their superiority to colour bars by their joyfulness, their good humour and their delight in living. People who imagine the ghettoes of white-dominated countries to be dreary and miserable places know nothing about the nature of the African people.

Worse than the colour bars, which are more dangerous and demoralising to the white people than to the black, for they live within a slowly narrowing and suffocating cage, like so many little white mice on a treadmill—worse than this is the fact that the Africans are being channelled into industrialisation in such a way that what is good in European civilisation cannot reach them. They are allowed to know only what is bad and silly. That is why I am so impatient that they should wrench themselves free before they have lost touch with their own rich heritage, before they have become exhausted by exploitation.

I long for the moment when the Africans can free themselves and can express themselves in new forms, new ways of living; they are an original and vital people simply because they have been forced to take the jump from tribalism to industrial living in one generation.

And yet—the stale patterns of white domination still exist. So because I was brought up in it I have a responsibility. And does that mean I must go on writing about it?

I have notebooks full of stories, plots, anecdotes, which at one time or another I was impelled to write. But the impulse died in a yawn. Even if I wrote them well—what then? It is always the colour bar; one cannot write truthfully about Africa without describing it. And if one has been at great pains to choose a theme which is more general, people are so struck by the enormity and ugliness of the colour prejudices which must be shown in it that what one has tried to say gets lost.

When I am asked to recommend novels which will describe white-settler Africa most accurately to those who don't know it, I always suggest a re-reading of those parts of *Anna Karenina* about the landowners and the peasants —simply because colour feeling doesn't arise in it.

For the interminable discussions and soul-searchings about 'the peasant' are paralleled by the endless talk about 'the native.' What was said in pre-revolutionary Russia about the peasant is word for word what is said about the Africans—lazy, irresponsible, shiftless, supersititious, and so on.

And in the person of Levin one finds the decent worried white liberal who is drawn by the reserves of strength, the deep humanity of the African, but yet does not trust him to govern himself. Levin, in Africa, is always dreaming of going native, of escaping from the complexities of modern civilization which he sees as fundamentally evil. He philosophizes; goes on long trips into the bush with his African servant to whom he feels himself closer than to any other human being and to whom he tells everything; half-believes in God; knows that all governments are bad; and plans one day to buy a crater in the Belgian Congo or an uninhabited island in the Pacific where at last he can live the natural life.

All this has nothing to do with colour.

I am struck continually by the parallels between pre-revolutionary Russia as described in Chekov, Turgenev, Tolstoy and Gorki, and that part of Africa I know. An enormous, under-populated, under-developed, unformed country, still agricultural in feeling and resisting industrialisation.

For a novelist based in Africa it is discouraging that so much of what develops there is a repetition of the European nineteenth century. Time and again one seizes on a theme, looks at it carefully, discovers that unless the writer is very careful it will merely repeat what has already been said in another context—and then, trying to isolate what is specifically African, what is true of Africa at this time, one comes slap up against that complex of emotions, the colour bar. I believe it to be true that what unifies Africa now, what makes it possible to speak of 'Africans' as if they were the members of one nation instead of a hundred nations, is precisely this, that white domination has given them one overriding emotion in common, which makes brothers of them all from Cape to Cairo. Yet behind this, perhaps, there is something else that is more important. Perhaps in a hundred years, looking back, they will not say: 'It was the century when we turned the white men out of our continent and regained our freedom,' but . . . 'I don't know. When a people struggles for freedom the struggle itself is always so much greater and more creative than what is being fought.'

Perhaps they will say: 'That is the century when we found we were not simply black men, but a company of peoples infinitely diverse, original, rich and varied. That is the century when we recovered the right to find out what we are.'

But now, for the writer, it is hard, because the infinite complexity and the richness always narrow into a protest against that monstrous thing, the colour bar.

In white Africa I do not think the Africans have yet produced types of people or forms of organisation that have not been produced elsewhere. African nationalists speak the same language as congress leaders in any country; political leaders must reflect white domination as long as it remains: Generals China and Russia of the Mau Mau would not have been possible without Colonel Blimp.

As for the British, they either live as if they have never

left Britain or proliferate into eccentrics or rogue elephants. Africa is full of colourful characters, adventurers, criminals, petty tyrants or solitaries. But I don't think it can be said we have not seen them before—or read about them.

I think it is the Afrikaner who is the original; something new; something that cannot be seen in any other continent. He is a tragic figure. The Africans are not tragic—they have the future before them; they are a suppressed people who will soon free themselves as Colonial people are freeing themselves everywhere in the world. The British are not tragic, they are too flexible. I think most of the British in Africa will be back in Britain inside twenty years. But the Afrikaners are as indigenous as the Africans. And since they insist their survival as a nation depends on white domination what possible future can they have? Yet they are not a corrupted people, as the Germans were corrupted by the Nazis—Afrikaner nationalism is not a falling-off from a high peak of national cultural achievement. The Afrikaners have remained unaltered while the world has changed, and that is their tragedy. Their history as a people has been a long, courageous battle for independence and freedom; yet they do not understand other people's desire for freedom: that is their paradox.

They are the most likable of people: simple, salty, tough, earthy, shrewd and humorous and hospitable. They are also childlike: like a child of seven they cannot understand that their own standards of right or wrong are not immediately acceptable to everyone else. And they are likely to go down to defeat as a nation in the black-white struggle supported by a proud consciousness of being misunderstood by the world in the nobility of their motives. For the self-pity that is always the basis of a false position is in their case half-justified: they feel aggrieved, and are right to do so, because the world fastens on them all the guilt for *apartheid*. But Malan would not have come into power without British votes; and *apartheid* is only the logical crystallisation of the segregation created by Smuts, the Afrikaner who became a spokesman for the British Empire, and his British-dominated United Party. Passes, segregation, farm-prisons, pick-up vans and the industrial colour bar were not introduced by the Afrikaner Nationalists: the system was created by the white people, Afrikaner and British together, and financed by British and American capital. But the Afrikaner has been made the villain of the scene; Smuts was called a great statesman, but Strydom is hissed in the streets when he comes to Britain.

And so the drive towards national isolation and self-sufficiency which is the basis of Afrikaner nationalism is strengthened.

Sooner or later it will be the Afrikaner and the African who will face each other as opponents in the southern tip of the continent. And they are very alike. I have yet to meet an African who does not say that he prefers the Afrikaner as a man to the British. 'The Afrikaner calls me a Kaffir, he says what he thinks, but he is more humane, he treats me better.' I have heard that very often.

And inevitably the two people are becoming fast mixed in blood—if one may use that convenient word—in spite of all the laws and the bars and the barriers. There is no sadder or more bizarre sight than to see a group of 'white South Africans,' each with the marks of mixed descent strong in face and hair and body-build, arguing about the necessity of preserving racial purity.

On an aeroplane in Northern Rhodesia I sat next to a young Afrikaner flying back home. He was immediately recognizable as one, first because of his open, simple face, and next because the marks of mixed parentage were on his hair and his facial structure.

We got into conversation.

'I am sad today,' he said, 'because I don't know what to do. I've just been up to the Copper Belt, and that's the place for me, man, you can earn money there, not the Kaffir's wages you get back home now. But if I go to the Copper Belt, man, my heart will break.'

'But why?'

'Because of my pigeons. They're my little sisters. How can I take my fifty pigeons all the way to the Copper Belt? They will be sad there. I'd have to sell them. I wouldn't like to do that. I'd feel sad all the time.'

'Perhaps you'd get over it? And you could buy some more pigeons?'

'How can you say that? That's not right. No, man, the way I feel now, I'll have to stay at home, even if I don't like it.'

I noticed he had broken his thumb.

'Yes, and that's another thing. I got that last year. On the job I'm a policeman. A man was beating up a Kaffir. He had no right to do that. The Kaffir hadn't done anything. So I broke my thumb on him. People shouldn't go hitting Kaffirs when they haven't done anything. Well, the next thing was I broke it again. You know how you have to beat up Kaffirs when you arrest them: they don't tell the truth if you don't give them a good hiding. But now I keep thinking about my thumb, and I can't do my work properly. You can't do the job without your fists. No, I'll have to get another job. Besides, the police is no good.'

'You don't like the work?'

'Hell, man, it's not the work. But things are bad now. I know you'll think I'm saying this because you're English and I'm trying to make up to you. But it's God's truth, I

like the English. There's an Englishman in the office, and
he's fair, and I like him. He treats everyone the same. But
our men there, man, but you can't trust them! They tell
you to do something, and then it goes wrong, and then it's
your fault. They don't stand by you. And they tell on each
other all the time. But the Englishman's going. He's going
back to England, he says. And so I'll leave, too. I'm not
staying where things aren't fair. Don't think I mean anything about South Africa; it's God's country. Why don't
you come and see it?'

This being after I was proscribed, I said his Government would not let me in and why.

He looked at me long and earnestly. 'Never seen a
commie before,' he said.

'There used to be plenty in South Africa before it was
illegal.'

'Never heard of that. Well, look then, tell me, what is it
about?'

'In South Africa, what is important now is that we are
against racial inequality.'

His face fell; he was a small boy. 'Now look man, hell!
I don't see that.'

'Sooner or later you'll have to.'

'But they're nothing but children, man! You must know
that. Look how they live! It makes me just about sick to
go into one of their locations. Besides, I don't like their
colour, I just don't like it.'

He paused, very serious, wrestling with himself. 'You
think I've just been brought up to be like that?'

'Yes, I do.'

'It's no good, I don't see it. Now look here'—and he
turned earnestly towards me—'would you let a black man
marry your daughter?'

'If my daughter wanted it.'

He slowly went a dark red. 'I don't like to hear a

woman talk like that. I just don't like it.' A pause. 'Then I can see why they didn't let you in, man. Women shouldn't go around saying things like that. No, you mustn't talk like that, I don't like to hear it.' His face slowly went back to normal. Then he said: 'But I've enjoyed talking. I always want to know about these things. I've never been out of South Africa before. If I can leave my little pigeons and get up to the Copper Belt and earn some money, then I want to come to England. They say that Kaffirs are just like everybody else there?'

'Just like everybody else.'

'I don't think I should like to see that. It wouldn't seem right to me. But hell, man, that means they can go with the women? Sorry talking like this, but it's not personal. But you can't have them going with the women. If I had a sister I wouldn't like. . . .'

This is the stock South African conversation; and it goes on just as if nothing had happened. But what is happening is that the poorer of the white people are becoming more and more like the poorer of the Africans.

*   *   *   *

In the Lusaka airport there was a five-hour wait for the connection south to Salisbury.

Sitting in the little garden were a group of white people, toasting themselves in the sun, carefully accumulating pigment under their precious white skins.

The mystiques of sun-tanning are becoming as complicated and irrational as those of food and sex. What could be odder than to see people whose very existence depends on their paleness of skin deliberately darkening themselves on the preserved 'white' beaches of the coasts, or on the banks of 'white' swimming baths? But in a country where anyone who works in the open must become dark-skinned, and where it is impossible to distinguish between deep sunburn and the skin of a coloured person, one acquires a mysterious sixth sense that tells one immediately if a person is 'white' or not.

Having been in Britain for so long, I had lost this sense; and, sitting in a café in Bulawayo, I was pleased to see a group of people come in who had dark brown skins. The spirit of Partnership, I thought, was really relaxing the colour bar. A few minutes later a man came in who I thought was indistinguishable from those already sitting there. He went to sit at a table by himself. At once the woman behind the counter came over and said: 'You know you are not allowed to come in here.' He got up and went out without a word. It seemed that the first group were Italians.

* * * *

In 1949, on the boat coming to Britain, where most of the passengers were elderly ladies playing bridge and knitting, were two attractive young women. They did not mix with the rest at all, were spoken of as 'Durban society girls.' One was a tall, slim, pale creature with smooth, dark hair and intelligent, dark eyes kept deliberately languid. The other was a plump little yellow-head, not pretty, but as it were professionally vivacious. They were American in style, as most South African girls are: very well-kept, self-possessed, independent.

I got to know the cheerful little one, who told me that her friend was called Camellia. 'She's done well for herself if you like. She was just an ordinary secretary, working in the office, but the boss's son married her. Then he got killed in an air crash. She's married into one of the oldest families in Durban. But she doesn't care. She doesn't give a damn for anybody.' It seemed that this quality of not giving a damn was the bond between the girls; for Camellia had taken her typist friend Janet with her into society. Janet had consequently also done well for herself: she was engaged to a cousin in the same family. It seemed that the young widow had gone to Uncle Piet, executor of the estate, and said: 'I'm fed up with life. I want a holiday in Europe.'

Janet said: 'That silly old bugger Uncle Piet said she had a duty to her position in society, and she should set an example, and she wasn't to go for more than four months. But he gave her a thousand. So that's how I came too. She's generous, Camellia is. And it's not that she's got all the money she wants. Actually she hasn't got any money. Her husband didn't know he was going to be killed, and anyway he was under age. They both were. When they got married the papers called it "the wedding of the beautiful children." Because he was good-looking. So Camellia doesn't get any money except what Uncle Piet lets her have, because she hasn't any money by will. But when Camellia said I must come with her, Uncle Piet didn't like it. He said it was my duty to stay with my fi-ance. But see the world before you get tied down with kids, that's what I say.'

The two girls spent all day lying side by side in two deck chairs in the shade, refused to take part in the deck-sports, and at night did the few young men there were a favour by dancing with them. At least, this was Camellia's attitude; though I think the little one would have liked to be less aloof.

Two years later I saw them in Trafalgar Square, sitting on the edge of a fountain. Camellia was with a man who was probably a West Indian; and Janet was tagging along. This set-up intrigued me for some days. Had they gone home to collect more money from Uncle Piet and then come back to Britain again? What had happened to Janet's eligible fi-ance? And above all, how could a Durban society girl, even if she didn't give a damn, get herself involved with a Negro? As I was on a bus when I saw the group, unfortunately there was no chance of finding out.

That was in 1951. In 1953 I was walking along the edge of the sea in the south of France, and there was the young man I had seen in Trafalgar Square with an extremely beautiful black girl. They were sitting side by side on a rock, arms and legs inextricably mixed, and on the sand watching them was Janet, who was her normal colour. Then I saw that the beautiful Negress was in fact Camellia. All that was visible of her—and she was wearing a minute red bikini—was burned a very dark bronze.

I went up to Janet and asked her how she did.

'Oh, it's you,' she said. 'You've been doing well for yourself since I saw you last.'

'I suppose so,' I said. 'And how goes it with you?'

She looked at the couple on the rock. No doubt but that she was very upset. 'It's all very well,' she said, 'my mind is much broader since I came to Europe, but what am I to do? Tell me that?'

'I can see your problem,' I said. 'But what's happened to your fiancé?'

'Which fiancé?' she said, and giggled. 'No, it's not that. I can look after myself, but it's Camellia. After we were here that time, we got a letter from Uncle Piet, asking when we were coming back. Camellia wrote and said she was still getting over her sad loss, so he sent her some more money. Actually, we were getting some culture. After all, you come to Europe to get some culture. South Africa has got everything, but it isn't very cultured. So we got mixed up in artistic circles. I made Camellia do it, because at first she didn't want to. There were coloured people, and she didn't like that. But then she met Max and he and she quarrelled all the time. Besides, it intrigued her, you know how it is, you come here from

South Africa and they just laugh at you. Max was always laughing at Camellia. The next thing was, my fi-ance came over, and said it was time I came home. But my ideas had changed. I said to him: "Now that I have been around a bit I am not sure that you and I are suited. My mind is much broader than it was." So we broke it off and he went home.

'Then Camellia and Max came here for a holiday. She said she couldn't stick it without any sun any longer. She started lying about in the sun. And at home she never goes out without a big hat, and even gloves if the sun is hot, because she is so proud of her skin. I told her: "You are crazy to ruin your skin." And Max said to her that the way everybody in Europe goes south to get sunburned every summer is an unconscious tribute to the superiority of the dark people over the white people. He said that a hundred years ago no one in Europe got sunburned. Max is very well educated and all that. But Camellia got mad, and they quarrelled badly, and so she and I went home. Camellia tried to settle down. Piet wanted her to marry cousin Tom to keep everything in the family. But Camellia said she wanted to go away to make up her mind about marrying Tom. So we both of us came back to England. Camellia met Max straight away. He is the son of a rich family from the Gold Coast. Did you know there were rich families among the natives in the Gold Coast? There are. He is a lawyer. Then they made it up and came here again for a holiday and when she came to England she might just as well have been born in the location. Just look at her.'

'Luckily,' I said, 'there aren't any locations here, so it doesn't matter.'

'Yes, but now Uncle Piet has written saying that if she doesn't go home before Christmas he will no longer consider her one of the family. No money, that means. And so she is going back. I'm taking her. I promised Uncle Piet I would take her. Next month. She and Max have decided that she would not be happy in the Gold Coast. For about one week they decided to get married, believe it or not. Then Max said she has not got the sense of social responsibility he wants in a wife—can you beat it? And she said that as far as she was concerned, he was primitive. They quarrelled, I can tell you!'

'So it has all turned out well in the end,' I said.

'Yes, but how can I take her back like that? The boat goes in a month. She says she is going to stay here until it goes. Everyone will think she's a Kaffir, looking like that. I can't understand her. The magazines used to call her the girl with the skin like petals. Actually Camellia *was* her christened name, believe it or not, but she was proud of them calling her that, even though she pretended she didn't give a damn.'

'There are bleaching creams,' I said.

Janet began laughing. 'It's all very well to laugh,' she said, and admittedly she sounded not far off tears. 'But if I take her back like that, Uncle Piet will blame me. And I'm going to marry a nice boy who is one of the family. I said to Camellia, "If you had fair hair," I said to her, then it wouldn't matter. "But you're crazy with your dark hair to have such dark skin."'

'Perhaps she could bleach her hair,' I said.

'She won't listen to anything I say to her.' She thought for a moment. 'But perhaps if I talk to Max, and explain it to him, perhaps he'll talk her into being sensible. He'll laugh himself sick, but perhaps he'll help me.'

And, a year ago, I saw a photograph in a South African magazine of Camellia, flower-like in white satin, being married to a stiff-looking dark-suited young South African with a proud, embarrassed grin.

*   *   *   *

On the plane between Lusaka and Salisbury, the misty powder-blue eyes of a large pink-coloured middle-aged woman teased my memory. At last, the turn of a heavy red neck on mauve-clad shoulder succeeded in setting those innocent blue eyes in the face of a frisking school-girl.

In my class at school there were a group of girls, committed to idling away the time until they were allowed to leave for the delights of the bioscope and the boys. The despair of the teachers and the envy of the girls, they set the fashion, which was to wear well-pressed gym tunics about half an inch longer than the bottom of one's black tights, long uncreased black legs, tight girdle, white blouse smooth as ice cream under the school tie, and the white school hat on the back of the head. No one's black pleats swung with such panache as those of the girls of this group, or gang; and Jane's, in particular, filled my heart with despair. She was very slim, and it was not a mode for the plump.

Several times a term the house-mother summoned us, and gave us a pep-talk which began invariably: 'Now, gals, I want you to take a pull on yourselves. . . .' For twenty minutes or so she would deal with the virtues of discipline and obedience; and then turned her whole person, which was whale-shaped and ponderous, in the direction of the intransigent group who sat, bored but bland, in desks at the back of the prep-room, meeting the stare of her full-blooded eyes and the jut of her dark jowl with calm but eager inquiry. 'There are gals here who are so stoo-pid that they are wasting their valuable school life in playing the fool. Life will never give them another opportunity. In two years' time they will leave to be shop assistants and clerks. While they are at school they think they are doing very well, because they mix with gals they will never see again once they leave. The system of education in this country unfortunately being what it is, they have a chance to improve themselves by mixing with their superiors. I want to plead with these gals, now, before it is too late, to change their low-class and cheap behaviour. I want them particularly to take a strong pull on themselves.'

This part of the good woman's lecture always went over our heads, because class language was no part of our experience. We resented, collectively and individually, all attempts to divide us on these lines, but the resentment was too deep to be vocal. There were teachers we liked, teachers who played the traditional roles of butts and villains; but this woman's self-satisfied stupidity repelled all myth-making. 'It was as if a savage spoke.' We recognized that hers was the voice of the Britain our parents had, in their various ways, escaped from. It was a voice peculiarly refined, holding timbres I did not recognize until I came to Britain and began to learn the game of accent-spotting.

But Jane's voice, when I heard it on the plane, was indistinguishable from that of the hostess: the anonymous, immediately recognizable voice of the Southern African female, which is light and self-satisfied, poised on an assured femininity which comes of being the keeper of society's conscience. It is the voice, in short, of Mom.

'Is that you?' said she to me, in her indolent voice—and it was really painful to see those pretty eyes unchanged among wads of well-fed flesh. 'I thought it was you. You've been doing well for yourself, I must say.'

'It looks,' I said, 'as if we both have.'

She regarded the solid citizen who was her husband with calm satisfaction. 'My eldest son,' she remarked, 'has just got his degree in law.'

'Jolly good,' I said.

'Do you remember Shirley? She's done well for herself;

she's married a High Court Judge.' Shirley was the most determinedly relaxed of the group.

'And Caroline?' I asked.

'Well, poor Caroline, she did well for herself, but her old man works with the Native Department, and so she's stuck in the middle of a Native Reserve. But she's always gay, in spite of having nothing but Kaffirs all about.'

'And Janet?'

'Janet didn't do well for herself the first time she got married, but he was killed in the war, and now she's married to a Civil Servant and her daughter's at Cape Town University. And have you heard about Connie?'

Connie was the odd-man-out of the group because her natural intelligence was such that she could not help passing examinations well even though she never did any work. This idiosyncrasy was regarded by the others with affectionate tolerance.

'Connie began to be a doctor because her dad said she must, but she did not really like to work much, so she married a Civil Servant and she's got a house in Robber's Roost. It was designed by a real architect.'

'It seems we are all doing fine,' I said.

'Yes, live and let live, that's what I say. But I think you are forgetting our problems being away from home so long. Do you remember Molly? She was the other swat besides you. Well, she's got a job on the *Star* in Johannesburg. She used to be a Kaffir-lover, too, but now she has a balanced point of view. She came up to visit last year, and she gave a lecture on the air about race relations. I listened because I like to keep in touch with the old gang. I think that as we get older we get mature and balanced.' And with this she gave me a lazy but admonitory smile and rejoined her husband saying, 'Goodbye, it was nice seeing you again after all these years. Time is going past, say what you like.'

II

SALISBURY WAS a wide scatter of light over spaces of dark. To fly over it is to see how fast it is growing—not vertically, save for a few tall buildings in its centre, but outwards, in a dozen sprawling suburbs.

I was reminded of the first time I saw Johannesburg from above by night. A few years ago one could not, even at one's most optimistic, compare Salisbury with Johannesburg: it was only a small patterning of lit streets in a great hollow of darkness. Now the regular arrangements of street-lighting—all these cities are laid out on the American plan, with streets regularly bisecting each other —confine the veld in sparkling nets of light.

The darkness of the earth at night is never complete in Africa, because even the darkest night sky has a glow of light behind it. And so these cities dissolve after sundown, as if points of strong, firm light were strewn wide over a luminous, dark sea.

To drive from the airport to the house I was staying in on the outskirts of the town took seven minutes. I knew that my sense of space, adjusted to sprawling London, was going to take a shock; but I was more confused than I had thought possible. If you live in a small town, you live in all of it, every street, house, garden is palpable all the time, part of your experience. But a big city is a centre and a series of isolated lit points on the darkness of your ignorance. That is why a big city is so restful to live in; it does not press in on you, demanding to be recognized. You can choose what you know.

But it was night; and the town at night was always to me a different place than the candid day-time town. Now the car swept up along avenues of subdued light, for the moon was full and hard, the stars vivid; the trees rippled off light; and the buildings were luminous, their walls thin shells over an inner glow, and the roofs plates of shining substance.

The garden of the house was full of roses, pale in the moonlight, and black shadow lay under the bougainvillaea bush.

I stepped from the garden into the creeper-hung verandah and at once into the living-room. It was strange to be in a house again that was pressed close to the earth, with only a thin roof between me and the sky. In London buildings are so heavy and tall and ponderous they are a climate of their own; pavements, streets, walls—even parks and gardens—are an urban shell.

But in Africa the wildness of the country is still much stronger than the towns.

But even so, this house was wrong; it was not this that I had come home to find. For me all houses will always be wrong; all bungalows, cottages, mansions and villas will be uncomfortable and incongruous and confining. I only like blocks of flats, the most direct expression of crammed town-living. I did not understand why this should be so for a long time, until I took to dreaming nightly of the house I was brought up in; and then at last I submitted myself to the knowledge that I am the victim of a private mania that I must humour. I worked out recently that I have lived in over sixty different houses, flats and rented rooms during the last twenty years and not in one of them have I felt at home. In order to find a place I live in tolerable, I have not to see it. Or rather, I work on it until it takes on the colouring suggested by its shape, and then forget it. If, in an unguarded moment, I actually see it, all of it, what it is, then a terrible feeling of insecurity and improbability comes over me. The fact is, I don't live anywhere; I never have since I left that first house on the kopje. I suspect more people are in this predicament than they know.

But that first house crumbled long ago, returned to the soil, was swallowed by the bush; and so I was glad after we had had dinner to go out again in the car, ostensibly to look for someone whose address we did not know, but hoped we might find by chance—in fact to get out of the town into the bush.

In five minutes we were there.

And now for the first time I was really home. The night was magnificent; the Southern Cross on a slant overhead; the moon a clear, small pewter; the stars all recognizable and close. The long grass stood all around, tall and giving off its dry, sweetish smell, and full of talking crickets. The flattened trees of the highveld were low above the grass, low and a dull silver-green.

It was the small intimate talking of the crickets which received me and made me part of that night-scape.

Before I left home seven years ago I used to walk

endlessly at night along the streets, tormented because there was a barrier between me and the steady solemn magnificence of those skies whose brilliance beat the thin little town into the soil. I saw them, but I was alien to them. This barrier is the urgent necessity of doing the next thing, of getting on with the business of living; whatever it is that drives us on. But on that first night there was no barrier, nothing; and I was effortlessly and at once in immediate intimacy with the soil and its creatures.

It was only so the first night; for at once habit took over and erected its barriers; and if I had had to fly back to England the next day, I would have been given what I had gone home for.

For to stand there with the soft dust of the track under my shoes, the crickets talking in my ear, the moon cold over the bush, meant I was able to return to that other house.

There are two sorts of habitation in Africa. One is of brick, cement, plaster, tile and tin—the substance of the country processed and shaped; the other sort is made direct of the stuff of soil and grass and tree. This second kind is what most of the natives of the country live in; and what I, as a child, lived in. The house was not a hut, but a long cigar-shaped dwelling sliced several times across with walls to make rooms.

To make such a house you choose a flat place, clear it of long grass and trees, and dig a trench two feet deep in the shape you want the house to be. You cut trees from the bush and lop them to a size and insert them side by side in the trench, as close as they will go. From the trunks of living trees in the bush fibre is torn; for under the thick rough bark of a certain variety of tree is a thick layer of smooth flesh. It is coloured yellow and pink; and when it is still alive, newly torn from the tree, it is wet and slippery to the touch. It dries quickly; so it is necessary to have several labourers stripping the fibre, with others ready immediately to use it for tying the trees of the walls into place. At this stage the house will look like a small space enclosed by a palisade—tall, uneven logs of wood, greyish-brown in colour, laced tightly with yellow and rose-coloured strips. The palisade will have spaces in it for doors and windows.

On this frame is set the skeleton of the roof. More trees have been cut, slimmer ones, and laid slantwise from the tops of the wall-poles to a ridge in the centre. They are tied with strips of the fibre to this centre pole, which is an immensely long gum tree or thorn tree made smooth and slim, lying parallel to the ground.

Now the house will look like an immense birdcage, set in the middle of the bush. For the trees have not been cut back around it yet; and the grass is still standing high all around, long swatches of grass, a browny-gold in colour. One cannot build this sort of a house save when the grass is dry, at the season for thatching.

Standing inside the cage of rough poles, the sun comes through in heavy bars of yellow. Strips of fading fibre lie everywhere in tangles; chips of wood send off a warm, spicy smell.

Now it is time to make the walls.

From an ant-heap nearby earth is cut in spadefuls and laid in a heap. Ant-heap earth is best, because it has already been blended by the jaws of a myriad workers.

It is not always easy to find the right ant-heap, even in ant-heap country; for even ants cannot make suitable wall-earth where the ingredients are not right at the start. And, having found a properly composed heap, there may be snags. For instance, when we were building our house, the ant-heap we were working had three skeletons laid side by side, in such a way that showed these were the bones of chiefs of a tribe. Earthen cooking-pots buried beside the skeletons still showed traces of white meal mingled with the earth.

Our labourers would not go near this ant-heap again, for they feared the spirits of their ancestors. So we had to choose another. But meanwhile, some of the earth had already been pounded into mud for the walls; and so the walls of our house had in them the flesh and the blood of the people of the country.

To make mud for walls, a great heap of ant-worked earth is built up and wetted. Then the feet of the builders squelch it into the right consistency. Also, in this case, the feet of my brother and myself, who were small children.

To lay the mud on the poles it is carried in petrol tins from the men who are softening it to the men who are plastering; great handfuls are taken up quickly from the tins, before it can dry out, and slapped on to the poles. Sometimes there are gaps between the poles too wide to hold the mud; and then handfuls of grass are caught up and inserted and worked in with the mud. The smell of this mud is fresh and sweet, if the water used is good, clean water.

Soon all the walls are covered with a thick, dark mud-skin; and this is quickly smoothed over with trowels or flat bits of tin. Now the house is a house and not a frame of tree-poles; for the walls cannot be seen through.

Next, the long, pale grass is cut from those parts of the farm where it grows best and tallest, and is laid in piles ready for the thatchers. It is laid swathe over swathe beginning from ridgepole and working downwards, and each swathe is tied into place with the bush-fibre. The grass is laid thick, 18 inches deep; and finally the loose, long tips that draggle almost to the ground are cut off straight and clean with long, sharpened bits of metal.

And now the roof of the house is a gleaming golden

colour, laced with rose-pink and yellow; and so it stays until the rains of the first wet season dim the colours.

Meanwhile, the doors have been hung and the windows fitted; and this is not easy when the poles of the walls are likely to be uneven. Nor are those doors and windows ever likely truly to fit; for the wood of lintels and frames swells and contracts with the wetness and the dryness of the time of the year.

The floor is done last. More ant-heap earth is piled, and on it fresh cowdung; and it is wetted with the fresh blood of an ox and with water, and is stamped free of lumps. This mixture is laid all over the earth inside the house and smoothed down. It has a good, warm, sweet smell, even when it dries, which takes about a week.

Now the house is finished and can be lived in. The mud-skin of the walls has dried a pleasant light-grey, or a yellowish-grey. Or it can be colour-washed. The mud of the floor is dark and smooth and glossy. It can be left bare, or protected with linoleum, for after a time this kind of floor tends to scuff into holes and turns dusty, so linoleum is useful, though not as pleasant to look at as the bare, hard, shining earth-floor.

A pole-and-dagga house is built to stand for two, three, four years at most; but the circumstances and character of our family kept ours standing for nearly two decades. It did very well, for it had been built with affection. But under the storms and the beating rains of the wet seasons, the grass of the roof flattened like old flesh into the hollows and bumps of the poles under it; and sometimes the mud-skin fell off in patches and had to be replaced; and sometimes parts of the roof received a new layer of grass. A house like this is a living thing, responsive to every mood of the weather; and during the time I was growing up it had already begun to sink back into the forms of the bush. I remember it as a rather old, shaggy animal standing still among the trees, lifting its head to look out over the vleis and valleys to the mountains.

I wrote a poem once about a group of suburban town houses; which I could not have written had I not been brought up in such a house as I have described:

THE HOUSE AT NIGHT

That house grew there, self-compact;
And with what long hopeless love
I walked about, about—
To make the creature out.

First with fingers: grainy brick
That took its texture from the earth;
The roof, membranous sheath
On rafters stretched beneath.

Yet, though I held the thing as close
As child's toy gathered in my hand—
Could shatter it or not;
No nearer truth I got.

Eluded by so frail a thing?
But if touch fails then sight succeeds.
But windows shadowed in
My face that peered within.

And through my shadowing face I saw
A room where someone lived, and there
The glow of hidden fire;
A secret, guarded fire.

Should I fail by closeness? Then
Move back and see the house from far,

Gathered among its kind,
No unit hard-defined.

And there a herd of houses! Each
Brooding darkly on its own,
Settled in the shade
That each small shape had made.

Till suddenly a mocking light
Flashed on from that one house I'd searched,
As if a beast had raised
His head from where he grazed.

And brilliant to my blinded face
As if with laughter openly,
These dazzling panes comprise
All dazzling gold eyes.

The house was built high, on a kopje that rose from a lower system of vleis and ridges. Looking from the windows you seemed on a level with the circling mountains, on a level with the hawks which wheeled over the fields.

My room was the third down from the top or end of the house; and it was very big and very light, for it had a large, low window, and a door which I kept propped open with a stone. The stones on the kopje were not of the quartz which cropped up all over the farm, but tended to be flattened and layered, and were brown, a light, bright brown, and when they were wet with rain, yellowish. To the touch they were smooth and velvety, because of the dust surface. Such a stone I used to prop my door open, so that I could look down on the hawks that hung over the fields, and watch them turn and slide down the currents of air with their stretched wings motionless. The great mountain ten miles off was the chrome mountain, scarred all over with workings; and it was part of the chain of hills and peaks over which the sun rose. The big field below the house was a mealie field. Newly ploughed it was rich reddish-brown, a sea of great, tumbling clods. From the path which ran along its edge, the field showed a pattern of clods that had fallen over from the plough-shares one after another, so that walking slowly beside it avenues opened and shut, lanes of sunlight and shadow. And each clod was like a rock, for the interest of its shape and colour: the plough-share cutting smooth through the hard soil left a clean, shining surface, iridescent, as if it had been oiled with dark oil.

And sometimes, from the height of the house, looking down, these clean, shared surfaces caught the sun all over the field at the same moment so that a hundred acres of clods glittered darkly together, flashing off a sullen light; and at such times the hawks swerved off, high and away, frightened.

Then the harrows drove over the field, side by side, the heavy, shining oxen plunging and scrambling over the great earth-boulders; they drove over it again and again, till the beasts walked easily, setting their feet down in soft tilthed soil; and the field was flat, without shadows, an even reddish-brown. And so it stood a while, waiting for the rains. During this time the air was full of dust, for the wind-devils danced and played continuously over the field; and sometimes columns of whirling, fiery red dust mingled with fragments of last year's mealie-stalks that glittered gold and silver, stood in the air higher than eye-level from the house; and the hawks were gone out of the dusty air into the clean air-currents over the far bush. Through the dust that shone a soft red at sunset and sunrise, the great soft-stepping oxen moved, two by two, in front of the planters; Afrikander oxen with their long, snaky horns; and behind the planting machines the small, white, flat seeds popped into the earth and were covered. The flocks of guinea-fowl moved down out of the bush at dawn and at sunset after those precious mealie-grains, flocks of sometimes fifty, a hundred, two hundred birds; and my brother and I, waiting in the bush with our rifles, saw them as industrious as farmyard birds over the hidden mealie-seeds.

Now the long tension of the dry season had built up into a crescendo of bad temper and irritability and anxiety that means the rains will come soon; and at night, lying in bed, I saw the lightning dance and quiver over the mountains while the thunder growled. The long stretches of bush and field were dark; this was the only time of the year the fields were dark, for all the light had gone into the electricity that darted along the edges of the cloud-masses.

And then, one night, I would wake and hear a rushing and a pouring and a rustling all around; the rains had come. Over my head the old thatch was soaking and swelling, and in the weak places the wet seeped through, so that from half a dozen patches of roof over my room came a soft dulcet pattering. I crept out from under the mosquito net to set basins and jugs to catch the drops; and looking out from the door into the wet darkness a battering of rain ricocheting up from the earth came as high as my waist so that I had to step back fast into dryness. But until the lightning drove down through the wet and broken cloud-masses it was dark; when the light came, it drove down the shining rods of white rain, and showed the trees crouching under the downpour and a thick dance of white raindrops like hailstones a foot deep all over the earth.

So I would go back to sleep, lulled by the roar of the rain outside and splash of the roof-leaks into the basins. In the morning I was woken not by the warmth of the sun on my bed but by a new intenser glare of light on my eyelids: the air had been washed clean of smoke from the veld fires and of dust, and the skies had lifted high and bright, and the trees were green and clean. The sun had come close again, shining free and yellow direct on to the big field, which was now a dark, rich, sodden red, a clear, red space among rich, sodden foliage. The thatch was still dropping long stalactites of shining water, and it was as if the house was enclosed by a light waterfall.

By midday the wetness had been whirled up into the air in clouds of steam; the big field steamed and smoked; and it was as if one could feel the growth being sucked up out of the mealie-grains by the heat and the wet.

During the first days of the wet season the storms and the showers advanced and retreated, and we watched the drama from the kopje-top; the now rich green bush stretching all around for miles would be blotted out suddenly in one place by a grey curtain, or the clouds would open violently overhead, enclosing us in a grey, steaming downpour. Below, the field was already showing a sheen of green. From the path beside the field, walking, the field was again opening and shutting, but now in avenues of green. Each plant was an inch high, a minute, green, divided spear, as crisp as fresh lettuce, and in the heart of each a big, round, shining globule of water.

Now the farmer would be pleased if the rain stopped for a week or ten days, so as to drive the roots down into the earth and strengthen the plants. Sometimes he was obliged; and the field of mealies stood faintly wilting, limp with thirst. But however the rain fell, the green film over the dark earth thickened, so that soon there were a hundred acres of smooth, clear apple-green that shimmered and rippled under the hot sun.

In the moonlight, looking down, it was a dim green sea, moving with light.

Soon the plants put out their frothy white crests; in the moonlight there was foam on the sea; and in the daytime, when the winds were strong, the whole field swayed and moved like a tide coming in. At this time the hawks hung low over the field with bunched, ready claws, working hard, so that from the house you looked down on their wide, stiff wings.

The rainy season passed; and the brilliant green of the field dimmed, and the sound of the wind in it was no longer a wet, thick rustle, but more like the sound of an army of tiny spears. Soon all the field was a tarnished silvery-gold, and each mealie-plant was like a ragged, skeleton scarecrow, and the noise of the wind was an incessant metallic whispering.

From the house now the field could be seen populated with black, small figures, moving between the rows and laying them flat. Soon the dark, dry earth was bared again, patterned with mealie-stooks, each a small, shining pyramid; and all over the soil a scattered litter of soft, glinting, dead leaf and stalk. Then came the heavy wagons behind sixteen oxen led by the little black boy who pulled six inches in front of the tossing, curving, wicked horns, with the driver walking behind, yelling and flickering his long whiplash in the air over their backs.

The field was bare completely, the stooks stripped of maize-cobs, the stooks themselves carried off to make manure in the cattle-kraals. It was all rough, dark-red earth, softly glinting with mealie-trash. In came the ploughs, and again the earth fell apart into the great shining clods.

This cycle I watched from my bedroom door, when I was not absorbed by what went on in the room itself. For after a decade or so of weathering, the house had become the home of a dozen kinds of creature not human, who lived for the most part in the thatch of the roof.

Rats, mice, lizards, spiders and beetles, and once or twice snakes, moved through the thatch and behind the walls; and sometimes, when the oil-lamp was flickering low, which it did in a steady, leaping rhythm till it flared up and out—in a way which I am reminded of by the pedestrian-crossing lights in the street outside my window, flicking all night on my wall in London—sometimes, as the yellow glow sank, a pair of red eyes could be seen moving along the top of the the wall under the thatch. A mouse? A snake perhaps? For some reason they seldom came down to the floor. Once I saw a pair of eyes shining in the light coming through the window from the moon, and called for my parents to kill what I was convinced was a snake, but it was a frog. In the wet season, the frogs from the vlei two miles away were so loud they drowned the perpetual singing of the night-crickets; and the irregular pattering of frogs on the floor of my room was something I learned to take no more notice of than the pattering of rain from leaks in the roof. It must not be imagined that I am a lover of wild life. I am frightened of all these creatures—or rather, of touching them by accident in the dark, or putting my foot on one; but if you live in a house which is full of them, then your area of safety contracts within it to the bed. I never went to bed without taking it completely apart to make sure nothing had got into the bedclothes; and once safely in, with the mosquito net tucked down, I knew that nothing could fall on me from the roof or crawl over me in the dark.

The family attitude towards the role of mosquito nets is illustrated by a dialogue I overheard between my parents in the next room.

It was the first rains of the season, and the roof had begun to leak in a dozen places. I had already lit my candle and set out the pails and basins; and I knew that my father was awake because I could see the fluctuating glow of his cigarette on the wall through the crack of the door which did not close properly.

I knew that he was waiting for my mother to wake up. At last I heard him say in a sort of hushed shout: 'Maud, Maud, wake up!' Nothing happened and the rain roared on.

'*Maud!*'

She woke with a crash of the bedsprings. 'What's the matter?'

'It's raining.'

'I can hear that it's raining.'

'The roof's really bad this year,' he said. 'Like a sieve.'

'When the grass swells, it won't be so bad.'

'It's worse than it was last year.'

'We'll get the thatching boy up in the morning,' she said sleepily, and turned over.

'But it's raining,' he said desperately.

'Go to sleep.'

'But it's raining on *me*.'

'You've got your mosquito net down, haven't you?'

'A mosquito net has holes in it.'

'A mosquito net will absorb a lot of water before it starts to leak.'

'It has already started to absorb the water.'

'What if I slung another mosquito net over the first?'

'Wouldn't it be easier to move the bed?'

'Oh. Yes. I suppose so.'

My father spent a large part of his nights sitting up in his bed smoking and thinking. Sometimes, if I lit my candle for something, he would say cautiously: 'Is that you?'

'Yes, it's me, I'm only just . . . .'

'Well then, go to sleep.'

'But I'm only just . . . .'

'You're not to read at this time of night.' And then, after a moment, 'Are you asleep?'

'No.'

'Hear that owl? It must be in the tree right outside.'

'It sounds to me in the bush at the bottom of the kopje.'

'Do you think so? You know, I've been sitting here thinking. Supposing we caught an owl and crossed it with one of your mother's Rhode Island Reds. What do you think would happen?'

'Almost anything, I should think.'

'I was being serious,' he said reprovingly from the dark room next door. 'I don't suppose *they* have thought of that, do you? An owl and a chicken. They could graft the seed somehow if they wouldn't do it naturally. A rat-eating chicken. Or a chicken-eating chicken.'

A stir in my mother's bed.

'Shhhhh,' my father would say hastily. 'Go to sleep at once.'

Or: 'Are you asleep?'

'No.'

'I've been thinking.'

'What about?'

'You know the centre of the earth is all molten, so they say?'

'Well?'

'Suppose they sank down a borehole and tapped it. Power. Much more effective than all these dams and things. Do you think *they* have thought of that yet?'

'Bound to.'

'You're not much good, are you? No imagination. Not a scrap of imagination between the lot of you, that's your trouble.'

*　　*　　*　　*

Walls are by nature and definition flat; and having lived for so long in London, when I hear the word wall I see a flat surface, patterned or coloured smooth.

But the wall that faced my bed was not flat.

When the workmen had flung on the mud, naturally it was a little bumpy because no matter how you smooth on mud over poles, if there is a knot on the pole where a branch was chopped off, or if the pole had a bit of a bend in it, then the mud settled into the shape of bump and hollow. Sometimes, because of the age of the wall, a bit of mud had fallen out altogether and had had to be replaced, much to my regret, for the exposed poles showed themselves riddled with borer holes and other interesting matters. Once there was a mouse-nest in the space between two poles. There were five tiny pink mice which fitted easily into about an inch of my palm. The mother mouse ran away, and I diluted cow's milk and tried to drop it off the end of a bit of cotton into the minute mouths. But a drop is always a drop; and for a baby mouse as if someone had flung a bucket of milk into its face. I nearly drowned those mice, trying to work out a way to make a drop of milk mouse-size. But it was no use, they died; and the jagged space in the wall was filled in with new mud.

The wall had been colour-washed a yellowish-white; but for some reason I have forgotten, after the brown mud had been filled in, it was not painted over, so that there was a brown patch on my wall.

I knew the geography of that wall as I knew the lines on my palm. Waking in the morning I opened my eyes to the first sunlight, for the sun shot up over the mountain in a big red ball just where my window was. The green mosquito gauze over the window had tarnished to a dull silver, and my curtains were a clear orange; and the sun came glittering through the silver gauze and set the curtains glowing like fire. The heat was instant, like a hot hand on your flesh. The light reached in and lay on the white wall, in an irregular oblong of soft rosy red. The grain of the wall, like a skin, was illuminated by the clear light. There were areas of light, brisk graining where Tobias the painter had whisked his paint-brush from side to side; then a savage knot of whorls and smudged lines where he had twirled it around. What had he been thinking about when his paint-brush suddenly burst into such a fury of movements? There was another patch where he had put his hand flat on the whitewash. Probably there had been something in his bare foot, and he had steadied himself with his hand while he picked his sole up to look at it. Then he had taken out whatever was in his foot and lifted his brush and painted out the handmark. Or thought he had. For at a certain moment of the sunrise, when the sun was four inches over the mountains in the east, judging by the eye, that hand came glistering out of the whitewash like a Sign of some kind.

It took about five minutes of staring hard at the walls where the light lay rosy and warm for it to turn a clear primrose-yellow. This meant that the sun had contracted and was no longer red and swollen, but yellow and its normal size, and one could no longer look at it without hurting one's eyes.

High near the roof, above the clear yellow sun-pattern, there were a series of little holes in the wall. These were the homes of some hornets, who like dried mud to live in. I don't know if hornets are like birds, returning to their nests, but there were always hornets at work on that wall. They were elegant in shape, and a bright, lively black, and they buzzed and zoomed in and out of the room through the propped-open door. One would fit itself neatly inside a hole and begin working inside it, and you listened to fragments of mud from the wall flopping down on to the floor.

And if the wall was in a continual state of disintegration and repair, an irregular variegated surface of infinite interest, then the floor was not at all the flat and even surface of convention.

Long ago, the good, hard surface of dung, mud and blood had been protected by linoleum; and this in its turn had hollowed and worn as the earth beneath had hollowed or heaved because of the working of roots or the decay of old roots. A young tree used to shoot up under my bed every wet season. There was a crack in the mud there; the linoleum began to bulge upwards, and then split; and out came a pale, sickly, whitey-yellowish shoot which immediately turned a healthy green. We cut it off; but it sprouted up once or twice every wet season. As soon as the rains stopped, the shoot sank back, sullen and discouraged until next year, biding its time. One year I decided not to cut it. The first thing every morning I put my head out from under the mosquito net, over the edge of the bed, to see how the shoot was getting along. Very soon it was a small, green bush, pushing up against the wire of the mattress. The next thing, it would have split the mattress as it had split the linoleum. I moved the bed, thinking it would be attractive to have a tree growing in the middle of my bedroom, but my mother would have none of it. She had it chopped down, and a lot of fresh mud laid and stamped hard and flat. Next season the shoot came up at the side between the fresh bit of floor and the old, near the wall. It came pushing up with a watch clutched in its leaves. This was because my father, who had many theories about life, had a theory about watches. Foolish, he said, to buy watches costing 5 or 10 guineas which, being delicate and expensive, were bound to break soon. Better to buy a dozen turnip watches at a time, at 5s. each, from the Army and Navy Stores; and then when they broke it would not matter. He ordered a dozen watches, but they never broke: they were indestructible. As a result we had watches propped all over the house; and I had one by my bed. When it fell into a crack in the mud, I did not bother, because there were plenty more. But it reappeared in the first rains of that year, from the mud of the floor, held in the green arms of the little tree, like a Dali picture.

The only creatures that were really a threat to this house were the white ants. All that part of the country was full of ant-heaps. They can be 10, 20 feet high. After the rains, a grass-covered peak of earth which has looked dead will suddenly sprout up an extra foot or so overnight of new red granulated earth, like the turrets and pinnacles of a child's fairy castle.

A good, hard kick will send the new earth flying and expose a mass of tunnels and galleries leading down far, far into the earth. There is always water under ant-heaps. People digging wells look for a good, old, well-established ant-heap. They follow down the tunnels. Sixty feet, a hundred feet, sometimes deeper, they are bound to come on water.

There was an ant-heap in front of the house, and another to one side; most of the time the ants remained there, but occasionally they sent outriders into the house.

On my white bedroom wall, for instance, would appear a red winding gallery, like an artery, irregularly branching. These galleries were wet at first, and granular, because each particle of earth is brought in the mouth of an ant. It is a mistake to wipe these galleries off while they are still wet, for all you achieve is a smear of red earth and crushed ants on the wall. Once dry, they can be easily brushed off, leaving only a faint, pinkish mark on the white. It is exciting to see a new gallery where none existed three hours before, and to shrink yourself ant-size and imagine yourself scurrying along under fragrant tunnels of fresh, wet earth.

It was the ants, of course, who finally conquered, for when we left that house empty in the bush, it was only a season before the ant-hills sprouted in the rooms themselves, among the quickly sprouting trees, and the red galleries must have covered all the walls and the floor. The rains were heavy that year, beating the house to its knees. And we heard that on the kopje there was no house, just a mound of greyish, rotting thatch, covered all over with red ant-galleries. And then in the next dry season a big fire swept up from the bush at the back, where the kopje fell sharp and precipitous over rocks into the big vlei, and there was nothing left of the house. Nothing at all; just the bush growing up.

One of the reasons I wanted to go home was to drive through the bush to the kopje and see where the house had been. But I could not bring myself to do it.

Supposing, having driven seven miles through the bush to the place where the road opens into the big mealie land, supposing then that I had lifted my eyes expecting to see the kopje sloping up, a slope of empty, green bush—supposing then that the house was still there after all?

For a long time I used to dream of the collapse and decay of that house, and of the fire sweeping over it; and then I set myself to dream the other way. It was urgently necessary to recover every detail of that house. For only my own room was clear in my mind. I had to remember everything, every strand of thatch and curve of wall or heave in the floor, and every tree and bush and patch of grass around it, and how the fields and slopes of country looked at different times of the day, in different strengths and tones of light. When I was working to regain that house from its collapse, I used to set myself to sleep, saying, 'Now you will dream of that room, or that tree, or that turn in the road.' And most often I did. Over months, I recovered the memory of it all. And so what was lost and buried in my mind, I recovered from my mind; so I suppose there is no need to go back and see what exists clearly, in every detail, for so long as I live.

Similarly, at that time when I dreamed only images of destruction, there was a terrible dream about Cape Town, an exact repetition of what I once saw, awake.

It was about fifteen years ago I went to Cape Town for holiday. Or, as we put it who come down off the high hinterland, where it is all drought and small, stunted trees and sand, and the rain gets sucked into the dry air as soon as it falls—I went to the sea. At the Cape there are pine trees and hillsides full of grapes, and the sea all around, a blue, blue sea, and miles of white, glittering beaches, and mountains.

One night I stood on that hill which is a flank of Table Mountain, looking down at the city. The sky was clear and full of stars, and the sea was a dark-bluish luminosity, and on it were dark shapes clustered with lights, which were the big ships from Europe and the world. The city was a glow of light. Behind me Table Mountain, black and straight against the stars.

On the left stretched some lower hills. There appeared a small white vapour glistening in the moonlight in a gap between the peaks. Over the edge of the gap came a wisp of white cloud, a small tendril, curling down. Then the sky on that side was a whirl of moonlit mist, and instead of one curling finger, cloud came pouring down and through the gap like a flood of celestial milk. It sank as it came, covering first the flank of the mountain, then blotting out the lights of the houses on that side. The lights went out swiftly, and the mist came pouring steadily in, and soon half of the city had gone, and the sky on that side was a high bank of white and shining cloud. Then all the city was gone and the ships and the sea, and below a great white floor of moonlit cloud heaved and rose, and over on the right side the stars were dimming. Then there was cloud overhead, and cloud at my feet, rising. The fir trees just below sank in mist till only their black tops showed. As the cold dampness came up the trees went.

It took only ten minutes, from the time that the city lay open and glittering to the time it had gone, gone completely.

And so, when this dream began to recur, together with the dream of the heap of red, sinking earth and dead grass with the trees growing through it, I first restored the house, and then forced the mist back, rolled it back off the city and the sea and the lighted ships and back through the gap in the mountains. It took a long time, but at last the city was free and illuminated again.

III

ON THE MORNING after my arrival the sun was warm all about the house, the leaves of the creeper on the verandah laid a black sun-pattern on the wall, the pigeons cooed under the roof, the roses blazed on the lawn. In the next garden, the garden boy was cutting wisps of grass even with a pair of rusted old scissors, and a plump black girl was strolling up and down, looking good-naturedly bored, holding a white child by either hand. Daddy was leaving for the office in one car; Mummy was off downtown in the other.

I would now get out of bed, knowing that all the housework was done and the breakfast ready. Imagine that I lived here for so many years and took this comfort for granted! Even worse, that for a period of months before I left, due to a moral compulsion I now think misguided, I insisted on doing all my housework myself.

'If I've got to live in this paradise for the petty bourgeoisie, then at least I shall take what advantages I can—
if I've got to be bored, then I shall at least be com-
fortable.' Thus a friend of mine, an old revolutionary from
Central Europe, sucked into Rhodesia by some current of
war. Until that moment he had been living on principle in
one room, studying and absorbing statistical information
about Africa against the day when he could go home to
Europe and civilisation and the class war. He lived in
complete isolation from the white citizenry, who filled him
with contempt. He then got himself a temporary job, a
pleasant flat and a servant, and continued to study. Two
years later he came to see me one evening. 'Please sit there
and don't say anything. I want to talk and listen to what I
am saying. I am in a moral crisis.' So I sat and made a
sounding board. He was saying that no one but a fool
could help making money here if he were white; he intended to spend five years making money and beating
these white savages at their own game. Then he would
take the money and clear out. This brief résumé of what
he said can give no idea of the prolonged and dialectical
subtlety of his argument. Having proved his case to his
satisfaction he became silent, frowning at me. Then, in a
quite different voice, with a small, unhappy smile, he said:
'This is a damned corrupting country. We should get out
quick. We should all get out. No one with a white skin
can survive it. People like us are too few to change
anything. Now *get out*,' he said. 'I'm getting out by the
first train.'

Three years later I met him in Bulawayo; he had made
a lot of money and was about to get married. He was in a
buoyant, savagely sardonic mood which I was easily able
to recognize. 'I want you to meet my fiancée,' he said. She
was a pretty, indolent girl, the daughter of a manufactur-
er, and on her finger was the apotheosis of all diamond

rings, which my friend J. insisted on showing to me, telling me exactly how much it cost, and how much cheaper he had got it than was probable, while she sat fondly smiling at him. He spoke in a voice that was a deliberate parody of a Jewish big-time huckster.

I hoped that this time I would run into him somewhere; but it seems he is now in Johannesburg, with four children and a whole network of businesses.

At breakfast that first morning I felt myself at home because four of us were having that conversation which I have been taking part in now for fifteen years: would he, would she, they or you, be given papers, passports, permits? This time it was about whether I would get into the Union of South Africa.

I had worked out a plan to get in, not illegally, but making use of certain well-known foibles of the Afrikaner immigration officials. But sitting there at breakfast in that comfortable house, it all sounded too melodramatic; and the conversation became, as it often does, a rather enjoyable exercise in the balance of improbabilities.

And besides, it was pleasant to be back in a country where everyone knows everyone else, and therefore gossip is not merely personal, but to do with the processes of government; a country where, unlike Britain, which is ruled by the Establishment of which one is not a member, one is close to the centres of administration simply because one is white. Here, journalists get their information straight from the C.I.D., with whom they have sundowners, and everybody has a friend who is a Member of Parliament or a Cabinet Minister. In this part of the world there are no secrets.

The information at my disposal was, then, that since Sir Percy Sillitoe of the British Intelligence had paid a helpful visit to the political C.I.D. of both Central Africa and the Union of South Africa, these departments are now closely linked and co-ordinated, not only with each other, but with their counterparts in Britain and America.

'In short,' we concluded, 'we are seeing a process whereby the countries of what is known as the free world have less and less in common with each other, and are linked only by the supra-national organization, the departments of the political police.'

But alas, the warmth of the sunlight, the smell of the roses, and the well-being that sets in when one knows there is no cooking, washing-up or housework to do for two months, had already done their work. I failed to draw the correct conclusion from this formulation, and decided to take my chance on getting into South Africa by the ordinary routes.

After all, I said, I could hardly be called a politically active person. For the business of earning one's living by writing does not leave much time for politics; and in any case, it is one of my firmest principles that a writer should not become involved in day-to-day politics. The evidence of the last thirty years seems to me to prove that it has a disastrous effect on writing. But I do not stick to this principle. For one thing, my puritan sense of duty which nothing can suppress is always driving me out to meetings which I know are a waste of time, let alone those meetings which are useful but which would be better assisted by someone else; for another, I find political behaviour inexhaustibly fascinating. Nevertheless, I am not a political agitator. I am an agitator *manquée*. I sublimate this side of my personality by mixing with people who are.

My friend N. listened to my hair-splitting with irritation and said that the C.I.D. would not be able to follow these arguments, and from their point of view I was an agitator. Much better not go to the Union at all, but stay here with my friends. And besides, Central Africa was in a melting-pot and at the crossroads and the turnings of the ways, whereas South Africa was set and crystallised and every-one knew about *apartheid*. South Africa was doomed to race riots, civil war and misery. Central Africa was com-mitted to Partnership and I had much better spend my time, if I insisted on being a journalist, finding out about Partnership.

But it was not that I wanted to be a journalist, I said; I had to be one, in order to pay my expenses. And besides it would be good for me to be a journalist for a time, a person collecting facts and information, after being a novel-ist, who has to go inwards to probe out the truth.

Well, if you are going to be a journalist, said my friends, then wait until you come back from South Africa. In the meantime, let's go on a jaunt to Umtali.

That was on a Friday morning, and we would go to Umtali tomorrow. Meanwhile a whole succession of old friends dropped in, either to make it clear how they had matured since I had seen them last, and believed in mak-ing haste slowly, or to say that a new wind was blowing in Southern Rhodesia; and things had changed utterly since I left, and segregation and race prejudice were things of the past.

Then I went downtown to do the shopping in the car, as one does here. Driving along the glossy avenues, be-tween the pretty houses with their patios, their gardens, their servants; driving in a solid mass of reckless, undisci-plined cars which half-remembered the old law of each man for himself, half-paid irritated but erratic attention to traffic lights and policemen—driving along the com-fortable streets of my home town, I understood suddenly and for the first time that this was an American small town; it is the town we have all seen in a hundred films about Mom and Pop and their family problems. I do not know why I had not perceived this before. Often, pursuing some character in a story I was writing, or describing an incident, I have thought: But this is American, this is American behaviour. But I had not seen the society as American. It was because I have been hypnotized by the word *British*.

Southern Rhodesia is self-consciously British; she came into existence as a British colony, opposed to the Boer-dominated Union of South Africa, although she has taken her political structure from the Union. Her turning north to federate with Northern Rhodesia and Nyasaland is an act of repudiation of the Afrikaner Nationalists, an affirmation of being British. Central Africa is British Africa. But even now the British are in the minority among the white people; there are far more Afrikaners, Greeks, Italians; and with all the people together, dark-skinned and white, the numbers of British people are negligible.

That would not matter: I do not think the numbers of a dominant class or group matter in stamping their imprint on a society. Portuguese territory is unmistakably Latin in feeling, though the Portuguese whites are a small minority.

What is it, then, that makes British white Africa American? What, for that matter, is that quality we all recognize as American? Partly it is the quality of a society where people are judged by how much they earn: it is the essence of the petty bourgeoisie: 'a man is a man for all that, because in this country there is no class feeling, only money feeling.'

Again, just as America is permeated with the values and attributes of the two groups of people supposedly non-assimilable—the Negroes and the Jews—so the white people here who think of nothing else, talk of nothing else, but the qualities they ascribe to the Africans are inevitably absorbing those qualities.

It is a society without roots—is that why it has no resistance to Americanism? Or is being rootless in itself American?

The myths of this society are not European. They are of the frontiersman and the lone-wolf; the brave white woman home-making in lonely and primitive conditions; the child who gets himself an education and so a status beyond his parents; the simple and brave savage defeated after gallant fighting on both sides; the childlike and lovable servant; the devoted welfare-worker spending his or her life uplifting backward peoples.

Yet these images have no longer anything to do with what is going on now in Central Africa.

On that first morning I went shopping to try to get the feel and atmosphere of the place.

First into a vegetable shop. Shopping has certainly changed: now the counters are refrigerated, self-service shops everywhere, and above all Coca-Cola has moved in. The Coca-Cola sign is on every second building, from the high new blocks of offices and flats to the scruffy little store in the Native Reserve.

In the vegetable shop were three white people and two Africans. Two of the white people were serving behind the counter; then two African men, with shopping baskets. Then me. I waited my turn behind the two Africans to see what would happen. The woman behind the counter eyed the Africans coldly, and then in the cool, curt voice I know so well said: 'Can't you see the white missus, boy? Get to the back.' They moved back, I moved in and was served. Another white woman came in; she was being served as I went out. The Africans patiently waited.

And for the thousandth time I tried to put myself in the place of people who are subjected to this treatment every day of their lives. But I can't imagine it: the isolated incident yes; but not the cumulative effect, year after year, every time an African meets a white person, the special tone of voice, the gesture of impatience, the contempt.

In the next shop, which was a bakery, a young girl in

jeans, striped sweat-shirt and sandals, was greeted by a
boy in sweat-shirt and jeans. 'Hiya, Babe!' 'Hiya, John-
ny.' 'See you tonight?' 'Ya, see you at the flicks.' 'Bye.'
'Bye.'

The main street is crammed with cars, with white wom-
en drifting along, talking, or standing in groups, talking.
They wear cool, light dresses, showing brown bare arms
and legs. The dresses are mostly home-made, and have
that look of careful individual fit that one sees in the
clothes of women in Italy and Spain.

These are the women of leisure; and, having been one of
them for so long—or at least expected to play the role of
one—I know that their preoccupations are in this order:
the dress they are making for themselves or their daughter, the laziness of their servants, and an infinite number
of personal problems. Or, as the Americans would say,
Problems.

Their husbands are now busily engaged in getting on
and doing well for themselves in the offices; and their
children are at school. The cookboy is cooking the lunch.
They will take back the car laden with groceries and
liquor, dress-lengths, bargains. Then there will be a morning tea-party. Then lunch with husband and family. Then
a nap. Then afternoon tea, and soon, sundowners. Then
the pictures. And then, bed. And, in the words of a
personal servant of a friend of mine: 'The white man goes
to bed, he makes love, twice-a-week, bump, bump, go-to-
sleep.'

Though this did not occur to me until later, at the end
of my trip, when my mind had cleared of the fogs induced
by the word Partnership, is it possible that the white men
of Central Africa are so anxious to create a class of
African in their own image, equally preoccupied with
getting on and doing well for themselves—is it possible
that one of the reasons for it is that other anxious white

myth, the potent and sexually heroic black man? Is it possible that (of course in a very dark place in their minds) they are thinking: 'Yah, you black bastard! You start worrying about money, too! That'll fix *you*!'

A group of these slow-moving, heavy-bodied women turned: one advanced towards me. Another school-friend. 'My old man heard it from his boss, and he heard it from a friend at the airport, so I knew you were back. Things have changed here, don't you think so? I hope you are going back to write something nice about us for a change. Hell, man, what have we done to you? You were always doing well for yourself before you left, weren't you, so what are you getting excited about? Hell, man, what have we done? I've had my cookboy for fifteen years, since I got married, and I've always treated him right. And what do you think of the lights of London? I was there last spring, did you know? But we went to Paris. Man, I don't know what they see in Paris. It cost ten pounds for a cabaret and a bottle of some champagne and some nightlife.'

'They were cheating you,' I said.

'Is that so? Well, next time we are going to Johannesburg. We've got just as good night-life there. And the Belgian Congo, too. They've got some night-life just as good as Paris. And if my old man wants to go and see some nudes, then he can go and see them there, because those nudes in Paris haven't got anything we haven't got. And it only costs half. Seen our new night club? Seen our new restaurant? Jesus, we've got as good here as you've got in London, I'm telling you. Things have really changed since you've left, they have. It's a fact.'

After this conversation, I walked down First Street. On the pavement, sitting with their feet comfortably in the gutter, five African women, knitting, watching life pass by. They looked relaxed and happy. They wore good print dresses, crocheted white caps, sandals. Clothes have changed much for the better in a decade. Gone are the old blue-printed cottons, which were almost a uniform for African women. A man I know who imports for the African trade said: 'The days of "Kaffir-truck" are over. Now we import quantities of cheap, bright stuff for the native trade. But already some Africans buy as good quality as the Europeans. In five or six years they won't be manufacturing special goods for the African trade.'

In Meikle's lounge, a place where I spent a good part of my adolescence, I drank beer and watched what went on. Women having morning tea, farmers in for the tobacco auctions, everything the same.

At the next table, two women, an American and an Englishwoman. It appeared they were both making trips through Africa, had met in Durban, were travelling back to England together for company. They knew each other previously. Now they were discussing some mutual friend who, it seemed, had come to no good.

AMERICAN: So now I don't know what he'll do. You can't start all over at fifty.

ENGLISH: It seems such a shame. And what can it have been? Yes, of course he always drank too much, but why *suddenly*. . . . I mean, he never drank *too* much.

AMERICAN: Well, dear, he had problems.

ENGLISH: But no worse than usual? And there was that nice wife of his. She always pulled him together when—I mean, I remember once, when they were over visiting us in London, he was rather depressed, and she pulled him together. It was not that they needed to worry about *money*.

AMERICAN: He was basically unstable, that's all.

ENGLISH: But *suddenly*? There must have been something definite, something must have happened. Of course, people don't drink too much for nothing. But everything must have suddenly piled up? Perhaps he was working too hard. He always did, didn't he?

AMERICAN: Now Betty, there's no point in going on. He had a character defect.

ENGLISH (*slightly irritated, but persistent*): I dare say, but his character couldn't suddenly have got all that much more defective? There must have been some reason?

AMERICAN: I keep telling you, he was psychologically maladjusted.

ENGLISH (*after a pause, drily*): You always put your finger straight on to a thing, dear.

AMERICAN (*very faintly suspicious*): What? But what more is there to say?

Walking out of the hotel I was looking for the lavatory where it used to be. Coming towards me, a middle-aged woman. I used to know her well. 'Where's the lavatory these days?' I asked. 'Really, dear!' she said. 'It's the powder-room since you left. Third door on the right.'

At the post office, it says *Natives* and *Europeans*. I went to my part of the building, and watched the long queues of Africans patiently waiting their turn to be served.

Then I went to get a copy of my driving licence, which I had lost. The office was in make-shift buildings on a waste lot; the growth of administration due to Federation has spread government departments everywhere there is room for them.

There was a long queue of about 150 white people, and another parallel queue of black people. The sun was burning down, and puffs of pinkish dust settled from the shifting, bored feet. Pleasant to see these sunburned skins, the red-brown, glistening, healthy sunburn of the highveld; pleasant to stand in the hot sun, knowing it would not withdraw itself capriciously in ten minutes behind cloud.

In front of me in the queue were two young farmers in for the day. Farm-talk: prices, cost of native labour; the Government favoured the townsfolk. This at least hadn't changed at all. They wore the farm uniform—short khaki shorts, showing yards of brown leg, bush shirts, short socks.

Time passed, nearly an hour of it; the queue had hardly moved forward.

They were now talking of one Jerry, and here, it seemed, was a matter they approved of, for the fatalistic shrug of the Government-oppressed countryman had given way to the earnest manner of two children swapping confidences.

'I'm with you. Jerry is a good type. Not like some magistrates. We are lucky to have him in our district.'

'Fair's fair with Jerry. He warns you—then he gets you, square and legal.'

'That's what I say. He came to my place one sundown— he said, "Now look here, man, that's the third time I saw you doing seventy through the township. Next time I'll see there's a fine." '

'Then he will. Because he does what he says. He sent a chit around to me. "Tom," he said, "it was nearly eighty you were doing today. You only have to slow down to thirty for a mile through the village. Is that so much to ask?" Yes, that's what he wrote to me.'

'Yes, that's Jerry all right. He said to me, "There's a school, too. The place is full of kids. Use your head," he said. "Think how you'd feel if you got a couple of those kids. Use your heart." '

'Yes, that's what he said to me when he came to see me. He gave me fair warning. Next day, that was yesterday, I got a summons. I was doing eighty, mind.' Here he paused and looked with dark solemnity at the other. 'Eighty. So I was summoned. Fair's fair.'

'Yes, you can always trust Jerry to do what's right.'

'Yes, he never lets you get away with it. Not more than what's fair.'

Which conversation may, perhaps, throw light on another: three weeks later, a friend of mine who inspects African schools, in that voice of exasperated affection which is common among liberal members of the administration who have to work constantly against their own beliefs, 'Damn it, man, they're mad. Say what you like. Yes, all right, we're mad, but they're madder. There are times I could throw the whole thing up. You know what? There's a teacher. He's been swatting and struggling for that ruddy Standard IV certificate for years, and then he got it, and he was in a kraal school at last, a big man with all his six years' schooling behind him and all's hunkydory. So then I went out to inspect. I found him there in that pitiful, bloody little school, next door to a whacking great church, needless to say, and he had his sixty kids sitting on the mud floor in neat little rows all chanting the A.B.C. in Shona, and there he was drunk as a lord and staggering around like a sick chicken. I said to him, "Aren't you ashamed, Joshua? Aren't you ashamed my man, with all these poor little kids dependent on you for their education?" He wept bitter tears and said, "Yes, sir," he would never do it again. "You'd better not," I said to him, and I went off in my fine government lorry to the next school 100 miles off. Then I heard it was time I went and had another look, so I packed myself into my lorry and off I went, 300 miles, and there was Joshua, lying on the ground under the tree outside the school, and there were his class, still sitting in neat rows in the hut on the floor, repeating after themselves, "Mary had a little lamb," maintaining perfect discipline in their efforts to get educated even without a teacher. So I lost my rag, I can tell you. I got him to his feet and shook him sobre and said he'd have one more chance. Six months later, out I went, there he was, drunker, if possible, so I gave him the sack. I gave him the sack there and then. The poor bastard wept and wailed and he said all his father's savings for fifteen years had gone into his getting Standard IV; but what could I do? I sacked him. Then I went off to stay the night at Jackson's farm, and I lay awake all night tortured—man, but tortured!—thinking of that poor silly bugger and his dad's life savings. Because, my God, if I was stuck out on that Reserve 150 miles from anywhere on £6 a month I'd drink myself to death in a month, man. Next morning I woke up more dead than alive, having decided I was going to clear out of this bloody country— no, really, I can't stand it, I'm going—when who should I see but Joshua on his bicycle? He had cycled 20 miles since dawn through the bush with a chicken. The chicken was for me. You could have knocked me down with a—I said to him, "Damn it, you poor fool, Joshua, damn it! I've given you the sack, I've ruined your life, now you'll have to go off and dig a ditch somewhere, and you bring me a chicken. Have a heart," I said, "don't do that to me." "Sir," he said. "It came into my heart last night to bring you a chicken. It is for you, sir. Thank you, sir." And with that off he went back to his bicycle. So I brought the chicken home, and here was my wife with psychological troubles, and my kids, damned spoilt brats who are so blasé and full of experience from the pictures they can't get a thrill out of anything, and the big baas, that's me. And the happy family, we ate that poor bastard's chicken, and I don't know why it didn't choke us.'

'Now, now, darling,' said his wife, 'you must keep a sense of proportion.'

* * * *

After two and a half hours I had reached the door of the office. It seems that this was the time of the year for renewing licences, and so the whole countryside moves into town for that purpose, and patiently queues behind the single counter that does duty for the ordinary run of business during the rest of the year. Then I discovered I was in the wrong queue, so I started again. At last, I was told I must go to an inner office; and the official invited me to do so through an inside passage, because otherwise I would have to pass through a crowd of natives, and I wouldn't want to do that, would I?

Inside there was a nice girl, who in the best tradition of the country, which is to have no respect for institutions, said, 'Well, I can't help you, because that silly lot of M.P.s we've got have absent-mindedly passed a law saying that everyone who loses his licence must take another driving test. I expect when they've noticed what they've done, they'll change it back again, but in the meantime I think you've had it, because there's queues miles long of people waiting to be tested for new licences and I can only hope there are some M.P.s among them.'

'But last time I lost my licence,' I said, 'all I did was to go to the office and they looked up a file and gave me a new one.'

'That was in the good old days. That was before Federation. No, things aren't what they used to be. And besides, it seems the files have got mislaid.'

So I went back to the house and telephoned the police at Banket where some time in the 'thirties I was given my licence by a young policeman who was not interested in the quality of my driving. But they said the records were always destroyed after five years, and they couldn't help me—the place I wanted was that office in town.

I fell into despair; but after reflecting that it was unlikely that the whole character—or, as the Americans would say, the *mores*—of the country had changed in seven years, I walked back to the licencing office, past the white queue that still waited, through the black queue, into the inner office, and said I had lost my driving licence. Whereupon a young man who had either not heard of the law just passed by Parliament, or who didn't care, charged me 1s. and gave me a substitute licence. And so the magnificent empty roads of the country were open to me.

*   *   *   *

Down the empty road to Umtali we drove. It is the road running east to the Portuguese border—a road that drives straight up one rise, down the other side, up again; first through hills tumbled all over with granite boulders like giant pebbles balancing on each other, sometimes so lightly it seems a breath of wind would topple them apart; then through mountains; for nearly 150 miles, and one looks down on Umtali from above, a small, pretty, sleepy town that never changes, in a hollow in the mountains.

It is hot there, very hot and steamy. This is not the high, dry climate of the bushveld; it is tropical, and after a few days there one becomes languid and disinclined to move. I know because I have stayed there for long stretches three times. Because those times were separated by periods of years, I know three Umtalis, and on that day I went back, dropping fast down the mountainside into it, those three towns remained separate from each other and from the town I saw then.

The first time I was eleven and I had never stayed away from home before except for boarding school. It was in a tiny house at the very bottom of Main Street, which is three miles long; the upper end of Main Street was respectable and rich, but the lower end was poor and near the railway. The house was of wood—wooden walls and floor, and lifted high off the earth on a platform, in the old style. It was in a small, fenced garden, crammed with pawpaw trees, avocado pear trees, mangoes, guavas; and around the fence nasturtiums grew as thick and bright and luxuriant as swamp-flowers. That garden quivered with heat and dampness. Under the thick shade of the mangoes the earth was sticky with fallen, decaying fruit and green with moss. The house was crammed, too; it was a large family; but I cannot remember the other children, only Cynthia, who was fourteen and therefore very grown up in my eyes. The others were all boys; and the two women, Cynthia and her mother, despised the men of the family utterly and all the time. Mrs. Millar was a big, dark, ruddy-skinned woman with heavy black hair and black, full eyes. She was like a big laying hen. Cynthia was the same, a dark, big girl, full-bosomed, with fierce red cheeks. The father was a little man, wispy and ineffectual and pathetically humorous, making bad jokes against his wife's bitter scorn of him because he had a small job as a clerk in a hardware shop. They were gentlefolk, so they said all the time; and this job and what he earned made it impossible to keep up the standards they wanted. And certainly they were very poor. I had always imagined our family was; but my mother's generous scattiness over money was luckily always too strong for my father's prudence; so that no matter how he laboured over the accounts, emerging on a Sunday morning with incontrovertible proof that we could not afford this or that, she would look at him with the stubborn wistfulness of a deprived small child and say: 'Why don't you get some out of the bank?' 'But, damn it, you have to put money into a bank before you can get it out.' 'Then get a loan from the Land Bank.'

'But we've already had a loan; we can't have any more.'
'Nonsense!' she would say at last with determination.
'Nonsense!'

Not so in the Millar household, where Mamma would
tell the guilty family the exact cost of the meal they must
be thankful they were about to receive—they were religious. Or rather, she and her daughter were. I had
imagined I was persecuted by religion, and had rebelled
against it; but religion with us never intruded too un-
comfortably into practical life.

But the difference between the Millars and ourselves
that made me most uneasy was this insistence on being
gentlefolk. It was a word that I had never heard before
out of novels.

Once again, it was the fortunate clash of temperaments
between my parents that saved us from it, for while my
mother was nothing if not conscious of having come down
in the world, my father was oblivious to all such things,
and had, in fact, emigrated from England to be rid of the
whole business of being respectable. And so, when she
was in one of her organizing moods, he would merely
listen, with irritable patience, until she had finished, and
say: 'O *Lord,* old girl, do as you like, but leave me alone.'

But the little house near the railway lines, which was
shaken day and night by the shunting trains, almost under
the great water-tanks which dripped and splashed over the
mango trees—that house which would have been a perfect
setting for one of Somerset Maugham's tropical dramas
was, in fact, saturated with the atmosphere of coy, brave,
decaying gentility that finds its finest expression in Louisa
Alcott's *Little Women.* Yet there were two women in that
house to, I think, five males.

Mother and daughter would sew, knit, patch, darn,
sitting together on the verandah, a unit of intense femininity, exchanging confidences in a low voice, while father

and sons would hastily slip out of the house, father to the bar, sons to their friends' houses.

And when the father returned, fuddled and apologetic, mother and daughter would raise their eyes from their sewing, exchange understanding glances, and let out in unison a deep, loud sigh, before dropping them again to their work, while the little man slunk past.

I was appalled and fascinated by the talk of the two females, for such confidences were not possible in our house. I would sit, listening, burning with shame, for I was not yet in a position to contribute anything of my own.

I was there six weeks. At night I used to lie in the bed across the tiny room from Cynthia and listen while father and mother argued about money in the room next door. One could hear everything through the wooden wall.

'Poor, poor, poor mother,' Cynthia would say in a burning passionate whisper.

I would fall off to sleep, and wake to see her in the light that fell through the window past the moonflowers and the mango trees, leaning up in bed on her elbow, listening, listening. Listening for what? It reminded me of how I used to listen avidly to her talk with her mother. Then a train rumbled in, and stood panting on the rails outside, the water rushed in the tanks, and Cynthia lay down again. 'Go to sleep,' she would hiss in a cross, low voice. 'Go to sleep at once.'

Before I slept I would think of my home, the big mud-walled, grass-roofed house on the kopje where the winds came battering and sweeping, and where I would fall asleep to the sound of my mother playing Chopin and Grieg two rooms off, against the persistent thudding of the tom-tom from the native village down the hill. When I woke the piano would still be sending out its romantic, nostalgic music and the drums still playing. I would imagine how in the compound the people were dancing around the big fire between the little grass-roofed huts while the drummers sat making their interminably repeated and varied rhythms on and on. But the other picture in my mind was not of my mother as she was now, middle-aged and tired, but of an early memory: her long, dark hair knotted low on her neck, bare-shouldered under the light of the candles set at either end of the piano, playing with shut eyes as she, in her turn, remembered something far off and unreachable. And the drums were beating, even then, as long ago as that.

The drums beat through all the nights of my childhood stronger even than the frogs and the crickets, ultimately stronger even than the piano, for when I woke in the morning with the sun standing over the chrome mountain, a single, tired, indefatigable drum was still tapping down the hill. And there came a time when my mother could not trouble to get the piano tuned.

But waking in the house near the railway lines, sweating with heat, half-sick with the sweet smell of the decaying fruit and vegetation outside, it was to see Cynthia and her mother standing together in the corner of the room, hands folded, heads bent in prayer. Then, with a deadly look at her husband Mrs. Millar would say in her womanly resigned voice, 'You can't have bacon *and* eggs—not on what you earn.'

I was badly homesick. I hated that house. I longed for my cool, humorous, stoical mother, who might sentimentally play Chopin, but would afterwards slam down the piano lid with a flat: 'Well, that's *that*.' I wanted, too, to lay certain questions before my father.

When I got home I went in search of him, managed to distract his attention from whatever philosophical problem was engaging him at the time, and remarked that I had had a lovely time at the Millars'.

'That's good,' he said, and gave me a long, sideways look.

'They have grace before every meal,' I said.

'Good Lord,' he said.

'Mr. Millar goes to the bar every night and comes home drunk, and Mrs. Millar prays for his soul.'

'Does she now?'

There was a pause, for I was very uncomfortable.

'Well,' he said, 'what *is* it?'

'Mrs. Millar came on to the verandah one morning, and said in a loud voice to Cynthia. . . .'

'Cynthia? Who's she?'

'Of course you know, she's been here to stay.'

'Has she? I suppose so. Lord, you don't mean *that* girl—very well, go on.'

'She said in a loud voice to Cynthia, "I've been praying Cynthia. O Cynthia, our *horrible, horrible* bodies!" '

I was hot all over. Never had anything made me as uncomfortable and wretched as that moment. But my father had shot me a startled look and gone red. He struggled for a moment, then dropped his head on the chair-back and laughed.

I said: 'It wasn't funny. It made me sick.'

'Lord, lord, lord,' said my father, lifting his head to give me an apologetic, embarrassed look between roars. 'Lord, I can see the old hen.'

'Very well,' I said, and walked away with dignity.

I was furious for him laughing; I had known he would laugh. I had come home a week earlier than was arranged to hear that laugh. And so I was able to put that unpleasant household behind me and forget it. My father could always be relied on in these matters.

*   *   *   *

Living down by the railway line, the upper part of the

town was represented by three houses where the Millars, mother and daughter, with the painful writhings of inverted snobbery, permitted themselves to be accepted—as they saw it. The inhabitants of the three houses were certainly innocent of the condescension ascribed to them. Living with the Millars, I knew the lower mile of Main Street and its shops, particularly the Indian shops which had cheap cottons and silks from the East. Mrs. Millar would send Cynthia and myself up to Shingadia's for half a yard of satin and a reel of sewing silk, and Cynthia walked proud and slow up Main Street, and into the Indian shop, her eyes busy for signs of the enemy, those girls who bought at the big stores farther up the street, and would certainly despise her if they saw her in Shingadia's.

And if one of these envied girls came in sight, as likely as not on her way to Shingadia's, she would turn to face her, head high, dark eyes burning, waiting to say in the voice of an exiled duchess: 'I have come to buy mother a yard of *crêpe de Chine*.' Then, the encounter over, we would walk back, and I waited for that moment when she would sigh and say: 'It's so horrible to be poor. It's horrible to have people despising you.'

Three years later I returned to Umtali to the upper part of the town for a two months' stay with a childless elderly couple who liked to have young people in the house. And the house by the railway line was part of an old nightmare, for the Millars had gone. White people are always flitting from town to town, as restless as the Africans who move from Reserve to town and back again throughout their lives. For most people are in the Service or on the railways, and must expect to be moved from one part of the country to another; most are in any case afflicted with wanderlust, or they wouldn't be in the colony at all. The Millars had gone to Bulawayo, a scattered town that does not have a long, central spine of a Main Street shading

from small, ugly, poor houses to big, beautiful ones—and
what material would those two women have now for their
fantasies of proud, persecuted poverty?

The elderly couple's house was large and darkened by
cedrilatoona trees that stood in clumps all round it, whose
glossy fronds of leaves kept up a perpetual susurration day
and night, as if one were on a green and murmuring island
on a lake. The golden-shower creeper that draped the roof
and the walls filled the rooms with its sweet honey-smell;
and blocked out the small light that came through the
massed trees. And inside books darkened every room. I
came, then, from the house on the kopje into a warm
darkness, where Mr. Boles, who was a journalist, lay in
bed until lunchtime under a heap of newspapers and
books; and Mrs. Boles lay in a bed opposite sleeping
endlessly under a vast silk eiderdown.

I was not permitted to disturb them until lunchtime;
but the night before I'd be given a list of shopping to
do by Mrs. Boles; and I spent the mornings sauntering up
and down Main Street, brilliant with its flame trees and its
bordering gardens, visiting all the shops and particularly
Shingadia's, because Mrs. Boles who had a thousand cousins, nieces and nephews was always sending them pres-
ents; and she would give me an extra pound note and tell
me to go and snap up any bargains there might be in
town.

When I knocked at the door of that dark room, at one
o'clock, she was sitting up in bed, an enormous mass of
loose flesh, with her grey hair straggling, exchanging
love-talk with her old husband across the room; she would
demand to see what I had bought, and as I spilled flowered muslins, bright cottons and sheaves of shining *crêpe
de Chine* all over her bed, she would snatch them up, hold
them to her face and cry: 'Oh, how beautiful! Oh, how

clever of you. Oh, no, I can't send them away. You must call in Miss Betty and she'll make you some dresses.'

Miss Betty, an old, frail English spinster, lived almost entirely off Mrs. Boles' generosity; and in the afternoons, when Mr. Boles had gone to the offices of the newspaper he worked for, the three of us stayed in the dim living-room, discussing the materials that lay glimmering and glowing over the floor and the furniture, and how they should be made, and if that would suit cousin Elizabeth, and this niece Jane.

They were very good to me, that old couple, and I loved them dearly; though it was not until long after that I understood the pathos of Mrs. Boles, that gigantic and hideous old woman who had wanted children and could not have them, and who had been beautiful and elegant, and now must direct her passion for pretty clothes and materials towards other people.

Mr. Boles always addressed her in the tenderest tones: 'My little dove, my little heart, my beautiful little girl'; and she spoke to him like a spoilt young bride. Once he saw my incredulous, embarrassed face, and, waiting until she had left the room, took out of a drawer beside his bed an old photograph of an exquisite young woman in full trailing skirts, and a big flowered hat, with the face of a cool young angel. After that, my puritan disapproval of the way they lived (for I knew what my parents would have said of them) vanished; and I could see that that photograph justified the way he sheltered her, protected her, inquired after her headaches and her aches and pains, for she was tacitly an invalid. There was nothing wrong with her save that she ate too much. They fussed and pampered each other's ailments endlessly, in between discussing what they would have for the next meal: I had never heard such expert attention being given to food; and Mr. Boles would send me two miles downtown to a certain butcher on a certain day of the week for a particular cut of meat. He knew everything about meat, as he knew everything about, it seemed, any subject in the world. 'Facts,' he would say, looking at me over the top of his spectacles. 'Facts. You should be ashamed to be so ignorant. If you want to get on—collect facts.'

All morning in bed he collected facts from books and newspapers piled all over and around and above him. He lived in a cocoon of paper. 'How many miles from the earth to the moon?' he would inquire sternly. 'How many miles is it around the earth? You don't know. I know you don't know. Well, read this. Do you know anything about the habits of the termite? Do you understand the chemistry of the soil? Of course not.' And he thrust into my hands half a dozen books and cross-examined me about them afterwards.

He wore a hat on top of his long, yellowing white hair, a thick jersey over his pyjamas, and between long, narrow, sarcastic lips was always clenched a pipe.

'My little bird,' he would say to his hulking old wife. 'Do you know how many miles from here to Venus?'

'No, my sweetheart, no, my angel, you know I don't.'

'No, I know.' And he puffed with satisfaction at his pipe.

Mrs. Boles was content to be stupid; and she would gaze fondly at her clever husband from her bed where she was reading some love-story. One of my duties was to read to her, but I never got farther than half a page, for Mr. Boles listened, his long, white moustaches writhing with incredulous scorn, while she gave him nervous glances and my voice faltered to a stop. 'You cannot fill that child's mind with that nauseating rubbish.'

'No, my heart, no, my dove.' And she took back the romance from my hand and patiently read it to herself with her weak red-rimmed eyes.

Mr. Boles was an old China hand, and spent many hours enlightening my political ignorance about the Far East. He was Far Eastern expert for the newspaper, and no crisis occurred anywhere beyond the Mediterranean without an illuminating article from him. It was he who greeted the Communist revolution in China with the words: 'There have always been war-lords in China,' and he who put Mr. Nehru in his place when he became Prime Minister of India with: 'Familiar as I am with Bombay bazaar agitators. . . .'

Several years later, in another town, just after I had read a paper to the Left Club on the Chinese Revolution, I got a message from him to go to his office in the newspaper building. I went at once, and found him behind his desk, his long hair on his neck, his long moustaches drooping as usual over thin, cold lips, his hat on his head and a scarf around his neck in case of draughts. It was a very hot afternoon just before the rains.

'Sit down,' he said. I sat, unwillingly, for if I say that at that time I was politically active the phrase can give no idea of the amount of agitation I and my fellow Socialists got through in a week. We considered a day wasted in which we had not been to at least four meetings, after we had done a full day's work in our respective offices.

Mr. Boles told me a long story about how a group of anarchists had blown up a power station in Japan in, I think, 1905. I listened patiently, critical of the deplorable tactics of these misguided revolutionaries, for I was at that time undergoing a thorough course based on the *Short History of the Communist Party of the Soviet Union* (*B.*).

When he had finished, I said, puzzled, 'Well?'

He was watching my face with cold, narrow, blue eyes.

'I wanted to let you know,' said he, 'that we have our eyes on the power-station.'

Since I was late for a meeting, I thanked him and hurried off; it was some days before I had time to think about what he had said; and even so it was months before it occurred to me that he had been warning me that the C.I.D., because of his vigilance and political *nous,* considered us likely blowers-up of the Salisbury power-station.

The third time I stayed in Umtali was just after the beginning of the war. Most of the young men of the country were being trained there; and the town was crammed with them and their wives. In the day-time we pushed our babies up and down Main Street in their prams, and bargained in Shingadia's; and at night there were enormous wild parties in the hotels. Umtali for the first and, perhaps, the only time in its life was no longer Sleepy Hollow; and my memories of the other two times I had stayed there disintegrated under the pressure of that wild, sad, angry six weeks of war.

But on that day, two months ago, when I saw the little town with its streets of flame trees, in the basin among the mountains, it was its wartime guise that seemed improbable and remote, and it was impossible to remember it full of drunken soldiery and excited, apprehensive wives.

Here I began the business of collecting facts: two of the people I met in Umtali were high in the administration for Native Education, and enthusiastic about Partnership. In the Union of South Africa, they said, opportunities for higher education were diminishing; the Nationalists had said education must fit Africans for their status as inferior beings. But in the Federation things were different. First I must remember, and write truthfully afterwards, that what education the Africans would get was exactly the same as white children got, and that they could work knowing that at the end of their labours there might be a place for them at the university, that the Government secondary schools now being built were as fine as any built for white children.

There is a five-year plan for African education. At the moment about 60 per cent of African children get some kind of an education, but mostly this means three or four years in a kraal school under a teacher with six or eight year's schooling. Last year, 1955, 5,000 Africans completed Standard VI—that is, what white children are expected to pass at the age of twelve.

The five-year plan will train teachers, some 4,000 of them, so that in the village schools 75 per cent will have teacher-training certificates and so that the children will pass Standard III—that is, five years of schooling.

I was instructed in the importance of this plan, this advance made possible by Federation and the new spirit, for some hours, and I became infected with optimism. In fact, I must confess that for about two weeks I was carried away by Partnership, partly because I wanted so much to believe in it, but mostly because the people who were selling it to me were so convinced by it themselves.

An ironical thing has happened: people who have been known for years as wild revolutionaries, dangerous citizens, are now sucked into Partnership. These two men in Umtali I remember being spoken of as Communists and rebels fifteen years ago; of course they were nothing of the sort; but old-fashioned liberalism in this part of the world is indistinguishable in the minds of the white voters from the extreme forms of sedition. And people who have felt themselves in a minority for so long, people called every kind of Kaffir-lover—how can they not see themselves as crusaders in some kind of a New Deal?

It was not until three weeks later that I saw this education plan in perspective, instructed by another member of Native Education thus: that this trumpeted figure of £12,-

500,000 to be spent over the five years is only £2,500,000 more than would have been spent in any case. That in presenting this plan to the outside world, the Government speaks of £12,500,000, while in soothing the resentful white people, they stress the £2,500,000. Because the white people resent spending money on African education, the poll-tax has been raised from £1 to £2 a head. This is felt to be unfair by the Africans, since white children are educated free.

Most of the education is still in the hands of the missionaries—without the missionaries there would have been no education at all until just recently—who charge small fees; whereas Government schools are free. So Africans try to send their children to relatives in the town, which is difficult, because the towns are so overcrowded. An African family often spends as much as £8 a year on getting a child educated, in addition to this increase in poll-tax, and the village schools are built by the parents themselves.

In short, it is a hardship and a sacrifice to get an African child educated; yet the white people are bitter because of money spent on African education; for it is taken for granted by white citizenry that all the wealth of the country is created by them and that whatever is 'done' for the Africans is a favour on their part.

It was on that first afternoon in Umtali that the note was struck which was sounded so often afterwards, and in so many keys, that I soon recognized it as the theme of Partnership.

The man who is running a Teacher Training College, the first in the country, who devotes fifteen devoted and enthusiastic hours a day to it, said: 'I supervise all the meals myself, I see that things are done properly, European food and proper china and cutlery, not the usual tin plates and maize porridge. *But I hope to God the white people don't get to know about this.*'

The architects of Partnership, which in essence is a last-ditch attempt to stave off an explosion of African bitterness, which is a policy of intelligent self-interest, lie awake at nights not because of the Africans, but because the white voters might suddenly put the brake on.

As I write (July 9th) I see that a 'Voice of the People Committee' has been formed in Salisbury, because they feel African advancement is being pushed forward too rapidly. 'We support African advancement at the right pace. But it is useless and dangerous to try to achieve in 60 or 100 years the level of advancement which it took the people of Britain 1,000 years to reach. It is our view that most people of this country think the same.'

This is the authentic voice of white settlerdom. But what the people of the country—that is, the Africans—think about matters like the doubled poll-tax or segregation at the university is that if the only way they can get education is to humour the spirit of white supremacy, then humour it they will. It is as if a mad dog lay sleeping, which both the Africans and the intelligent among the white people watch fearfully, thinking, 'Perhaps it might die in its sleep!'

It is a phenomenon which never ceases to fascinate and puzzle me, this unreasoning spirit of self-destruction that is seen at its clearest in white-settler countries. How is it that a tiny handful of white people, surrounded by a mass of black people who could overwhelm them if they wanted—how is it that they persist in a policy that led to the massacres of Kenya, to the slow, bitter stalemate of racial antagonism in the Union?

I remember hearing Lord Malvern, then Dr. Huggins, addressing a farmer's meeting in Lomagundi when I was a little girl. He said that the white people must create a class of privileged blacks to act as a bulwark against revolt.

They shouted at him: 'Who's going to pay for it?' And 'Get back to the operating table.' And 'Kaffir-lover!'

What Partnership is actually doing is to give a few privileges, raising the standards of a minority of Africans above their fellows, *without altering the basic structure of segregation, which is identical with that of the Union,* in the slightest. And even this is regarded by the white people as 'going too fast.'

*   *   *   *

Another conversation in Umtali: we sat on a hilltop from which we looked down over Portuguese territory, and discussed the brutal nature of the Portuguese Government.

There is an agreement between the Governments of the two territories, British and Portuguese, by which the police of either country may cross the borders to regain Africans who have escaped one way or the other.

'My cookboy,' said my hostess, 'crossed the mountains into Portuguese East, the police went after him, and found him in a Portuguese prison. He had got up to something he shouldn't. The prisoners had their hands tied behind their backs with wire. To feed them the police emptied buckets of mealie porridge on to the ground inside the prison gates, and the prisoners had to go down on their hands and knees with their hands still tied and eat it off the earth like dogs with their mouths. They are savages, these Portuguese. Can you believe anybody would treat human beings like that? You'd think that after living next to us, next to British territory for so long, they'd have learned to behave decently. After all, I think we treat our natives nicely.'

I transcribe here a conversation I had later with Dixon Konkola, President of the African T.U.C. of Northern Rhodesia, President of the African Railway Workers'

Union of the Federation. Dixon was describing what he had experienced in prison when he was arrested during the campaign against Federation. While he talked, I made notes: the result was published in the *Tribune,* to which thanks are due for permission to reprint this.

'What were you charged with?'

'They arrested me so as to get me out of the way during the campaign.'

'Yes, but what was the reason?'

'Because I was telling my people the truth about Federation.'

'Yes, but they must have made a charge?'

'They call it breaking the peace. Yes, I believe that time it was inciting to breaking the peace. They arrested me and took me to the train at night. They wanted me out of Broken Hill away from the people who knew me. They put me on carefully so no one would know. I was handcuffed. I was put on to the top bunk and I lay there for seven hours of the journey with my hands hitched up to the rope that goes across the top of the compartment. It was cold because it was winter and I only had shorts on. In the early morning a white woman came down the passage and saw me up there and she was sorry for me and wanted to give me some tea, but was told that it was not permitted to give tea to prisoners.

'I was in the general prison doing tailoring. It was not hard work, but for the men doing work outside it was very hard. But I would not eat because they gave us nothing but hard lumps of cold porridge and black beans. So they put me into the punishment cell. I was alone. I had one blanket and only shorts on. Sometimes they threw buckets of cold water on to the floor where I was because I was being punished. I was there some days, then I went back to the general prison. After a few days there were protests among the prisoners about the food, and I was told, "We know who is making the trouble. You are a trouble-maker. If you don't stop you won't ever leave here alive."

'I said: "If I die here my people will know who killed me, they will say you killed me." Then the District Commissioner came to see me. He is the official charged to watch prisons; but he is also a judge in his own courts. He asked what I was complaining about. I said we worked from six until one, and then the food was lumps of cold porridge and black vegetables, and then from two until six or seven, and more cold porridge and sometimes that thick prison cocoa. I said we had only one blanket and we were crowded in our cells. I went on protesting so they put me in solitary confinement. I was two weeks in the general prison and about four months in solitary. I had nothing to do and I asked for something to read and they gave me the Bible. I read that and said it was not enough, and they gave me a book by a priest who was in Russia during the Revolution describing all the horrors he had seen. But the worst was that my cell was next to the cell where they hang people. They hanged six people while I was there. Usually they take all the prisoners away from that part of the prison when they hang someone, but they left me there to frighten me.

'The first time I was awake all night, it was so terrible. That man came in singing, he was singing hymns right until the moment that he dropped. He had a big sad voice. When they hang someone there are two African warders, and a District Commissioner and a doctor and the Superintendent and a priest. The Roman Catholics are always there. There is a hole in the corner of the cell where they hang the man up and then they let him drop and they all run away. I heard their feet clattering as they all ran away down the passage because they didn't want to stay. But I was next door listening. Half an hour later they came back to make sure he was dead. When you hear a man being hanged—it's not something I can tell. I kept thinking, that is a man's life ending, that is a life ending. I could never sleep in that place.

'I did not serve my full sentence in spite of their threats.

'But for political people like me it's bad enough, but what about those who are there always? I keep thinking about the people I saw in prison. There was a man there who got in when he was a young boy and he may be there all his life. He was an animal after all that time. And I saw an old man let out after many years, and he didn't know what to do or where to go. They let the relatives come, but relatives forget you if you are in so long. The old man stood outside the gate frightened of everything he saw. I often think of him. And the women—that's even worse, how the women get when they are a long time in prison. And the prison is so crowded, so many people in a cell. Terrible things happen. I am embarrassed to tell you because you are a woman.

'But what is worse than anything, what hurts most is that even in prison there is colour discrimination. Even there. The white prisoners are in one place with good food, and they aren't treated roughly. When I found that even in prison we were treated according to colour then I really understood injustice.'

The other matter we discussed was how the Portuguese administrator just over the border takes money from Southern Rhodesian farmers to press-gang Africans for work on the farms.

Before I left Umtali I was finally instructed thus:

'I would have no time for any journalist who did not make a point of the two following facts: (1) The system consists of vicious circles: for instance, that the Africans are poor, and therefore their education is poor, and therefore they are poor. (2) Those countries in Africa which are most poor are those without a white administration: Bechuanaland, for instance, is miserably poor. In this country every man, woman and child (white) is taxed £10 a year for African education. For God's sake don't tell them so, or they'll go up in smoke. Of course you can say that it is the labour of the Africans that provides the money and that sort of thing, but suppose the white population of this country doubled, it would double the number of people who have to pay £10 a year.'

I transcribe this direct from my notes, without altering a word of it, because the man who said it is known as a Socialist, and it is an example of how a colour-bar society pressures economic thinking into strange, strange shapes.

IV

BACK IN SALISBURY again. A gathering of people, members of the new interracial society, who are very advanced because they invite Africans and Indians and coloured people to their homes.

One interracialist was very angry because the Government is importing Greeks and Italians, 'wops and dagos, the scum of the earth,' into the country, instead of advancing the Africans, the people of the land.

'I don't mind being considered the equal of an educated African, but I object to any dregs from Europe being my equal simply because they have white skins.'

This is an interesting and typical example of the phenomenon of Displacement. In a country where people are always conscious of other people's colour or kind, hatred and prejudice are never restricted to coloured people only: you may be sure that a person has passionate views about the dirty Japanese as against the decent Chinese, or vice versa, or the fine, clean Northern European peoples like the Germans, as against the loathsome French and Italians, and so on. And of course there is anti-Semitism; or a complicated anti-anti-Semitism, thus: The Jews are all right; the Indians are the Jews of Africa.

The business of inviting Africans to dinner, which was begun by members of the interracial society, leads to infinite and intricate argument. Later, when I started interviewing people on what I hoped would be economic policies, this question of inviting Africans to dinner never failed to arise; and I was astonished at the ingenuity of the reasons for disapproving of it. They ranged from the uncompromising old-fashioned 'I don't want my daughter to marry a black man,' with its variations and refinements, such as 'I don't mind if my daughter wants to make a fool of herself, but I'm not having my grandchildren going to segregated schools,' to 'It's not fair to invite a minority of Africans just because they are educated, it's hard on the others,' or 'I don't mind eating with Africans but I'm not having them use my lavatory,' or 'They don't want to be invited, it embarrasses them,' or 'If I invite Africans, it's not fair on my servants, they wouldn't like it,' or 'It's artificial to invite Africans to a meal when you can't take them to a restaurant, and you couldn't take them to a show afterwards,' or 'The Africans who get invited to dinner are the political Africans, the Government show-pieces they keep to impress foreign visitors with, and not because of what they are as people, and I don't invite white people to my house on the basis of their politics,' or 'It's nothing but a red-herring, this business of inviting Africans socially, what they want is higher wages and not social condescension.'

There are infinite variations on this theme; in short, it is not possible simply and naturally to invite Africans or people of colour to visit.

I heard a story of a white woman who invited an African teacher to drinks and a meal. As it is illegal for Africans to drink European liquor—a law which intelligent people simply ignore if Africans are guests—she served him with ginger-beer, while her white guests drank ordinary liquor; then she sent him to the kitchen to take his meal with her cookboy while her other guests ate with her. She was overcome by her progressiveness and deeply hurt when the teacher refused her next invitation—he was ungrateful, she felt.

Wanting to visit an old friend of mine in Harari, the African township near Salisbury, I had to apply for permission to the Native Department, and was told: 'We do not encourage visiting between white and black; besides, there is a lot of immorality going on, there oughtn't to be, but there is. If you want to meet natives socially why don't you get them invited to a white house and then there is no problem.' And finally, when I insisted on meeting my friends in their own house: 'If you wanted to hold a meeting, we'd give you a permit for the whole day.' This rather surprised me, until the obliging official hastened to explain: 'We always have our men at the meetings so that we know what is going on, but social visits are discouraged, they lead to all sorts of complications.'

I got my permit for two hours, which I treasure as a souvenir of Partnership.

*   *   *   *

I flew down to Johannesburg trying to recapture the mood I went south in, in the past, the many times I entered the Union. For me going south was going to the big cities, for I was locked in Southern Rhodesia for years, wanting all the time to know something bigger, to know Europe. For years it was impossible to leave, and so going to the Union was a small form of escape. Johannesburg was then the big city to me; and Cape Town meant the sea, for living land-locked in the highveld I used to hunger for the sea so that it became a mania. That moment when, after five days in the slow, hot, dusty train I smelt the sea at last, and a blue stretch of water and the masts and funnels and hulls of ships appeared between the factories at water-level on the Cape Flats—that moment was always an explosion of relief after a long stretch of tension and nostalgia. I used to travel towards South Africa like someone being allowed, briefly, out of prison.

Although this time I was not sure whether I would be allowed in, it is hard to believe one can be kept out of a country that has meant so much to one as South Africa has to me; and in any case that frontier at the Limpopo has not seemed to me important, since it is at the Zambezi that the frontier between segregation and the Protectorates has always been; and so when I saw the great mine-dumps of the Reef, I thought that soon I would be seeing my friends, whom I have not seen for a long time, since they are mostly not allowed out, being either former Communists or people 'named' as Communists.

The atmosphere in the Jan Smuts airport immediately warned me; every person in it is a member of the Special Branch of the police, down to the girl selling cigarettes, and one feels the tight, suspicious watchfulness of the place at once. We sat waiting in the outside room while the plane-lists were checked against the black lists of the police. Then my name was called first, and I went into the room next door, and I knew I was already on the way out. There were two tables in the immigration room, one with a pleasant young man behind it, who dealt fast and politely with respectable people and one manned by the worst type of Afrikaner official—and there is no worse type of official, rude, overbearing, boorishly sarcastic.

Since they already had my name from the plane-list, he went through my immigration form and my passport as a matter of form, though the fact that I was born in Persia caused him particular annoyance: the first time I went into the Union in 1937 I was taken off the train while the immigration officials telephoned Pretoria for a ruling as to whether I was an Asiatic or not: the movements of people from Asia are strictly controlled in Southern Africa, and had I been one I would not have been allowed in without special forms, if at all.

Finally this man went off to telephone Pretoria again, and I sat and waited, watching men in plain clothes emerge from various strategic points. It must cost the Union Government a great deal of money to keep so many policemen on hand for those comparatively rare occasions when they have to throw somebody out.

Finally I was told I was a prohibited immigrant and must go back on the same plane I came in on. I said to the man who told me this, a tall, thin, worried-looking individual, obviously embarrassed by the situation, that it would be better if the Union published a list of their prohibited immigrants so that we would not waste money, whereupon he said that 'this sort of thing happens in other countries, doesn't it?'—by which he meant to say that since movement in and out of Communist countries is controlled his Government is entitled to do the same, an argument one does not have to travel to South Africa to hear.

Meantime, the first official, grinning with spiteful delight at having caught out another enemy of the State, was nudging me on towards the plane, and thus, escorted by a posse of plain-clothes men, I was put back on the plane, and instructed to sit by myself and away from the

window. Presumably this last was in case I might jump
through it, or throw a bomb through it—I don't know,
but it annoyed me.

I was, in fact, very upset. Particularly as, not being a
romantic about politics and thinking, as so many people
apparently do, 'the greater the oppression the sooner the
day of liberation,' I believe that the present regime in
South Africa will last a very long time. It will be a long
time before I can go back. It is a State which is designed
on every level to prevent the Africans from rebelling, to
keep them as helots; it is a completely logical and very
efficient system—that is, it is politically efficient, for
apartheid will keep the country poor and backwards and
will slowly corrupt it. *Apartheid* means, inevitably, isolation from the rest of the world. It means that the white
people, increasingly soft with that self-pity which I have
already mentioned, and which is the most remarkable symptom of 'white civilisation' on the defensive, will become
more and more brutal and warped.

I have asked several people recently, liberals from
South Africa, if they thought there was any chance of the
Nationalists being thrown out. None by parliamentary
means, they said. Or by an effective revolt from the Africans? No—the state is too efficient. Then it will all go
on indefinitely? No; it will collapse under the burden of its
corruption. How do you define corruption here? For one
thing, crime—the figures for violent crime are staggering,
higher than anywhere in the world. Everyone is afraid all
the time. There are no standards in public life; everything
is bribery and chicanery. The white youth are by definition corrupt, drinking, drugging, interested in nothing but
pleasure.

All this is bad but does not necessarily destroy a
State.

It can't go on; it simply can't go on like this, they say.

Personally I think it can go on. The forecast I agree with is this: the value the Union has to the power centre of the world—America—is that it now produces uranium in large quantities. Also gold. Provided uranium and gold continue to come out of South Africa, the Nationalists will be free to do as they like. South Africa will become poorer, more backwards, intellectually and morally corrupt, a place of sporadic race riots, violence, crime, prisons, internment camps, fear. I believe that we tend to think in terms of dramatic alternatives: 'The Africans will revolt.' 'Liberal opinion will throw the Nationalists out.' But a country can just as well dwindle into decay and stagnation.

I do not believe that South Africa can save itself; it is in a deadlock. But it could be saved by economic pressure from outside: it might be forced into sanity if progressive opinion abroad took forcible action. Even so, I think the Nationalists would prefer to become backveld peasant farmers in complete isolation from the rest of the world, rather than give up their dream of racial purity.

To understand the Nationalists, one must read a history of Paul Kruger. Having once grasped the essential fact that this shrewd, grasping, bigoted peasant is their national type or ideal, one should read Harry Bloom's *The Incident* which is an absolutely accurate description of the miserable racial conflict which goes on in the Union now. Then one should have a good enough idea of the sick, suffering flesh which clothes the bones of the country— uranium, gold, diamonds.

And it is such a beautiful country—beautiful, and potentially so rich.

Well, so I went back to Salisbury and consoled myself

with the thought that there was, after all, plenty to see in Central Africa, plenty to do in the short time I had.

Almost immediately I was rather deviously summoned by a man in a high position for an interview. Unfortunately I cannot describe this ironical and interesting encounter, for I promised I would not; but the essence of the thing was that I was only in Southern Rhodesia at all because of the personal intervention of this high personage and that if I crossed the Zambezi to Northern Rhodesia and Nyasaland I could expect to be deported at once.

This upset me a good deal. To be refused entry into a country one knows and loves is bad enough, but to be told one is on sufferance in a country one has lived in nearly all one's life is very painful.

I am, of course, considered so undesirable in these parts because I am a Communist. But I would not, very likely, be a Communist if I had not lived for twenty-five years in Central Africa. I can easily see why people who have lived all their lives in Britain do not easily take to Communism. Nor do I think they are likely to do so until Communism has proved itself to be as genuinely democratic as it has been claiming to be. I believe that in a decade the Communist countries of the world will be freer, more democratic (in the political, as well as the economic sense of these words) than the Western world, which is rapidly becoming less free, less democratic. If I did not think this I would not remain a Communist. Too many people have been prepared to die for liberty and freedom in the last five hundred years for these words to become mere symbols of an outdated economic system.

For if the first need of a human being is for three square meals a day and a roof over his head—and it is the most sickening hypocrisy to believe anything else—then the second need is the freedom to say what he thinks.

Sometimes it is the first need, more important than food or a roof.

But if one has been brought up in one of those outposts of British democracy, a British colony, it is no education for believing in the middle way, compromise and the rest of the phrases which still have emotional force in Britain—and in no other country in the world.

In short, whatever I am, I have been made so by Central Africa, but this is not the way political police anywhere in the world are likely to reason; and during the next few days I was very impressed by the efficiency of the C.I.D. As I have already said, this is a country where one always knows everything that goes on, because of the smallness of the white population; and I was being continually informed by friends that the C.I.D. had made this or that inquiry, or had said this or that. Not, one would have thought, that they needed to make inquiries, since they seem to have the most detailed information about everything I have done or said since I left home.

All this put me into an uncomfortable frame of mind. Of course, as a Communist one is used to living as if one were plastered all over with labels that have nothing to do with what one thinks or feels; but I have never felt this so strongly as on this last trip home. For the backwardness of these countries is such that the sort of work a Communist does in them (as, for example, the work the South African Communist Party did before it was banned) is exactly the same sort of work a liberal or a progressive churchman does. It is a fight for basic human rights. If I were not a Communist I would be doing exactly the same kind of thing.

It is another parallel between white-settler countries and the United States, which gets into such a state of hysteria about its small Communist Party, and destroys its own civil liberties in the determination to destroy Communism. What sort of a precarious state can Central Africa be in that it gets so excited at the prospect of having one Communist inside its borders for seven weeks? And what —with the worst intentions in the world, and of course I had them—could I do in seven weeks?

But now that I was under high though invisible patronage, officials that had been stuffy and suspicous now became guardedly helpful; and I set out on a round of interviewing and inspection. I spent most of my time doing this for some weeks; but what soon became evident was not the diversity or variety of what was said, but how a single thread ran through what seemed at first to be complicated.

For all these officials said the same things. It is a commonplace that a certain political epoch will feed the same words and phrases into the minds of people who are probably convinced they have thought them up for themselves; but it is a remarkable experience to see this commonplace take flesh.

When I left home the slogans and catchwords were different. Then, everyone was saying that the natives must be advanced slowly; the time was not ripe; you cannot civilise barbarians in under a thousand years. These are the things the majority of white citizens are still saying; but since the recent events in Kenya, which were like a burglar alarm in a rich house, the intelligent whites are frightened and they are all with one voice, but in a variety of phrases, saying: 'We must create a small privileged class of Africans to cushion white supremacy.' It is what Huggins has been saying for years; now it is official policy.

And once having grasped this basic policy, all the contradictions and anomalies fall into place.

Ten years ago the Africans who protested against being described as barbarians with barbaric needs were called agitators and troublemakers; now it is the Africans who demand political rights *for all Africans as distinct from rights for a privileged minority* who can expect to be deported, threatened, imprisoned.

In all these interviews there were two interviews—one during which the phrases of the policy were offered to me; and an unofficial interview which I was asked not to quote. But what was said off the record was always the same: 'We have a small, a very small chance of avoiding a racial flare-up, of making Partnership work. If African nationalism does not become unmanagable, if the spirit of white settlerdom does not revolt against Mr. Todd and his enthusiasts, then perhaps we may avoid what is happening in the Union, what has happened in Kenya. We must create a middle-class of African quickly.'

And so with the white trade-union leaders, who, having accepted a policy whereby Africans are workers by law, and thus able to join multi-racial trade unions, so that African trade unionism may be controlled and directed—these men are frightened that the mass of the white trade unionists may flare into hostility, refusing to accept Africans as fellow-workers, even in their own self-interest.

The chief block to African advancement in Central Africa, as in the Union of South Africa, is organised white labour. A white artisan is a white man first and a worker second. The proud traditions of the British Labour Movement suffer a strange transformation in Africa. There are no more colour-conscious people than the white artisans; yet, if reproached with their attitude towards the Africans, they reply: 'All we say is that any job must be paid at the same rates.' Which sounds fair enough. But an African labourer, in 1956, in Southern Rhodesia, earns about £3 or £4 a month, plus food and housing which cost the employer about £2 10s. a month. A white artisan can earn £70 or £80 a month. On the Copper Belt the comparable figures are: African workers £6 to £10 a month, white workers £150 to £200 a month. Impossible for an employer to pay an African 'white' rates, for it would cut at the root of the colour structure. Therefore the white trade-union demand for equal pay preserves skilled work for white workers. In Southern Rhodesia it is impossible for an African to do skilled work, except in the building industry; and then only outside limits within which it is saved for white artisans. In June the Government enforced a law saying that any African employed by a building firm within these territorial limits must be paid the same rates as white workers: the opposition came from the African building workers—immediately, rather than pay the same wages, employers began sacking their African workmen.

And so there is the anomalous position where the chief support for abolishing or modifying the industrial colour bar comes from the industrialists: even if wages were three or four times as high as they are now, it would be much cheaper to employ African labour than white labour. A slow battle goes on between the Government (expressing the needs of the industrialists) and the white workers, who are being forced, step by step, to release certain categories of less skilled work to Africans. A category of work is 'released' when there are enough Africans skilled enough to take over all that class of work within a particular industry. For it is degrading for the white worker to work alongside an African. Recently, on the Copper Belt, the copper companies forced the white mineworkers' union to release twenty-four categories of semi-skilled work. Next week the white workers came out on strike: the employers had put on three African pipe-fitters when there were still white pipe-fitters on the job. This was an insult to white labour. The strike succeeded; the companies have agreed to keep these categories 'white' until they can be taken over entirely by Africans—no mixing of the colours on the job.

And yet on the Copper Belt I was told by a mine official: 'And after all that fuss, on such and such a mine Africans are actually doing pipe-fitting, and the white workers are saying nothing. One never knows when they are going to lose their tempers and strike.'

There is no place where it is easier to see that colour-feeling is basically money-feeling than here, in spite of all the rationales of racialism. On the building sites one can watch white artisans and black artisans working together: the black men mix the cement and the mortar, lift the bricks and carry them to the white men, who fit the bricks into place on the wall. The black men will be earning a tiny fraction of what the white men earn. And on the Rhokana mine, I saw a great furnace being opened to let the molten waste flow out: five black men on the crowbar, and one white man, working together. The white man would strike if they were paid the same, while they still worked together.

In Southern Rhodesia the white artisans say that Africans are incapable of doing skilled work, as a moral justification for keeping them out; but in Northern Rhodesia, where white labour is concentrated on the Copper Belt, the Industrial Colour Bar is confined to mine-work. There Africans have done skilled building, plumbing, surveying and clerical work for decades.

The white trade-union case is self-contradictory: if the black man is so obviously inferior, why create so many barriers to keep him out? In reply, the white trade union uses the classic language of British trade unionism: the capitalists will exploit the African by paying him less than the rate for the job unless we keep up standards.

The leaders of the white trade unions in Southern Rhodesia are in exactly the same dilemma as the more intelligent of the white politicians: they will not remain in their jobs unless they are voted back into them by white votes; but the majority of their following consider them 'soft' towards the Africans. And it is a fact that many of the white artisans are right to be afraid. Many of them are poor human material; not only are their standards of skill very low, but they are degraded by their attitude towards the Africans, who are, after all, their fellow-workers. Faced with competition from Africans who are avid for education and new skills, with all the irresistible energy of a suppressed people, they know they will go to the wall unless they are protected: white trade-union policy is in essence to protect that section of the white workers who intend to rely not on their skills or their industry or their education, but on the colour of their skins for their standard of living.

The more sensible of the leaders know this, know their position is untenable. Therefore, the difference between what these trade unionists said to me privately, and what they could say publicly, was greater than in any other group of people I interviewed.

'Our white kids,' said one, 'they leave school the minute they legally can, and all they are interested in is the pictures and sport and their girl-friends. In the meantime, these natives are killing themselves to get educated. Well, our white kids have got to pull their socks up or they've had it.' But that is not what they can afford to say to their union members.

In Northern Rhodesia, however, there was an interesting reversal of what was said for publication and what off the record. An official of the white mineworkers' union, of whom the rumour goes that he is an ardent Afrikaner Nationalist and a supporter of *apartheid*, spent three-quarters of an hour putting himself across to me as an old-fashioned liberal interested only in African advancement. It was a most impressive performance; and if I had not previously read his evidence to various commissions and committees, where his voice was the traditional voice of white trade unionism, I might easily have been convinced by him. But the point is that on the Copper Belt there is a vigorous and well-organized African trade union, and he cannot afford to be quoted as an opponent of African advancement. So here the public voice is a liberal coo, mixed with execrations against the machinations of the capitalists who want only to exploit the poor Africans; and the private voice is savagely reactionary.

It was during this interview that the door into his office opened, and an African appeared saying: 'Baas, I want work.' Whereupon the official shouted at the top of his voice: 'Get out of here, go on, get *out*.' At which point, recollecting the presence of the enemy, he hastened to assure me that had a white man entered that door he would have spoken to him in exactly the same tone of voice.

The evening before this interview I spent talking to another of the union officials, who spoke of the Africans in a way in which most white citizens are becoming too self-conscious to speak: filthy, dirty, ignorant, savage, immoral—it was a stream of abuse. The point is that this man was not a South African—for there are thousands of Afrikaners now on the Copper Belt, forming a solid block of white reaction—but an Englishman. He was one of those who became officers during the war and was unable to return to artisan status when it ended; therefore he very logically emigrated to the Rhodesias where he could be a baas.

Time and again it was said to me, either jubilantly or with regret: 'If you want to see the natives badly treated, then you should see the people just out from Britain: they are worse than anyone, much worse than the old Rhodesians.' And: 'We thought that a big influx of immigrants from Britain would strengthen liberal opinion, but not a bit of it.'

In Bulawayo I met a group of young women who had left £7 a week typing jobs in London and were now earning £60, £70, £80 a month. In the accents of the more refined women's magazines, they were complacently exchanging the phrases I have been hearing all my life: 'These Kaffirs are so backwards.' 'In Britain they don't understand our problems.' 'It has taken *us* two thousand years to become civilised. . . .' and so on.

*   *   *   *

Another kind of immigrant: a white man, newly arrived in Southern Rhodesia, full of indignation at the colour bar, goes to the Matopos to Rhodes's grave. He finds two African watchmen on guard.

He says reproachfully: 'How can you allow yourself to guard the grave of the man who enslaved you, who tricked your ancestors out of their land?'

A guard interrupts him: 'Mind, baas! You are treading on the grave.'

*   *   *   *

While the post-war immigrants are not a sympathetic lot, there are no more touching group of people than the white workers who left Britain during the hungry and unemployed 'thirties. In Africa they found, for the first time in their lives, a good standard of living and some sort of security. They were white men. They were baases. At immense cost, often borrowing the money to do it, they left their own country with their wives and families. They had to conform, if they did not have the money to leave again. Some couldn't stand it, and left. They were the best or the luckiest. Some said they would leave when they had saved the money. But when that time came, if it ever did—for if wages are high then so are the standard and cost of living—well, it is a beautiful climate, and in Britain one does not have servants. So they stayed and conformed. And in order to drown their consciences, for they are after all products of the British Labour Movement with its traditions of brotherhood between man and man, they adopt the shabby phrases which justify the colour bar and shout them louder than anyone else.

And the big industrialists, who are all liberals to a man—for to hear them talk one would imagine that the copper mines, gold mines and industries are there solely for the philanthropic purpose of uplifting the African, and it takes quite an effort of will to remember the millions of pounds that flow out to overseas investors—these liberal industrialists never cease to complain about the reactionary white trade unions. Yet the privileged white worker was the deliberate creation of earlier industrialists; and it is a policy which has boomeranged, for there he stands, blocking the path to cheap black labour.

Not, I should imagine, for long: I was told that when the representatives of the World Bank were out reporting on the investment possibilities of Federation, their chief doubt was the shortage of African labour. In a decade, they said, industrialization would be hamstrung for lack of labour, because the industrial colour bar keeps Africans unskilled and inefficient, because it keeps wages down and restricts the internal market and perpetuates poverty, disease, and early death. So far the private investor has not shown much interest in the Federation; it is the public funds which make Kariba and other enterprises possible. Federation considers its future depends on a strong flow of investment—therefore I think the gap between black and white worker will very rapidly narrow. It is already narrowing. Already people are saying that in such and such a factory the white apprentices have been talked into accepting a coloured apprentice; there is a place where an African is working on the same bench with white men; and—most significantly—in such and such a factory all the work is done by Africans. And then, inevitably, with the small grimace of a naughty schoolboy: 'Luckily the whites don't realize what is going on, *or*. . . .'

Oh, these naughty schoolboys, these pleasant amateurs of politics! They are pushed into public life simply because there are so few people available for it. At this moment there are four or five political parties forming to oppose Garfield Todd's men. Looked at from outside, their policies are virtually indistinguishable; they all rest, just like the Federal Party and Mr. Todd's party, on segregation and the Land Apportionment Act. It is the spirit of white settlerdom, still uncertain and wavering, blowing up to form an opposition to even the modified interracialism that exists. But the real difficulty is shortage of men. A party may form, collect half a dozen members, and disintegrate because of the defection of one. This is a place where a man's personality may still count far more than the policy he is supposed to be standing for. Here a man may become a politician scarcely knowing himself how it has happened.

In Central Africa men are not carefully groomed for seats in Parliament, as they are in Britain; they do not serve long apprenticeships on committees and subcommittees. The farmer who speaks more often than most at the farmers' meetings, the businessman who is vocal about some grievance, the man who is in the habit of writing indignant letters to the newspapers—they will find themselves sucked into the legislative assemblies by the sheer force of the general shortage of ability and public experience.

These enthusiastic amateurs, flushed with surprise and success, each with his grievance or hobby which brought him here to sit in the councils of the state, find almost at once that the spirit of the time is welding them all into a body with a single soul. The needs of this time being to give the Africans just enough to keep them quiet, they all become Paternalists.

The Paternalist says that the Africans must be given a square deal; they must have fair play; they must look forward to a place in the sun. The Paternalist, however, does not intend to abolish the Land Apportionment Act or end segregation: such ideas have most likely never entered his head. He wishes there were more money to spend on clinics and hospitals and schools for Africans; the fact that he wishes it makes him feel warm and virtuous; but he does not mean to go so far as to tax the white voters who put him into power so that there should be more public money. The Paternalist will do everything in the world for the Africans short of losing his seat or giving the Africans an equal vote with the white men.

Similar to the kind-hearted Paternalists are the Useful Rebels, public figures in the politics of Central Africa. One, whom I met in Lusaka, is a man known to the white citizens as a Communist; he is, however, a Minister of Government. A very dangerous man, this—he mixes socially with Africans.

We had a conversation; he was explaining to me how wicked Communism was because it did not respect the liberty of the individual. I agreed that I hated as much as he did the massacres and atrocities that have occurred under Communism; but I thought there was a certain incongruity between his belief in liberty and the fact that the administration of which he is a member imprisons Africans by the dozen for being Congress members. I pointed out that Mr. Konkola, President of the T.U.C., had just done time for some political offence. I said that the two Congress leaders, Mr. Nkumbula and Mr. Kaunda, had recently done spells of hard labour for simply being in possession of seditious literature. Whereupon he exclaimed—and this is the immediately recognisable voice of the Useful Rebel—'If I had been here it wouldn't have happened. I was away. When I came back I said how could they be so short-sighted as to imprison these men; it makes such a bad impression.'

Note that the Useful Rebel does not consider himself part of government; he disapproves utterly of it, although he has probably been of it for years. He consents to work with it because he thinks that by doing so he keeps a bad reactionary out. Thus, at every crisis, when he has to do something against his conscience, he never resigns because he thinks: 'No, I must stay, I am at least a Progressive.'

In the meantime he modifies a law slightly here, puts in an oar there, uses his influence somewhere else; but he is never responsible for the wicked things his Government does. And as for the Government, he is a feather in their cap; because if such a well-known Progressive consents to work with them, they can't be so bad, after all.

The Useful Rebel always plays another role, which is that of the Respectable Patron. In any particularly repressive society there are always half a dozen small organizations of people who are an angry minority of critics, but who have to adjust their criticism just this side of the line which will lose them their jobs or get them deported. The Useful Rebel is on the committee or is chairman of these societies. He is necessary, because they have to be respectable. To his Government reactionary friends he says half-laughing, but showing his integrity: 'No, no, they have some very good people, you are wrong. I think they should be supported.' A pause. 'Besides, one should keep an eye on them in case the hotheads take over.' Whenever the society wants to go too far, to pass a forthright resolution, or write a letter to the newspaper which is strongly worded, the Respectable Patron threatens to resign. Now the society is in a difficult position: if their Patron resigns, it means they will be branded in the eyes of the citizens as dangerous and irresponsible. On the other hand, if they continue to give in to their Patron's threats of resignation, then there might just as well not be a society; it is a society without teeth.

In this situation the Patron always wins, and the society either becomes so respectable it has no force at all; or it simply dwindles and dies.

A classic example of this is what happened in an interracial club recently. When the interracial club was started it was considered very advanced and dangerous, but now it is tolerated by the white citizens as perhaps rather eccentric.

People in Britain are shocked because the new University in Salisbury will be segregated. But even more shocking is that, unique among the universities of the world, there is provision that the Government of the day, through the Minister of the Interior, can dismiss any African student at any time without giving reasons for doing so. This provision is expressly and openly for the purpose of getting rid of any agitators that the University might inadvertently produce.

The interracial society wished to pass a resolution against this law; but a Useful Rebel, in his other role of Respectable Patron, said no; the time was not ripe. Of course it was a shocking outrage against liberty and freedom, but if the society pressed on with this resolution, it would get into disrepute with the white citizens which it wished to educate into liberalism. Therefore it was his regrettable duty to resign if the resolution was passed. So the resolution was not passed.

I have known now a good many Useful Rebels. The

end of such a man—that is, if he does not by some political development which makes him particularly useful become Prime Minister—is always a sad one. For the white citizens he remains that Red, that Socialist, that extremist; and when a scapegoat is needed, there he is, ready to be cast out. And cast out he is—if he does not have the sense to resign in good time—bitterly conscious of ingratitude, and rightly so, for without him white supremacy would never last half so long.

As for the Africans, of whom he, of course, considers himself the spokesman—he is the spokesman of African *advancement* as distinct from African independence—the Africans will have no more of him, and say aloud what they have been thinking for so long, that he is the most disgusting hypocrite and a much more dangerous enemy than a forthright opponent like Mr. Strydom.

Luckily, however, he is able to retire into private life. I have never known a Useful Rebel who did not have some job to go back to, or a private income. It is not a role that can be played out without a cushion of some kind. And therefore the bitterness of the ingratitude of mankind is at least suffered in some sort of comfort.

* * * *

Here is a 'profile' which appeared in the newspaper *The African Weekly*, June 6, 1956, published in Salisbury for Africans. Every week there is a feature called 'Prominent Central Africans,' dealing with some African who has distinguished himself. I think this one is particularly interesting, not only because of the story it tells, but because it illustrates the theme of the Useful Rebel in another way. The Federal Party mentioned in this piece, being that which stands for the forcible imposition of Federation against the wishes of the Africans, is boycotted by all but a few of the Africans:

A boy who was appointed prefect at a new school a week after his entry and was made senior prefect after another week, and then boasted to his classmates, 'I shall become great,' has literally become great. He is Isaac Samuriwo.

Starting life as a poor herd-boy who attended calves on a European farm, and who could boast of nothing but 'royal' blood which flowed in his veins, he has risen to become one of Central Africa's most successful African businessmen. Instead of the herds of European cattle he tended as a youngster, he now runs a fleet of buses (three, including one just sold), he is a cartage contractor (with five lorries, three of them new), a building contractor (believed to be the only African operating in the heart of Salisbury), a greengrocer and provision merchant (with wholesale vegetable trade) and general dealer. On top of it all, he is president of the Southern Rhodesia African Association, first president of the Southern Rhodesia African Chamber of Commerce, president of the Southern Rhodesia African Transport Contractors' Association, etc.

Isaac Henzi Samuriwo, son of Chief Samuriwo, was born in October 1913 in his father's kraal in what is now known as the Chihota Reserve, Marandellas District.

His mother, Nvowa Nhora Tshekede, daughter of a brother of Chief Siwundula, now living in the Que Que District, was one of Chief Samuriwo's twenty-six wives.

There were eleven children in Isaac's house, of whom seven were girls. Isaac was the sixth-born.

Isaac first went to school in 1928, attending his kraal school (Samuriwo School). After passing Sub-B he left to work on a European farm. He tended calves for a Mr. 'Folera' in the Enkeldoorn District. Folera was nicknamed 'Gandakanda' by his African employees 'because he was harsh and cruel and beat his workers.' Isaac stayed on the job for five months and progressed from tending calves to leading oxen, 'despite the beatings.'

He returned home, stayed a few months, then went to work in a tobacco barn at a place called Chamboko in Wedza. Here he was joined by two of his half-brothers, both older than himself. But they could not endure the treatment the European farmer meted out to them and they ran away. Isaac stood it for eight months, then returned home to resume his schooling.

After passing Standard I he went to Domboshawa Government School. With him went his elder brother, Chiyangwa. Being sons of a Chief, they were given attendants to accompany them to school, as was then customary. Isaac's attendant was his cousin named Shadrack Kariwo. Chiyangwa failed the entrance-examination and had to return home. Isaac and Shadrack passed and were admitted.

In Standard II Shadrack failed and fell out, leaving Isaac to continue.

Isaac proved a good student. He passed his examinations well. He was ambitious.

While he was doing Standard IV a strike took place among the students and Isaac was suspected of engineering it. The students were sent home. After a while some of them were re-admitted. Isaac received a letter from the principal forbidding him to return. Isaac returned to Domboshawa and pleaded with the principal. He was taken back.

Isaac's influence among the students was dynamic. He formed a group known as 'The Band of Outlaws' which held debates after school hours. The principal naturally looked upon it with disfavour and did not like Isaac very much for it. But the boy did his examinations well and was very loyal to and popular with the teachers.

After doing post-Standard VI in agriculture he went to teach at Jonas School in the Epworth Circuit, at a wage of £2 5s. a month (being an untrained teacher). After three months he left and took up the post of agricultural demonstrator at the Government Experimental Farm, Msengezi, Makwiro. Old demonstrators resented this meteoric promotion of a junior. There were protests and Mr. Samuriwo was transferred to the Gatooma Cotton Ginnery Station. Jealousies followed him there, and he did not last more than three months.

Going to Kwenda he taught agriculture for two years. Then he went to Tjolotjo as a builder, quarrelled with a European over accommodation and was fired. He came to Gwelo and became hide buyer for the Bata Shoe Co. at a wage of £6 10s. a month. He saved some of the money, got a passport and went to the Tsolo School of Agriculture in the Transkei, Cape, for further training.

That was July 1943. He arrived at the school on a Tuesday. The following Monday he was made a prefect. A week after that he became head prefect. He told his class-mates: 'I shall be great.'

Two years afterwards he wrote the final exams and passed in the first class, with a percentage of 80.3. That was in June 1945. In July came his marriage, which he was arranging as he was preparing for the examinations. The bride was Miss Rotina Ntuli, daughter of the head of the Hlubis at Etyeni, Tsolo.

He returned home with a certificate and a wife.

The Education Department offered him a post at Domboshawa as an agricultural instructor. He turned it down, saying, 'I want to be a land development officer.' The Government would not give him that post, which was for Europeans only. Samuriwo went to work for Mr. Meikles at Leachdale Farm, Shangani. He received good pay and treatment. After a year he left and bought a secondhand lorry, which he drove in Harare, Salisbury, carting sand, bricks and firewood. He made money and bought a new bus for £2,300. Before it was fully insured he drove it home to the Chihota Reserve on a third party cover to show it to relatives. A half-brother out of his senses set fire to it, and it was completely destroyed.

Mr. Samuriwo came back to Salisbury and drove his old lorry. He rebuilt the business, sold the old vehicle and bought a new one. Then he bought a diesel bus. Then another bus. Then he built two stores—one at Mt. Darwin, one at Chiweshe. Soon afterwards he established two stores in the Chihota Reserve, one in Salisbury, and a service station in Chihota. Recently he has acquired three new lorries.

He says he owes all this success to truth, hard work and fearlessness.

In politics he is not unknown. Soon after his return from the Cape he took an interest in the Southern Rhodesia African Association, whose membership includes a number of chiefs. Before long he was appointed its vice-president, eventually president. When a branch of the Federal Party was established in Harare he was chosen its first chairman. For some time he was a member of the Harare location advisory board and one of the location's streets is named after him.

Mr. Samuriwo is the first president of the Southern

Rhodesia African Chamber of Commerce and is now president of the Southern Rhodesia African Transport Operators' Association. He is an agricultural and horticultural advisor in Salisbury, a building contractor, a cartage contractor, greengrocer and provision merchant and general dealer.

V

FOR TWO WEEKS I had been meeting Partners, Useful Rebels, Interracialists and supporters of the new anti-colour-bar society, Capricorn. I had attended a Capricorn meeting addressed by Colonel Stirling and Laurens van der Post and seen something that would have been impossible eight years ago: a white audience applauding a black man. In 1943 a few members of the Labour Party held a meeting in a Native Township where such matters as the Passes Act and the Destocking Act were discussed. This meeting caused such a furore among the citizenry, such a flood of newspaper leaders, angry letters signed 'Pro Patria' and anonymous letters that ultimately it led to the breaking up of the Labour Party. A decade ago the Labour Party split on the issue of whether there should be an African Branch of the party. Now, in 1956, I heard five hundred applauding speeches about racial harmony;

and all the political parties court African membership. Day and night I had been besieged by people who wished me to report that Partnership was an honest policy—people who believed, or rather wished to believe, that it is.

I never did believe it to be true that one has to live in a country to understand what is happening in it. I believe it even less now. One cannot be brought up the daughter of a white settler with impunity; and it is hard to withstand the persuasions of old friends whom one not only likes but respects.

In short, I was on the verge of succumbing to the blandishments of what must be the most effective public relations officers in the world, both official and self-appointed, when I met an old African friend to whom I confessed my state of mind.

He listened with the sardonic good humour with which Africans meet the involuted defences and rationalisations of their white allies, and told me to go off and have another look at the Land Apportionment Act.

He also said that having worked in the Union as well as in Southern Rhodesia he infinitely preferred the Union; and so did most of the Africans he knew who had the opportunity to compare them. '*Apartheid*,' he said, was an honest word, exactly describing the segregation patterns of the Union and also of Southern Rhodesia. 'Partnership' was a typical bit of British hypocrisy. There was nothing he disliked more, he said, than the British liberal, having his cake and eating it; give him the Nationalists every time—they said what they thought and meant. They were honest opponents.

This upset me. I had not suspected that the ghost of a perverted patriotism still lurked among the meshes of the stern pattern of my Socialism; I did not like to think of British Africa being worse than Nationalist South Africa.

But I exorcised the ghost, and set myself to ask all the Africans I met, who knew South Africa, which they preferred. They all said that within the segregation patterns, which were identical, there were much better amenities for Africans in the south: they could shop, for instance, being served on equal terms with the whites. The colour bar was much less rigid. There were hotels and restaurants on a civilised level—only a few, but better than nothing, and there was nothing in Southern Rhodesia.

So I restored myself by a couple of evenings with the Land Apportionment and other Acts.

Briefly, then: Southern Rhodesia has modelled itself on the Union: a law passed down south is always passed within a year or so in Southern Rhodesia, under a different name. The Land Apportionment Act is the basis of Southern Rhodesia policy, as the Group Areas Act is in the Union. In both countries land is parcelled out into areas called Native and European. In Southern Rhodesia only 46 per cent of the land still remains to the Africans. (Whereas in Northern Rhodesia and Nyasaland about 5 per cent has been taken from them.) Since Partnership, this basic segregation has been hardened, not relaxed. Thousands of Africans have been forcibly moved off 'European' land, where they had been living for generations, into Reserves.

Here I quote from that revealing document, the Report on Native Affairs, 1954, signed Mr. J. E. S. Turton, Chief Native Commissioner, Secretary of Native Affairs, and Director of Native Development.

.. It is little appreciated what is involved in one of these mass movements. Land has to be provided to accommodate the Natives, and as prerequisite to the movement, the land has to be developed with roads, water supplies, village sites, dipping facilities and

medical services ... the preparation for movements
have, at the dispatching end, entailed patient expla-
nations to the Natives, and arrangements of minute
precision regarding the timing and loadings with
goods and families, of the Government and private
motor vehicles engaged on the problem of transport.
In some areas where approaches to Native kraals are
limited it has been necessary to set up collecting
areas or transit camps from which the Natives are
collected by Organized Transport. Similar provision
has to be made at the destination, so that all the
Natives moved were subject to as little inconvenience
as was possible in the circumstances. Most movements have been done during the period August to
October, that is after crops have been reaped and
before the onset of the rains, and in all respects
maximum attention has been given to the human
aspect. Thus it is that, although some opposition was
experienced in some districts when movements were
first organized, Natives moved from Crown lands
and other areas have been in fact co-operating extremely well with the administration. It was often
noticeable that the women were the first to put their
shoulders to the wheel in assisting with the preparation of the household and domestic baggage. The
remarks of the Native Commissioner, Gokwe, typify
the attitude of the administrative official and the
Native:

'The never-ending movement of Natives to this
district continues at high pressure. Administrative
and field officers are fully extended to cope with the
necessary developments of virgin areas to accommodate the annual movements. The tempo for settle-
ment is such that we have neither staff nor finances to
launch protective work which is so vital ... the

movement of some 1,500 people with 3,000 head of
cattle was carried out without a hitch and was completed within approximately four weeks.'

. [I would give a good deal to know what those
three dots represent in the report of the Native Commissioner at Gokwe—Author.]

There has been the call for the utmost tact and
consideration from the Native Commissioners concerned to ensure that these Natives settle down without rancour or bitterness towards the administration,
who *alone in their eyes are responsible for the
upheaval.* [Italics mine—Author.]

No major incidents have occurred; and the smooth
running of these mass movements, unnoticed by the
general public, redounds to the credit of the administrative officials.

This note of self-congratulation, almost self-commisera-
tion, is typical of Government publications during this
era. I suspect that at the bottom of their hearts the officials
are sorry for themselves because the Africans are not
grateful for being moved off their land with such tact and
consideration.

Another interesting piece from the same Report: 'October 1954 saw the completion of the first year of Federation, and the Native population for the most part have
accepted the metamorphosis with complete indifference.
There have been the usual vociferous few who have made
the occasion one of maligning the motives of the Europeans, but this was only to have been expected from mal-
contents who in the aggregate live, not by an honest day's
work, but on what they can squeeze from a simple and
credulous Native population who generally see, too late,
hard-earned money passing into the pockets of thieves and
rogues who filch it from them on the pretext of "taking

legal advice or other suitable steps to safeguard the interests of the Natives." Never once has a society or organization of this type published a statement detailing the manner in which donated funds have been spent, and experience has been that they shun any publicity on this aspect of their affairs.' Officials always complain about the venality of African leaders; sometimes they are venal or careless. But this is not a weakness confined to Africans.

Conditions in the cities of Central Africa exactly mirror those in the Union. Around the 'white' centres are African townships and squatters' camps. These are completely segregated. Africans may not use restaurants, hotels, or bars in the white areas. They have special counters in post offices, banks and public buildings. An African leaving his Reserve must carry a variety of passes—his registration certificate in any case, which is a sort of certificate of identity; then his certificate of residence, of work, and—if he is employed as a servant—he must have a 'pass' to go visiting. Thousands of Africans are fined or imprisoned every year for not being in possession of one of these passes.

A few privileged Africans carry a pass exempting them from carrying passes. One of these told me a story of how he had been picked up by the police, since he had left his pass at home, and was taken to the police station where the official said: 'What! They've picked *you* up? They don't know yet you're an old Rhodesian? Off you go.'

It is always a question of grace and favour, the disposition of a particular official. Thus, Salisbury is repressive in the matter of pass offences; whereas in Bulawayo, under the liberal Dr. Ashton, things are much better.

Africans were amused in Salisbury when I was there because Colonel Hartley, the Superintendent, had been complaining that Africans were not to be trusted with money, and therefore he could not allow them to act as gatekeepers for the location football matches. The European gatekeepers he appointed having mislaid a sum of money, Colonel Hartley exclaimed from the depths of his paternal heart: 'How can our people be so irresponsible as to act so, setting such a bad example to these backward natives?'

I quote here a letter to the *African Weekly* which explains how Africans feel about the curfew regulations:

SIR,

The curfew regulations in all the main urban centres of S. Rhodesia which prohibit an African from passing through town after ten o'clock, sometimes nine o'clock, are bringing untold harm to Africans. They restrict all their movements after dark and virtually put them in a 'social box.'

What type of social life is the African expected to have in urban areas? He is expected to go and see bioscope in the Welfare halls. Often he has not got the money to pay at the door, and at times he is not very interested because bioscopes are a new thing to him. We like to play (particularly those of us from Nyasaland) our own games, and dances. To do this we want to get together after work—cookboys, houseboys, garden-boys, and general workers—at a central spot and play our own dances. The problem is how will some of us cross the town after ten o'clock so that we return to our rooms on the other side of the town. We cannot. In that way the curfew regulations are making it difficult for Africans to enrich their social life and organize the dances they used to partake in before coming to town. The cooks and garden workers who do not reside in urban locations are the ones most affected by this.

The argument that Africans would steal a lot of property if permitted to pass through town at night is groundless. They should be permitted to move on the road and pavement. If someone leaves the road and starts getting on to private premises, that one should be arrested and dealt with severely. Even in Europe, America and anywhere in the world no one is permitted to linger in someone's premises without permission.

*   *   *   *

Conversation overheard on a bus:

WHITE CHILD (*aged about* 12): Is your dad going to let you go to the Kaffir college?

WHITE CHILD (*about* 15): Nah, I'm going down to the Cape.

LADY (*from back seat, leaning forward*): My dear children, there have been *Africans* at the Cape Town University for years.

WHITE CHILD: Nah, the Nats have kicked all the Kaffirs out.

*   *   *   *

The Land Apportionment Act has been amended to allow Africans and other people of colour to reside at the University, which is on 'white' land.

It has also been amended to allow representatives of the Indian Government to live in white areas—provided it is understood that the local Indian community does not do so.

As soon as I arrived I was canvassed for support against an Indian couple, official representatives, who had insisted that their child had the right to go to the local white Government school. One man, a journalist, said sourly: 'Yes, and as soon as they had their way, and made a fuss, then what? They haven't even sent their kid to the school. They just wanted to fight on principle so as to make us look silly.'

Later, meeting representatives of the local Indian community, I was told that the parents of this child had had so many anonymous threatening letters that they had not dared send her, for fear of what she might be made to suffer.

The Indians of the three federated territories suffer all the hardships that the Africans do, with minor differences —for instance, they may drink 'European' liquor.

I was told they have petitioned both Lord Malvern and Mr. Garfield Todd for a revision of the colour bars on the grounds that their treatment was inconsistent with Partnership. They got no satisfaction. Easy to see why not: administration, terrified above all of the white voters, would not consider the satisfaction of the comparatively small Indian communities worth losing their seats.

The Indians here, as in the Union, have always been the sore spot of the colour bar. One cannot say of Indians, who have a much older history of civilization than Europeans, that they are barbarous and backwards, yet they are treated just as badly, sometimes worse, than the Africans. The excesses of the colour bar are always due to a bad conscience; and it is the Indians who excite particular venom in the white people.

Mrs. S., the wife of one of the Indian Government representatives, being advanced in pregnancy and feeling tired, attempted to use the lift in one of the big stores. She was pushed out and made to use the stairs.

A charming and cultivated girl, used to intelligent society in New Delhi, after two years' residence in Southern Rhodesia, she showed signs of strain. Mr. S., however, on the evening I was at their house, told anecdotes about the colour bar with zest.

'Imagine, what people!' he said. 'I want a hair-cut. I am told I can only have a hair-cut if I come in after hours through the back door so that no one can see me. So I do, and then I'm charged extra. Fascinating! Extraordinary! Wonderful!' And with savage joy he darted off on another expedition to collect evidence of white imbecility.

* * * *

A trip to a Native Reserve. The office is the same as that which during the war was the Aliens' Office. I know it well, because during the war I was technically an enemy alien by marriage. I was supposed to report once a week, my fingerprints were taken, and I was not allowed to move without permission beyond 50 miles around Salisbury. My husband was a refugee from Hitler, and passionately anti-Nazi; but this made no difference to officialdom.

This was a very interesting experience: first, becoming an enemy alien because of my signature on a bit of paper; then being policed and restricted in my own town; and then ceasing to be an enemy alien because of another bit of paper. The labels stuck on me in this case were so arbitrary, bizarre and incongruous that I could never quite believe that the thing was happening at all. Now, of course, the law has been changed.

But it was certainly a useful apprenticeship to living in the world today.

The official of the Native Department enthusiastically explained to me the provisions of the Native Land Husbandry Act. Its aim is to break the tribal system, under which land is communally owned and distributed through the Chiefs. Land is now being given on the Reserves in plots of one, two, three, four acres to Africans, provided they have given evidence that they are willing to learn husbandry. And, in the words of my guide: 'They have to

be good types, you know; we don't like troublemakers.'
This policy is quite different from what is happening in
South Africa, where Strydom intends Africans to remain
based on the Reserves, going into town to work in the
industries. Under the Husbandry Act, which is regarded
as the key to the new policy, Africans who cannot support
themselves on these plots are expected to leave the Reserves and go into town to work. This is deliberately
creating an industrial proletariat. The land is expected to
be allocated by 1961. As there is a shortage of surveyors,
a scheme is worked out by which the land is photographed
from the air; it is said boundaries can be judged by these
photographs to within a foot either way.

Within the framework of segregation this is a far-
sighted policy. For one thing, since the plots can be left to
only one heir, it will prevent the infinite subdivision of
land among children which has taken place on poor white
farms in the Union, leading to dust-bowl conditions. And
they can be bought and sold, which means, inevitably,
that the efficient will acquire larger plots, and the inefficient must leave the land for the towns. This policy will
save the soil. There are too many Africans for the amount
of land left. They cannot all be supported on it, even with
the policy known as 'destocking' which has caused more
bitterness among Africans than any other.

Cattle traditionally play an important part in the rites
of tribal life. For years the Government has been forcing
the people to sell the beasts which cannot be supported on
the land available.

The Africans hate the Land Husbandry Act. It is a
blow at their traditions, and will divorce them from their
soil. Ninety per cent are still tribal people, who think of
themselves as village folk who make trips into town to
earn some money, from whence they can return to their
own people, their own way of living.

Progressive Africans told me that they could see it was inevitable that their people must become either village or townspeople; what they objected to was the fact that this policy consolidates segregation: 'If they gave us back some of our land, they wouldn't have to force so many of us off. Nor would they have to make us kill so many of our cattle.'

From the point of view of maintaining white supremacy it is a brilliant policy: creating a class of small peasant farmers who are traditionally conservative. To quote again from the Report on Native Affairs, 1954, in a succinct paragraph called 'Political Situation': 'Rapid implementation of Government policy by application of the Native Land Husbandry Act, right throughout all the Native Reserves and areas, is vital to establish and ensure a contented and progressive Native peasant, who, having been divorced from the present communal system of land tenure will, with his individual allocation of land, become aware of a new pride of ownership and aware of a new incentive to adopt better husbandry methods for his own progress. Inevitably he will disregard the political sirens of the industrial areas, who themselves are making no headway with their self-aggrandisement schemes.'

I was taken to the Chinamora Reserve, near Salisbury. We knew the moment the Reserve began, because the road abruptly turned into a sandy, rutted track. As an African said to me: 'No vote; no roads.'

The official was enthusiastic about the Act as it had affected this Reserve. Three years ago, he said, there was not a blade of grass on the place; now the grass was growing up again and erosion had been arrested. There were small dams here and there, and evidence of contour ridging. The villages were of the familiar mud huts, each with its tin-roofed little store and its church.

This is not a typical Reserve because it is so near

Salisbury. Most of the men go into Salisbury to work; the women do the farming. The official said that a class of prosperous small farmer was already emerging, growing vegetables or flowers for sale in Salisbury. They might earn £50 or £60 a month. They were beginning to build European-type houses—brick houses with two or three rooms. Some had proper furniture and ate European-type food.

This official, a pleasant young man obviously very enthusiastic about his work, said: 'It will take three thousand years for them to get civilized.' And then: 'We must create a middle-class with some property.'

Next day I visited a Native Purchase Area. On these, Africans may buy plots of 50 to 200 acres. It is intended that these areas, at present for what the Native Commissioner called 'the upper-class of Native who thinks himself every bit as good as we are,' will ultimately merge with the Reserves, when the small peasants there have consolidated themselves and weeded out the weaker, and enlarged their units of land.

I saw several houses on the Purchase Area. They were like a poor white man's house, brick-walled, with a corrugated-iron roof, and a minimum of furniture.

In each house was the basic family and many sons, daughters and cousins of allied families. The clan pattern is breaking up very slowly into the individual family pattern.

The first house we entered was owned by a friendly fat lady, curtsying at every second step, 'Yes, Madam; no, Madam'; obviously well used to showing off her home to visitors. She had a little orchard of citrus trees, a run of fowls, and was very house-proud.

In the next house was an old man, who said deprecatingly: 'We are very poor people here.' Whereupon the Native Commissioner said sharply: 'But you are much better off than you were.' 'But we are very poor people,' he insisted.

He told me he had paid £10 a year to send his son to Domboshawa Mission to be taught the trade of building; and in return his son had built him his house for nothing. 'My son is very good to me, very good to me,' he insisted, and showed me the photograph of his son and his new daughter-in-law who would come to live in another little house next to his, to help him with his farming.

He earned £100 gross in a good year, £80 in a bad year; grew maize, rapoka, nuts, rice. He sold his rice and maize to the neighbouring European farmers for food for their labourers.

Another homestead was half-way between the African pattern and the European. It was a scattering of half a dozen brick huts, thatched, allocated among the twelve people who lived on this farm. They grew Turkish tobacco, munga, maize. The sons were employed in town. One son ran a lorry service, and helped his parents with the proceeds.

At the back of these houses young women were pounding grain in old-fashioned mortars, or spreading grain on racks to dry.

On one plot, under a light thatched roof open at the sides, about a dozen young women were sorting tobacco. They were hired from a neighbouring Reserve at 1s. a day. Work was going on with much laughter and enjoyment, until we appeared. They obviously resented us.

Employment of Africans by Africans is new. On the Reserve I saw a work-party in progress, which is a traditional way of getting a rush of work done quickly: the host family brews beer and cooks something specially good to eat, and invites friends and relations to do the job. But wages are ousting the work-party.

On another homestead the farmer, who was single and

more prosperous than the others, said that he had employed two men but they had left him. 'They didn't like working for another African,' he said. 'Although I paid them as well as a European farmer, one £2 a month and one £4 a month; and they ate the same food as I did.'

He said he ate mealie porridge, with vegetables he grew, and a fowl for special occasions.

Points made by the Native Commissioner: That all these people had savings-bank accounts. That none had beasts up to the amounts allocated—in this area they are allowed forty-nine beasts each. That all the children went to school up to Standard III—that is, five years' schooling. That the women owned sewing machines.

Both Purchase Areas and Reserves are always under the eye of the Native Commissioner; nothing can be done without his advice and permission. Under the Native Commissioners work the agricultural demonstrators, especially trained Africans who are the backbone of the Husbandry Act, and whose task it is to exhort and advise and demonstrate proper methods of farming.

When we had finished seeing the homesteads, the Native Commissioner and I had a sandwich lunch under a tree near the Women's Centre, whose foundation-stone had been laid, but which was not finished for lack of funds. The two Africans who were with us, the demonstrator and the interpreter, wandered off tactfully to find their own lunch. As usual I felt bad about this; and as usual could say nothing—it was not as if I were an ignorant visitor who did not know it was impossible for them to sit and eat with us. And I felt bad, too, about this official, who was kindly and helpful; just as I felt embarrassed the day before by the other Native Department official, who was so pleased because the grass had grown up over the eroded land. For so deeply ingrained in these white people are the ideas of segregation—that it is right and proper for a white farm to be thousands of acres, and a black plot one acre, or, for a few, a couple of hundred, that any discussions taking place can only be on this accepted basis. Therefore we sat under the tree and talked about the role women were playing in these Purchase Areas. It seemed that in this case it was the men who had pushed the women into starting a Women's Association—because it made their wives more house-proud, better cooks and better mothers.

I wished very much I could have had the chance to be alone with the two Africans for an hour without the Native Commissioner; not, I must emphasise, that he was concealing anything from me.

Before we went in search of the two Africans, he said that Mr. Todd was a wonderful Prime Minister, and that if only they were given time to create a middle class. . . .

Going back in the car, passing a clutch of straggling poverty-stricken huts, I asked the interpreter how many of these farms had good houses, such as we had seen; and he said eagerly, as if he had been waiting for me to ask it: 'Only eleven, Madam.' And the Native Commissioner said quickly: 'We have seen the better houses, of course.' As if he were saying: 'If you were me, wouldn't you have shown the better houses?'—Well, of course I would.

I asked the interpreter if there was a library. He said there was not. No, the people did not read newspapers. He added that there was no electricity in the whole area, no telephone, no laid-on water. He said that to reach Salisbury, the people had to walk a minimum of seven miles to the bus-stop; the bus made the journey on the main road, once a day, in and out of town.

There are now 5,000 of these better farms in the Colony. One eighth of the land available for purchase has been allocated. There will be 40,000 farms; but the Purchase

Areas will not be settled as quickly as the Reserves, because they are being surveyed properly.

'And why can't they be photographed, like the plots on the Reserves?'

'Because if people *buy* a bit of land, they have the right to be fussy about their boundaries; and because the Reserves are more urgent—we've got to save that soil before it blows away.'

There is a waiting list of tens of thousands for these farms. To own one is the summit of ambition of most Africans.

*   *   *   *

A conversation which illustrates the Native Land Husbandry Act from the grass-roots:

A friend and I had made a trip into Marandellas to buy stores. It is a pretty little village. The sun glistened off the leaves, the wall of the post office glared white.

An old African, passing the parked car, stopped and said:

' 'Morning, baas.'

'Ah, that you, Thomas? And how are you?' He settled down for a talk, one foot on the running board, while the African stood on the pavement, hat in hand.

'Ah, baas, things are very bad.'

'Ah? And how's that?' (This talk is in kitchen Kaffir.)

'Baas, baas, the Government is shupa-ing me meninge.' ('The Government is pushing me around.')

'Yes? And what is the Government doing to you, Thomas?'

'Baas, I have just come from my kraal. The Government says I must put my cattle into a house in the winter and feed them.'

'Well, Thomas, and what is wrong with that?'

'But baas, there is only my wife when I've gone to

work. And how can a woman all by herself put the cattle into a house and get all the food they need all through the winter? Why can't the cattle graze as they have always grazed?'

'Thomas, you do not understand this business.'

'No, baas, I do not understand. Explain it to me, baas.'

'Your soil on the Reserve is no good.'

'Ah, baas, that is so. Very bad land on the Reserve, not good land like you have, baas.'

'Yes, but the land is bad land because there are too many cattle on it.'

'Ah, *baas!* And how can there be too many cattle when the Government has made me sell my cattle so now I have only three cattle?'

'But, Thomas, the Government has made you sell your cattle so that there won't be too many cattle on your land.'

'Then why cannot they graze as they always did?'

'Thomas, it is like this.' And my friend takes his foot off the running board, stands up, and raises his finger in admonition. 'And now listen well, Thomas, for now I will explain the Government to you.'

'Thank you, baas. I am listening well.'

'When you let your cattle run all over the veld in winter looking for grass they cut the land into dust, and the cattle and the grass both get thin and no good.'

'Yes, baas?'

'Now you put your cattle into a house, you cut grass for them and you carry the grass to the cattle, and they do not make the soil into dust.'

'But baas, the soil is no good, not like your soil.'

'It is because you do not shut up your cattle.'

'But baas, the Mkiwa do not shut up the cattle, they let the cattle run.' (Mkiwa—the white men.)

'The farmers that are good farmers, they shut up their cattle and feed them in the winter when the grass is no good.'

'But if the Mkiwa do not wish to be good farmers, then they can let their cattle run, because they have plenty of land.'

'But, Thomas, you are not using your head.'

'Yes, baas, I am using my head well.'

'Now, Thomas, you must do what the Government says.'

'Yes, baas, that I understand. But the Government is shupa-ing me. For how can my wife, who is a woman by herself, do all the work?'

'Then you must leave your work for Mkiwa and help your wife, otherwise the Government will say you are not a good farmer and take your land.'

'Ah, *baas*. And how can that be?'

'Because now the Government says all the natives must farm well.'

'But how can I and my wife and my small children eat if I do not earn money from Mkiwa?'

'The Government says this, Thomas—now listen well. It is a new law.'

'I am listening well, baas.'

And now my friend stands on one foot in the dust of the road and says: 'Now, Thomas, this one foot of mine, it is in the Reserve.'

'Yes, baas?'

And he plants down his other foot and says: 'Now this other foot of mine, it is in Mkiwa.'

'Yes, baas?'

'Now the Government says the natives must either be Reserve or they must be Mkiwa,' and he lifts up his feet alternately, and with vigour, so that puffs of glistening pinkish dust go off into the hot sunlight. 'Either one thing or the other. But *not* both Mkiwa and the Reserve.'

Thomas says nothing. Then: 'That is not a good law.'

'Yes, Thomas, it is a good law, because now you must either be a good farmer, on your land, or you must work for Mkiwa. But if you work for Mkiwa and just go home at week-ends, then you will be a bad farmer and the Government will take your land.'

'Ah, baas!'

'Yes, Thomas, it is so. That is the new law. It is the Native Land Husbandry Act.'

'Thank you for explaining it to me, baas.'

The two men stand facing each other for a while. I see that there is something more to be said. After a pause, however, Thomas says: 'May things go well with you, baas.' And moves off.

My friend stands looking after him.

'That's the only boy,' he said, 'that I've ever known who can cut a hedge straight. But I sacked him for smoking dagga.* I wish I could get him to come back.' A pause while Thomas, a straight, thin old man, retreats along the pavement. 'I suppose he can cut a hedge straight because he was in the army for so long during the war.' A pause. Thomas is walking very slowly. My friend calls: 'Thomas!' Thomas turns. He comes back again. 'Baas?'

'Thomas, you are the only boy I have ever known who can cut a hedge straight.'

'That is so, baas.'

'My hedges need cutting.'

Thomas says with dignity: 'I will come to you on Sunday afternoon and cut your hedges.'

My friend hesitates. 'I can do with a good boy, Thomas.'

Thomas says: 'Ah, baas, but now that the Government

---

* Dagga is a hemp drug.

is shupa-ing me, I must be with my wife in the kraal. But because you ask me I will come and cut your hedges next Sunday afternoon.'

And with this he departs.

Going back in the car my friend says, half-admiringly, half-annoyed: 'Damn the old bastard. It's all very well, but did you hear that? Mkiwa, Mkiwa—the white man. It used to be Mlungu, which is a term of respect, but now it is just "white man." All the same, I don't see how we could have him back really, even though he can cut a hedge. He can do all kinds of work, lay bricks, do metal-work and carpentry. He used to live in the compound with his wife. Then she had a still-born baby, and we had to find her another hut because she said her baby had died of witchcraft. Another baby died, and now she said she could not live in the compound at all, because the evil eye was on her. So she went back to her kraal. So Thomas took to going home every week-end. It's 50 miles. Then he took to coming back at lunch-time on Mondays, and I didn't say anything. Then he came back drunk. Then he started smoking dagga. I gave him fair warning. I said to him if he didn't stop smoking dagga, I'd sack him. But he started coming back Tuesdays or even Wednesdays, drunk or sodden with dagga. So I sacked him. But for all that, he can cut a hedge. He can really work, that boy. Perhaps, if I don't push him, I can talk him into coming back when he pitches up on Sunday.'

*   *   *   *

My friend and I have many discussions about the colour bar.

'The trouble with you,' he says, 'is that you're out of touch with our problems. You don't understand our problems.'

'But I was brought up in the same way as you.'

'But you've been out of the country for six years and you've lost touch.'

'But all my childhood these feudal baas-and-boy conversations went on; and I come back, and they are still going on.'

'The boys I work with, they are the real natives, not those agitators you mix with.'

'After all that's happened,' I said in despair, 'you can talk about agitators! Any minute you'll have another Kenya on your hands, and all you farmers will be heroically defending your isolated homesteads and, I may add, feeling very sorry for yourselves.'

'I do not see,' said he, after thought, 'that there is anything heroic about doing your duty. And besides, it won't happen here.'

'Partnership will save you from it?'

'Partnership? Oh, old Todd's racket. Well, he's sincere enough I expect, but the boys I work with would not know how to spell Partnership. I wish you'd understand, they're primitive people.'

At this point a message arrived that one of the men wanted him in the workshop, so together we went to the workshop.

'Baas,' says a young man, 'when you have time I wish to speak to you.' This is not an old and dignified man like Thomas of yesterday, but a young man with a keen, sharp, intelligent face.

'Speak.' My friend settles down on the table, one foot propped on a chair, while the other faces him. It is a palaver.

'It is a question of that old car you are selling.'

'Yes?'

'If you lent me £100 I could buy it.'

'Why do you want to buy it?'

'So that I can use it to take my vegetables in to the market.'

'You earn £6 a month, and when will you pay the £100 back?'

'From the money I earn from selling my vegetables.'

A silence. 'And now listen well, for you are being very foolish.'

'And how is that?'

'That car is nearly dead. That is why I am selling it.'

'I can mend that car.'

'No, you cannot mend a car that is nearly dead.'

'But why do you not wish to sell me that car? Who, then, will you sell it to?'

'I shall sell it to a white man who has the money to mend it.'

'But if you lent me the £100 I should have the money.'

'Now listen, if I were your enemy, if I wanted to kill you, then I would sell that car to you for £100. For inside one year, the car would be dead and you would owe not £100 but £200, £100 to me and £100 to the garage for repairs. And you would have nothing.'

'But I would have the money I had earned from the vegetables.'

'When I go into Salisbury, all along the roadside there are dead cars lying, the dead cars that foolish natives have bought from bad white men who know the cars are nearly dead. And the Nkoos Pezulu' (The Chief Above—God) 'only knows what happens to these foolish natives.'

'Baas, the Nkoos Pezulu may not know, but I know.'

'How is it, then?'

'They have made money out of the cars before they die and so they can buy another car.'

'Sometimes they have made money and sometimes not. If not, then they owe the money.' A long silence. 'You would owe *me* the money if the car dies. And is that good?' The young man looks straight at my friend and waits. 'But now this is very serious, a very bad thing that I should hear you talk like this. You talk like these bad and foolish white men who have no sense.'

'But how can such a thing be, baas?'

'Do you know what goes on at the station? The butcher, the store, the garage—they tell me they are owed thousands of pounds. All the tobacco farmers owe them thousands of pounds. That is credit. That is what you are asking me for. It is a bad thing. And the Nkoos Pezulu only knows what will come of it.'

'Baas, I do not see that the Nkoos Pezulu is involved in this matter. The storekeepers know that the farmers will get money from the bank on the very day that the tobacco is sold. And that is why they get credit.'

'This credit is a very dangerous thing. It is money that is not there.'

'Yes, the money is there. It is still growing in the earth, where the tobacco is. Where my vegetables are.'

'You do not understand this question of credit and money.'

'It seems to me that I understand it well.'

'But if there is a slump, what will happen to the farmers?'

'Then they may sell some of their land, for they have so much, or the Land Bank will give them credit.'

'But I am not the Land Bank. I am a man, only.'

'But now I grow my lettuce, I grow my tomatoes. And because I have no lorry I cannot take them into the village to sell them, and so they go bad.'

'So now I will explain to you where you do wrong. It is because you grow vegetables like lettuces and tomatoes. You must grow potatoes or onions that do not go bad in a few days. Then you must put the potatoes in a hut and keep them and sell them a little bit by little bit.'

'But the Mkiwa do not pay so much money for potatoes as they do for the vegetables like lettuces and tomatoes. On my small bit of earth—no, that is not for potatoes. Potatoes are for big farmers, with plenty of land. I would make no profit.'

'But I cannot lend you the money.'

'Then, baas, there is nothing further I want to say.'

' 'Morning, James.'

' 'Morning, baas, go well.'

We went back to the house.

'That boy has a hard life. The trouble with him is that he is always wanting to make some more money. Of course, we cannot blame them for wanting to make money when we are all so money-minded.'

'No,' I said.

'He is a very good worker. He can do all kinds of work. He came to me and said he wanted some more money. He earned £6 a month. I said I knew he deserved to earn more, but I could not pay more. I have a certain amount set aside for wages and that's that. But I said if he liked I would give him a couple of acres of soil and he could grow vegetables and make up the extra.'

'But surely that is against the Land Apportionment Act?'

'What? Oh, don't be silly. And besides, the Native Commissioner knows all about it and about this native. He is a native with a record. When he came to me he told me, fair and square, that he had been in prison for forging a cheque. I talked it over with him, and it was perfectly obvious he had had no idea what a cheque was. He thought it was a kind of magic device by which white men get money for nothing out of banks. Or at least, I hope so. But I took him on, and the next thing was old Smith from across the river came to say, did I know that I had a man with a prison record working for me? I said to Smith, I thought that was a dirty trick; and in our law once a man has served time, he has paid for his wrong-doing. Old Smith was upset. He meant it for the best. The next thing was, James started smoking dagga and the Lord knows what. But I talked it over with him, and found that once he was a Christian, because he was at a mission school once for a couple of years before his father's money ran out and he had to stop his education. I got him back to going to church, and he took an oath not to drug any more. Or drink. But it didn't last long. He could hardly stand up on a Monday morning sometimes. So I got him in front of the padre to swear a solemn oath on the Bible to give it up, and he was forgiven on condition he gave the names of his drug-ring to the Native Commissioner. So at the moment he's in the clear. But probably not for long, because he's heavily in debt.'

'You could pay him another couple of pounds a month?'

'I can't. I'm only the manager here. I have a certain sum given me for wages. Besides, he's lucky to find anyone who'll take him on. Though he's a good worker and he really works. Not like most. The trouble with these natives is they are too backwards to understand the simplest things in modern life. Only yesterday I had to talk to a new lot I took on last month. There they were loafing around. I had them up and I said to them: "Now look. I will explain to you this business of a contract. When I take you on, I say I will pay you £2 a month. I pay you £2 a month in return for your labour. Do you understand?" '

'And do they?'

'They say, Ah, ah, ah, *baas!*—as if I were cheating them. I say to them, very well then, go. But if you stay, you work. £2 a month for your work. That's a contract.

And please. . . .' And with this he turned to me, 'please do not tell me that £2 a month is not enough. They have good brick huts. I give each of them a plot of land for their wives, because they like to have their women kept out of mischief. I give them proper rations. And I pay a teacher for their kids. All the kids on this place go to school, and they go to school properly all day, Government inspected, not this hole and corner business that goes on on the big farms. What do you want me to do? Well, go on, tell me. I know it all stinks. I know it. It's all a bloody mess. But is it my fault that the poor damned savages aren't £10-a-week skilled workers with semi-detached houses filling in their football coupons, all nice and tidy like Britain? Well, is it?'

'No,' I said, 'it isn't. But tell me, what do you think is going to come out of all this?'

'I'm coming more and more to the conclusion that unless the Almighty steps in and takes a hand there isn't any solution to anything. The whites are as bad as the blacks. It is a case of the blind leading the blind.'

*　　*　　*　　*

About two years ago I was visited in London by an old friend from Salisbury, who told me it was time I came back home to see how things had changed, how out of date and unfair my books were since Partnership and Federation. 'Natives are doing very well now,' he said. 'In towns they have to be paid £4 a month, and the employers have to pay for the accommodation. Everything is being done for the natives and nothing for the Europeans. And they aren't grateful.'

I felt bad about this. The reason that I felt bad was that this man had had the advantage of four years' solid Socialist education in our Left Club; and it was hard to admit that this wasn't enough to insulate him against becoming so rich. For his story is a familiar one: a refugee, he arrived on the shores of Africa before the last war with not much more than the clothes he stood up in. Now he owns shops, farms and enterprises of one sort or another in large quantities.

In Salisbury he at once demanded that I should go out to his place, or one of his places, to see how well the natives were being treated these days. I was naturally anxious to do so.

On a fine afternoon, then, we drove out to the grading-sheds, 30 miles through the beautiful green countryside of an African autumn, for the grass still stood high and green, undimmed by the dry season, and the skies were high and fresh. There are two Africas, and I do not know which I love the best: the green, lush, bright country when the sap is running and the earth is wet; or the dry, brown-gold wastes of the drought, when the sky closes down, hazy and smoke-dimmed, and the sun is copper-coloured and distorted. Hard to imagine, on an afternoon in April, that in two months this expanse of green and soft-coloured earth will have been beaten by the sun into the colours of metal; and how every lungful of breath will taste of veld-fires.

All the way out we talked about Parnership and gratitude and how unjust journalists are to Federation.

The grading-shed was familiar to me, a great, high barracks of a place, sultry and rancorous with the strong breath of tobacco.

It was five in the afternoon: the men had left their work, but the women and the children were just finishing theirs of tying the tobacco into bundles.

They sat in two lines on the brick floor. The women sat on one side, some with their babies tied on their backs, some with small children playing beside them. On the other side were the children, aged from six years to about twelve years, boys and girls.

My host said that as this enterprise was some distance from town, too far for these workers to travel in and out, they lived here in a compound he had built for them. There were about 160 men, some with their wives and children. The men earned £2 10s. a month, which with overtime came to about £3 10s. a month. The women earned from 15s. to £2 a month. The children earned 15s. to £1 a month.

They worked from six in the morning until twelve; and from one until four or five.

'And I am not unreasonable,' he said, 'for I let the women go off at eleven to cook the porridge for their men and the children.'

The air, in spite of the ventilators, was oppressive, and I could not have borne it for long; but my host said one gets used to it. The women and children were coughing all the time.

'And in addition to this, I give them rations and accommodation.'

'And what rations do you give them?'

'The rations laid down by the Government.'

I quote, then, from a handbook printed by the Government designed to attract settlers to the Federation, and it is called: *A New Life in the Federation of Rhodesia and Nyasaland*.

This is from the section on how one should feed one's servants:

(*a*) 1½ lb. of mealie-meal a day.

(*b*) ½ lb. of meat a day. This used to be the usual ration, but although the native still looks upon it as his right, the meat position no longer allows it. Other protein foods will then have to be substituted.

(*c*) Vegetables at least twice a week. This will be found difficult as the African does not understand the meaning of vitamins. He usually likes the more pungent vegetables. Onions, potatoes, cabbage and spinach in limited quantities are recommended.

(*d*) 1 lb. of sugar per head per week.

(*e*) 1 lb. of dried peas or beans. These the African does not like. He will always prefer ground-nuts, which are usually obtainable. For some months green mealies are available and could be provided.

(*f*) As much salt as required.

(*g*) Slice of bread and jam and tea or coffee remaining from the table.

As these workers were not domestic servants, slices of bread and jam and tea or coffee remaining from the table would not be available; and what they actually lived on, it seemed, was mostly mealie-meal.

Then we took a walk around the accommodation.

There were three of us, my host, one of his farm managers and myself. On a couple of acres of soil were crowded a hundred or so tiny mud huts, roughly thatched. The floor was of damp earth, with blankets lying directly on it, cooking pots stacked up beside them, bits of clothing hanging from nails. In one hut there was a bed made of strips of cowhide laced on unbarked tree-trunks stuck direct in the mud floor and a very small deal table but no chairs. My host said: 'Look, you see they are doing themselves well.' Among and around the huts were planted mealies; and chickens wandered in and out of the hut doors. The huts were very small and so low that a full-grown person could not stand upright in them.

A broken-down motor car was settling into its parts among the mealies. 'You see—they are getting rich—they have motor cars these days.'

I have seen many bad compounds, but never one as bad as this; and when my host said: 'They are picturesque, aren't they?' I said I didn't think they were picturesque.

Whereupon he said that this was the first time he had actually taken a look at this compound; and if one had farm managers one expected them to take the responsibility; one had to see to everything oneself these days, or nothing was done. But perhaps some brick huts could be built here—yes, it was time there were some brick huts.

The farm manager looked a little quizzical at this, but said nothing.

In front of the compound, between it and the grading shed, were a big water-tank and a water-tap, which was the sole supply for all these people; and the women and the children were standing in the mud puddles around the tap waiting for their turn to draw water.

The whole place smelt bad and wet; it smelt of heavy, damp vegetation, of chicken droppings, of souring porridge. There were no latrines or showers in the compound.

I asked the boss-boy privately if there was any one thing that the people of the compound wanted more than another, and he replied with simplicity: 'Higher wages.' So I said, 'Yes, but apart from that?' He said: 'We want the doctor to come, because our children cough all the time.'

In the meantime my host was urging me to go and see how the children were being educated. For he was paying a teacher £6 a month so that the children could be taught.

In a corner of the grading-shed was the class. About twenty children sat on the floor among piled bales of tobacco. They were of all ages, girls and boys, in their ragged pants and shirts, their ragged dresses—barefooted, of course. They were the children we had already seen working. The teacher, a cheerful and enthusiastic peda-gogue, was repeating the syllables of the Shona language again and again, while the children chanted them after him. He wrote the syllables on the blackboard, which was the top of a packing-case, with a bit of chalk. The children had pebbles for the purposes of counting, and bits of torn schoolbooks lay about. They had to pay for their own books.

There was a single yellowish electric-light bulb glowing down from the rafters of the shed.

It was a very cheerful class; both teacher and scholars were proud to have visitors, and the little hands were shooting up in answer to every question: 'Yes teacher,' 'Me teacher,' 'Please teacher.'

It seems that these children go to class every afternoon at four or five o'clock after their day's work for a couple of hours' education; but my host said it was a pity I could not see them at the week-ends, when they are at their best, for they do marching and games under the teacher.

'And so,' he said, 'you must not say that nothing is being done for the children, because all the tobacco farm-ers have schools on their farms now.'

I tried to get the figures later from one of the publicity men for child labour, but was unable to do so. It appears there are no figures. Child labour is extensively used on the farms; and in the towns children work as house serv-ants. But it is expected that within five years all the children in the towns will get some sort of education.

I also asked the publicity man if there was any sort of control of these private compounds; he said there was regular inspection, and the conditions were 'pretty good' these days.

When I paid a visit to my own district, Lomagundi, some weeks after this, I was on another tobacco farm, and asked how many children were employed. My hostess did not know; she thought sixty or seventy children. 'But these days all the tobacco farmers provide schools. You can't get the children to come and work at all unless you pay a teacher for them. And you have to pay at least £6 a month for a teacher. On some farms the children don't work in the afternoons at all. They work in the mornings and go to school in the afternoons.'

We were driving through the compound as we talked; it was of brick huts, but a squalid broken-down place, and everywhere were ragged, barefooted children with the pot-bellies of malnutrition.

'Look,' she said. 'They look happy enough, don't they?'

My host of the grading-shed was also convinced of the happiness of his natives; but he did say that they were an unsatisfactory lot, very unstable, because they went off at the end of the season back to their kraals, and they never came back, although he offered a £2 bonus to any who would. He always had to recruit his natives afresh every season.

After the visit to the class, we went off to have supper in the farm manager's house. It all made me feel as if nothing had changed and nothing ever could: the big, bare, brick room, with the stars shining more brilliantly through the window than the light inside the room; the soft, hot air coming in; and the talk, which was, of course, about the colour problem.

But we had to hurry the meal, because there was to be a film show for the natives, and they didn't like it to be late, since they had to get up at five in the morning.

At eight o'clock, then, we were back in the big grading-shed. We, the white people, sat on chairs beside the projector, and the women and the children sat forward, on the floor under the screen which had been erected; and the men stood on either side, leaning on tobacco bales or against the tobacco racks.

The farm managers were whooping up an atmosphere, shouting 'Su-pair!' For we were to show films of Superman, which it seems are popular with the Africans.

The lights went down; and the film began. It was about some wicked men in a skyscraper office in America somewhere, plotting against Superman. The villain appeared to be some sort of Beetle; but as Superman himself was, in his human guise, an undercover man inside the Beetle gang, the whole thing was very confusing to me; and the only person whose role was quite unambiguous was the beautiful blonde's. There was a big fight at the top of the skyscraper, where Superman was throttling people and banging them like limp sacks against the walls; and at this point the audience was growling and roaring with excitement. The only points in the film where this audience showed unmistakable appreciation were when Superman was beating up someone.

There was a ramp from the top of the skyscraper to the street; and the blonde, who had passed out from stress and strain at the wheel of an immense car, was whizzing around and down this ramp, while Superman fled down the sky after her. He caught her at the bottom just before the car crashed into a wall, and then the lights went up.

The two white managers got up from their chairs and began clowning and throwing themselves around, shouting 'Su-pair! Su-pair!' while a few of the Africans laughed and played up, shouting back 'Su-pair!' Most looked embarrassed and sullen, however. All the time the reel was being wound back, the two white men were diving head first over bales, staggering around shaking their hands together over their heads, or, pointing their joined hands upwards, made as if to fly off upwards, like Superman.

To cries of 'Su-pair!' the lights went out; and we were

now in the bowels of a mountain, where Superman was plotting against the Beetle for some good and noble end, but what this end could be was never made clear. At the end of this reel, the Beetle had thrown a switch which dissolved the mountain into lava; and Superman was wading waist-deep through red-hot lava thousands of feet under the mountain.

For five minutes or so the white managers clowned and postured, shouting 'Su-pair!' while my host explained he had these film shows every fortnight; it was expensive, of course, but he liked to do something for his workers.

The next instalment began without explaining how Superman got out of the red-hot lava; but he was now rushing around some place like Texas with the blonde on a horse, while the two managers, now in a perfect frenzy, were shouting 'Su-pair!' at every bound of the horse, and capered and pranced over the bales in the dim light, while about three hundred Africans watched the screen in silence.

After Superman, a film was shown about skiing in Switzerland. Skiers whizzed down the snowy slopes one after another, and I heard an African mutter just behind me, half in admiration, half in disgust: 'Those Mlungu! Look at them!' ('Those white men! Look at them!')

Now the film show was over, and time for the people to go back to their damp and filthy huts for the night.

They piled in silence out of the doors of the grading-shed, while the indefatigable managers yelled 'Su-pair!' and made a few last dives and capers among the bales.

My host asked the boss-boy if he had understood what the last film was about, for snow never falls in this part of Africa; and he replied with extreme politeness: 'It shows how the white men slide on sticks over ice.'

We then drove back the thirty miles to Salisbury, extremely fast. Twice something dark swooped from the stars down towards the windscreen, there was a soft squashy bump, and an owl fell in a struggling mass of feathers on the roadside.

VI

ABOUT THIS TIME, three weeks out, I found myself succumbing to my own private form of the colour mania.

After those endless morning tea-parties, those sundowner parties where, if the talk does manage to leave 'the native problem' for five minutes, it languishes, the intolerable boredom of this narrow, provincial place settled on me like an illness, and I found myself back at my old post, at a back window, watching the lively social life that goes on around the native quarters and in the sanitary lanes. I went around Harari, the African township which, if squalid, is gay and noisy and vital—and I went there as a white person whose very appearance freezes the spontaneity and the gaiety.

Supposing I were given permission to live in one of the townships? I would still be a white person and very properly resented by the Africans themselves. I could never live among black people without any notice being taken of me. And besides, it is against the law. Supposing I were given permission to live on one of the Native Reserves, then. . . .

All this is madness. Not only is it inconceivable that I should be allowed to do anything of the kind, basically it has nothing to do with colour. If I were in a white country where the people had not yet been exhausted and confined by industrialism I would still be looking out of the window and envying them. Since I seem to have 'chosen this damned profession where you have to use your brains all the time,' naturally I feel sentimental about those who do not.

Late night fantasies: When I was a child I used to think 'Supposing I blacked my face, and then. . . .' Half-asleep I think of the German General Lettow-Vorbeck who, during the First World War in Tanganyika, blacked his face and reconnoitred as an African in the enemy lines. So it is possible. But not without its difficulties, for a woman. When I am middle-aged, then all these problems will vanish, and then. . . .

This fantasy of blacking one's face is not confined to white people. A novel sent to me to read by an African had an episode in it where a kindly white man, wishing to share with his black friend the experiences of night life in Salisbury, blacked his face and went the round of the shebeens and dance-halls. He was not discovered.

This novel was very interesting to me. It had two heroes, a good white man who defied the colour bar and adopted the other hero, a black youth, as a servant or friend. When he went out in the evenings he would say to this youth: 'And now, when you have swept the room and washed up, if you are tired you may lie down on my bed and sleep.'

The white man suffered no ill-effects among his own kind for this behaviour: he seemed to have been a forerunner of the members of the interracial society. Later he said to his servant: 'You are a good and clever boy, I will send you to university.' But at the end of the book the youth gets killed in an accident where a white man half-deliberately and half-accidentally runs him over, being drunk and wishing to show off to his friends.

This was the only touch of realism in the book.

The book was particularly a lesson to me because its author, once a violent and uncompromising nationalist, is now a supporter of Capricorn and of Moral Rearmament.

These fantasies of mine, if unchecked, will lead me straight into the role of the Useful Rebel.

But it is intolerable never to be able to know, from the inside, the life of the people of one's own country. . . . It is three in the morning; everything silent, everyone asleep: the only people allowed by the Government to live in such a way that there is no unpleasant strain between white and black are the missionaries. But unfortunately I have not the benefits of religion. Supposing I became a missionary, would I then be permitted. . . .

Enough now, it is time you went back to England and sanity! Four in the morning: what a pity I have had my sound political education. If I didn't understand these matters, I wouldn't know how the patient gets worse before he gets better; I wouldn't always be croaking like Cassandra and finding my most unpleasant prophecies coming true; I could be a happy member of the inter-racial society, or a pleasant Capricornite.

Once a painter said to me that when his picture went wrong and he didn't know what was wrong with it, he used to creep out of bed in the middle of the night, go to his studio, and very quickly and suddenly throw on the lights—*so that he could catch sight of his picture before it could see him.*

Well, I wish I could switch on a new light so that I could see me before I saw myself.

I am bored with my own contradictions. If, as a Marxist, I say certain kinds of people are bound to behave in a certain kind of way, according to the type of society they live in, or what part of that society they are, then there should be nothing emotional about this; it is certainly no theme for moral indignation. One can and should be morally indignant about the form of the society, but not about the behaviour of the people in it. Yet these comfort-loving, pleasure-satiated white settlers make me angry and disgusted. And the way the Africans are forced to live makes me angry and miserable because of the waste and the stupidity of it.

But I don't approve of any of these emotions.

If only, just for half an hour, I could be fitted into a black skin, to see what the world looked like from there. Quite different. Everything different? Lord, how many centuries before all this colour nonsense dies away.... Five in the morning. I get to sleep, and immediately dream of the Garden of Eden like a Blake engraving with the Undying Worm, looking sly and mean and satirical, offering me a large apple marked: Communism, or the Knowledge of Good and Evil.

*   *   *   *

I have now been sent six novels by Africans. None of them was good enough to be published. But they all had the vitality and freshness of language of people who still use natural imagery in ordinary speech, and translate these images direct into English.

It was not the writing which was poor; at best it had a Shakespearean vigour and country directness. But the construction was bad.

In each of these novels the action ceased for several pages at a time, while this kind of talk went on:

[Two men are sitting at the hut-door at evening.]

'How, then, can we Africans advance while the Land Apportionment Act still applies? Consider, my friend, the Land Apportionment Act as just amended by our Legislative Assembly. It is a wicked blow to African hopes and aspirations.'

'And consider, too, the Native Pass Laws. Until they are revoked, there will never be freedom of movement in our country.'

'And do not let us forget the Destocking Act, which makes the hearts of our rural Africans heavy indeed.'

'And then, my good friend, there is the Sedition Act, an Act which is not easy to understand.'

'No, I would say it is easy to understand. But should we not consider, too, that Act which is called the Subversive Activities Act, and that Act which is cited as the Public Order Act? For these Acts are indeed a yoke around our necks.'

'Ah, truly, it is time the hearts of the Europeans changed towards us.

'It is time they turned their hearts towards good will and understanding between the races, yes, my friend, I agree with you.'

These novels all had the same plot; it is the story of an African who comes from his village in the Reserve into the white man's town, and—I make a point of this for the benefit of reviewers, one of whom complained of a novel that 'it had the South African plot'—this is the story of the African in modern Africa. If art, then, is to have any relation to life, stories about contemporary Africa are likely to be based somehow on this plot. And is it not, after all, one of the world's ten—or is it twelve?—basic plots?

Another thing I was taught by these novels. It was to be suspicious of that warning which all white writers from colour-bar countries get from their white progressive friends. 'Do not attempt,' this admonition goes, 'to write about Africans, for no white person can understand the African soul.'

For a long time I paid heed to this, until it occurred to me that it might well be another type of Displacement; another way of shifting colour-bar emotions on to an apparently harmless point.

For when I read these novels, I saw that there was nothing of the mysterious African soul in them at all. They could all have been written of Britain in the late eighteenth or early nineteenth century. It was all there, the warmth, and the space, and the humour; the religious and moral earnestness, with many warnings against that solace of the oppressed and poverty-stricken, the Demon Drink.

But the most extraordinary thing about these novels was that I saw, suddenly, my home town Salisbury, that peaceful, cushioned, pretty, boring little town, from the underside. Here it was, a wild, police-ridden, precarious, dangerous place, lit most luridly by fires of crimes and alcohol and drugs, beguiled by wicked women and evil men, among whom the good people of the town lived from one moment of hard-won security to the next. These novels were all picaresque. Tom Jones might have been the hero of any one of them; Joseph Andrews might be met round any corner. Moll Flanders would have found herself perfectly at home; and Fagin's gang of bad lots could swap one set of narrow streets for another with nothing to astonish them but the sunlight.

In the *African Weekly* there is a serial story about two

young men called Hatichke and Munhira. Hatichke is a
rogue, and Munhira tries to keep him out of trouble and
prison. The author, someone called 'Nhaudzimere,' is in
the great tradition of English moral writing; that is, he
writes of wickedness so entertainingly that it sounds much
more interesting than virtue.

Here, by permission of the editor of the *African Weekly,* are two instalments of this tale (not continuous)—one
where Hatichke goes to prison; and one where Munhira
goes home to his village, where he tells Hatichke's parents
of their son's misfortunes:

Hatichke, Billy and Mubaiwa found life in the
Prison Reserve unbearable. They were used to white-
collar jobs, good food and suitable sleeping accommodation. Here the position was just the opposite
and contrary to their expectation. Above all, after the
first two days of admission they had gone through
solitary confinement and had spare diet for three
days. On Saturday they received three strokes with
the cane each.

Munhira was anxious, in fact very anxious, to
meet Hatichke. After obtaining the necessary
documents to visit the Prison Reserve, Munhira met
Hatichke there on Sunday afternoon. 'Now, Hatichke! how much money did you make by your grand
scheme?' Munhira asked. 'It was not my idea,
Munhira. It was Billy's idea and I must say life in
jail is intolerably bad,' Hatichke said. 'But what did
you say when I condemned the scheme, Hatichke?'
Munhira went on. 'I must admit that I was too
foolish to see your point of view when you advised
me,' Munhira blushed. 'Let me tell you that solitary
confinement and spare diet is really hell on earth,'
Munhira said. 'And the treatment of prisoners is

simply horrible, my friend,' Billy joined in, but Munhira ignored him. 'It is you who devised this notorious scheme which landed us in a mess, Billy.' Hatichke turned red. 'But you were not forced to follow him in brewing the concoction, especially after my repeated warnings,' Munhira pointed out. 'You were free as anybody to say no. But because you are stupid you just follow any move without questioning and unreasonably,' Munhira reprimanded his friend.

'Billy and Mubaiwa! who gave you two permission to talk to that visitor?' a tall, robust gaol warder dreaded by all prisoners exclaimed. 'All I know is that this gentleman had permission to talk to Hatichke. Come with me and I'll show you how to keep the regulations,' he said. Billy and Mubaiwa, after receiving some strokes, were taken to a ward to polish the floors. 'By five o'clock I want to see my own shadow here.' The warder left them there.

'These fellows as well as yourself deserve this punishment, Hatichke,' Munhira said scornfully. 'I have no compassion for people who are mischievous,' Munhira said. 'When are you supposed to come out?' he asked. 'I hope to be out by Saturday this week. But one never knows because there are several regulations to observe here. I understand my friends will remain here because they were found smoking two days ago,' Hatichke said, shedding tears. 'Well, goodbye. I'll see you on Saturday when you come out.' 'I really need good food at home on Saturday, Munhira,' Hatichke sobbed. Munhira left.

'Good heavens! I nearly landed into a mess! Now how shall I explain this to Hatichke's parents? I was certainly an accomplice in this mischievous operation. It was just by sheer luck that the travellers failed to identify me,' Munhira murmured to himself, hurrying away from the Magistrate's Court. 'Although I have no money on me now, I must get home, right to Hatichke's parents as soon as possible before false rumours spread to them. I know they will not believe my story. However that cannot be helped. It is human nature to disbelieve true stories,' he said to himself.

As he trotted talking to himself a Policeman on duty gazed at him. 'You have all the qualities of a habitual criminal, my dear boy!' the Policeman said in a rough voice. 'I beg your pardon! Are you addressing me, Sir?' he asked frightfully. 'Let's have a look at your Registration Certificate or Town Pass, please,' the Police demanded. After searching through his pockets Munhira retorted: 'It appears I have left it at the Police Camp where I was working as a scavenger. I have just been discharged and I am hurrying home to explain that my comrade had landed into trouble,' Munhira said shivering. 'Whom do you think will believe that story?' the Police was getting impatient. 'You need a foolish Policeman to believe it and not me,' he said in a mockery. 'Please, Sir, take my word for it,' Munhira said. 'You are lucky because I am hurrying to go off duty. I would have taken you there to get at the bottom of the story. However do go and get your papers now. Next time if I meet you without them you will certainly be in serious trouble,' the Police warned. Munhira pretended to return to the Police Camp but when the Police was out of sight he took a sudden turn homewards. He ran as fast as his thin, long legs could carry him, falling headlong thrice within a distance of five miles and lo! there was another Policeman checking passes of loafers. 'I must change direction and walk home through the forest,' he said. From this point onwards he travelled through thick forests until he arrived. On his arrival Hatichke's parents came to find out what was happening with their son who never visited them for a long time. 'How is your friend Hatichke?' the mother asked. 'He is very well indeed, except that he landed into trouble two days ago for impersonating the Police,' Munhira explained. 'He was sentenced to six months' imprisonment without option of a fine. Fortunately three months were suspended for two years on condition he behaved well,' he said. 'But were you not working together?' she asked. 'We were but he has been so mischievous during the past years that this is his third time to be imprisoned, ma'am,' Munhira said in reply. 'Hatichke was never mischievous from childhood. You must have been the cause of all these troubles. I shall hate you more than I hate the devil, you swine!' Hatichke's father joined in. 'Look, my dear friend! my son was not your son's keeper. You either ask him nicely or do not ask him at all,' Munhira's father was annoyed by the last dirty remark. 'Get out of my house immediately before I change my mind, you fools!' he mocked. 'Since when has your son been a well behaved man? Out you go this very minute or else I shall make use of this sharp axe,' Munhira's father remarked. 'We will meet again at a beer drink,' Hatichke's father warned.

I was not surprised, when I said to an African lady how much I liked this adventure story, that she replied: 'I don't see why they find room in the newspaper for a story about common urban rascals instead of printing material that would be of interest to respectable people.'

'But,' I said, 'I've now read six novels written by Africans, and all of them very respectable men, and they all had this same atmosphere that makes the story of Hatichke and Munhira so attractive. To me, at least. It surely can't be an accident that all the creative writing that has so far come out of the colony by Africans deals with these matters?'

'They give the impression,' she said, folding her hands before her on the band of her apron, 'that we are not a law-abiding people.'

'You have, I am afraid,' said her husband, 'anarchistical tendencies, otherwise you would not like these immoral stories. And besides, they put wrong ideas into the heads of the youth.'

'I do not see,' I said, 'why it proves I am anarchistical if I prefer the light-hearted breaking of wicked and unjust laws, to suffering them in resigned patience.'

We argued about this for some time, but came to no conclusion.

*   *   *   *

An evening with my friends, the African schools inspector and his wife:

HE. Of course, like all you damned journalists, all you are interested in is the towns. You are interested in what is going to happen to the urbanized African. Oh, yes, I know, but shut up a minute about your proletariat. You've been looking at housing schemes and night-schools. The point is that all the white people, progressives or what-nots, have got a vision of this country that is dependent on something the poor Kaffirs haven't got.'

'Money?'

'No, the motor-car. Take a look at the map . . . the road running north and south, from Beit Bridge to Chirundu, taking in Bulawayo, Gwelo, Gatooma, Hartley and Salisbury and Sinoia; the road running east to Umtali. The road from Bulawayo to Wankie. All the *Herrenvolk* spend their lives rushing up and down these roads in their motor-cars. But behind these roads and the white farms that lie along them there are thousands and millions of acres of sweet bloody nothing. Nothing. In other words, the Native Reserves. And do not tell me that you have seen Reserves around Salisbury and Bulawayo, that's something different.'

'Then,' I said, 'please describe for me in your words, so that I may record them for interested readers, what the Native Reserves are like in their natural state.'

'Good. I get into my lorry and I drive 200, 300 miles into the bundu. I don't need to ask when the Reserves begin, because they begin at that point where the roads become of interest to my insurance company. They aren't roads, they are dust-tracks. Then I see a double row of thatched mud huts stringing out a mile, or two or three miles, with some miserable patches of mealies and pumpkins and rapoka around them.'

'Why a string of mud huts and not a cluster, as is natural to a village?'

'For two reasons. First to save fencing; the cattle are supposed to graze on one side of the huts, and the crops are grown on the other. But secondly, because it is more easy to keep people in order if they live strung out, nicely arranged, two by two.'

'But,' I said, 'the Reserve near Salisbury had its huts in natural groups.'

'Quite so. The Government has decided this martial arrangement of huts is bad, partly because it depresses the poor natives to live so, and because, now we have the Native Land Husbandry Act, we are going to have a fine, healthy individuality, and competitive individualism is much more effective than policing. But—there is no money in the Reserves. And there isn't likely to be, and so for a long time things will go on as they are. If you fly over the country, what do you see? You can pick out a Native Reserve because instead of miles of empty bush, which is a white farm, there is a long line of single huts, with close-packed strips of cultivation beside it, not an inch of soil wasted. And please remember that the vast majority of natives live like this. It is the minority who are in the towns. So I come to the first of the long line of miserable huts, and out swarm a million ragged children, shouting and laughing and pleased to death to see me, shouting, "Sir, Sir, let us show you the way to the school." They perch all over the car like tick-birds on an elephant. We drive over the ruts at the edge of the cultivated land because there isn't a road, passing half a dozen nice churches. Because a life and death struggle goes on all the time between the different churches about who is to convert who. Sometimes one cuts another's throat; so there's only a couple of churches, and sometimes they live side by side in happy harmony, only bickering a little, five, six, seven of them, competing for the souls of the heathen. And then we come to the school, which is a shack of some sort, mostly built by the parents of the children, in the intervals of their other work, which is to keep body and soul together. Sometimes the kids are sitting on the mud floor, and sometimes they are sitting on the benches; sometimes they have a blackboard, and sometimes they haven't. And there they all are, happy as anything, being educated by a Standard IV teacher. And in all the Reserve there is no telephone, there is nothing. Neither telephone, nor radio, nor electric light, nor running water, nor books, nor newspapers. Nothing, nothing. They might as well be on the moon. There is a choice of churches and mealie-porridge to eat, and a whole lot of visiting Government officials like myself, telling them they must become civilised. So I inspect the school, very efficient and uplifting, and I leave that Reserve accompanied by a million happy kids, waving and shouting good-bye. So I drive to the next Reserve in a very bad temper, where another batch of a million kids swarm around shouting, "Hello, Sir; good morning, Sir!" '

'Now, dear,' says his wife, 'you aren't being positive.'

'Well, I don't feel positive. I'd like to shake the lot of them. What right have they got to be so bloody happy living like that?'

'You wouldn't want them to be miserable, surely?'

'No. Yes, I would. No. But what gets me is now they are getting educated they are going to be miserable and full of complexes like us. When I walk into a room full of teachers I can pick out all the Standard Sixes because they look so damned serious and full of responsibility. And when I say to them, all formal and inspiring: "What do you want to do with your lives?" up shoot their hands and they say, "Please, Sir, we will devote our lives to uplifting our people." And they all look as miserable as a lot of wet cats.'

'But, dear, you aren't being consistent.'

'Why should I be consistent? But look at *us*—we make me sick! But those poor bloody little kids are as happy as anything. They have a whale of a time, being backward and miserable.'

'That isn't a progressive way of thinking at all, dear.'

'Provided I act progressively I don't see it matters how I think. Aren't I educating and civilising the African? Lord, am I not. But I'd like to spit.'

'The reason why we white people aren't happy is because we suffer from a guilty conscience.'

'Guilty conscience my foot! They never think about the poor Kaffirs. They only think about the colour bar and Partnership and all that. That's different. The more civilised people get, the unhappier they are. Are you happy? No, God knows you are not. Am I happy? No. Is Doris here happy? Well, if she is she has no right to be. Do we know anyone who is happy?'

'Well, dear, we are learning to be happy on a higher level.'

'Is that it? Well, in that case, you have my best wishes.'

*   *   *   *

Father Huddlestone has just begun his campaign in Britain: someone told me today that in the Stock Exchange news on the South African radio it said: 'Kaffirs are down two points, due to the activity of certain clerics in Britain.'

*   *   *   *

Long conversation about politics, or rather the colour bar, with a man who was described to me as 'another of you blasted Communists.' An Englishman who has lived in South Africa most of his life, he has been in Southern Rhodesia five years.

'Communism,' he said, 'is ruining Britain.' He meant the Labour Party.

Then he said: 'I wish all you blasted people would shut up. You and Father Huddlestone and the rest of you. You'll only frighten off the whites who are taking Todd and his Partnership quite quietly at the moment. It'll be your fault if they get cold feet and clamp down.'

(Similarly, Lord Malvern blamed the Reverend Michael Scott for the bloodshed in Nyasaland when there was rioting over Federation: the deaths, he said, were on Michael Scott's head.)

'Of course I have no colour feeling myself. I don't mind any man educated to my level coming to my house. In the Club they call me a Red. But I wouldn't ask the plumber's mate to dinner in England, and I wouldn't here, white or black.'

Finally, after pursuing this line for some time, he concluded: 'Your kind of talk makes me tired. You've got to have some loyalty to your own kind. *My friends are Europeans.*'

*   *   *   *

I have been hearing a great deal of talk about a novel, written by Donald Leavis of Bulawayo, called *Voices in Every Wind.* It is described as very seditious. No one has read it, and it is not in any of the bookshops.

At last I ask an old friend of mine who works in a public relations job if he has a copy. He says: "You won't find a copy of that anywhere. The C.I.D. came to me when it came out, because I am supposed to be a literary type, and said they were going to ban it. They said it had sex in it between black and white—a rape scene. I told them not to be silly, it would only draw attention to it. They just went round the bookshops and had a word with the managers. The book disappeared from sight, as it were.'

Later I managed to get hold of a copy of this book. It is an intelligent novel, describing what might happen in Central Africa if things went the way they did in Kenya. It has been deliberately killed by silence and the helpful co-operation of the booksellers.

In South Africa, which is supposed to be so much less liberal than Central Africa, books like Gunther's *Inside Africa,* and others equally critical of the Nationalists, sell openly and in large numbers. I have been asked why it is that the Nationalists are so tolerant about the kinds of books they allow to be sold. They will pounce on books that suggest sexual equality between black and white— their mania causes the oddest books to be confiscated: *Black Beauty,* for instance, until it was suggested they should read it to see what it was about. But the most critical books are on sale, provided they are not tinged with Marxism.

Perhaps the words of a Nationalist publisher I met seven years ago in Johannesburg might suggest an answer: 'You Kaffir-boeties can go on talking,' he said, good-naturedly enough. 'We've got the police.'

And, from another Nationalist: 'We don't mind books. The Kaffirs don't read books, they read the newspapers. And we don't mind what the whites read.'

In Salisbury I was told by someone trying to buy Gunther's *Inside Africa* that the bookseller had only produced it from beneath the counter with great reluctance. 'But he says horrible things about us,' said this good lady indignantly. 'It isn't a nice book.'

There is no real need for a censorship in Southern Rhodesia.

* * * *

An African trade-union leader tells me about his difficulties getting a passport in 1953 to come to Britain for a trade-union conference. First they asked him for a large deposit; then, when he had managed to raise the sum (I think £150), said they would consider the matter.

At last they called him in and asked, 'What route would you take?'—meaning did he intend to visit Communist countries, as he did once before. He said: 'The same route as before—Nairobi, Cairo, Rome, London—unless the air company has changed its route.'

'And are you going to visit Caux again?' (Caux is the headquarters of Moral Rearmament.)

'No, I do not plan to visit Caux this time.'

He did not get his passport and is not hopeful of getting one.

About Moral Rearmament: 'All they are interested in is getting hold of us trade-union leaders. They come to see us, night after night after night for months. They aren't interested in ordinary people, it is the political leaders they concentrate on. Once I asked one of their men: "If Moral Rearmament is so necessary for good relations between white and black, why don't you sign on Mr. Fletcher" (Minister of Native Affairs), "then perhaps his heart will change towards us and he will repeal the Land Apportionment Act." And another time they came and said they had been guided in a prayer during a Quiet Time that I should go to Caux again. I said: "That's very strange, because I have just had guidance in my Quiet Time that I must not go to Caux." So now Moral Rearmament leaves me alone.'

This man is a Roman Catholic. Long ago he was threatened with excommunication if he went on with his trade-union activities. He told the priest: 'Then excommunicate me. But I have God in my heart, you cannot take Him from me.'

* * * *

A party where some people who have left South Africa because they are afraid of what will happen there and are now settled in Southern Rhodesia, talk to another South African whose last visit this is to Salisbury: his passport has expired and he knows he will not be given another one.

To his ex-compatriots he says: 'When Central Africa goes the way of the Union, where are you going to emigrate to then? Britain?'

'There's just a chance Central Africa may not go the same way.'

'Why? How? Have even one of the basic laws been changed since Federation?'

'The atmosphere is much more pleasant here.'

'It may be more pleasant for the whites, but not for the

Africans. I'm going back to Johannesburg tomorrow, and I know I shan't get out again. I'm in it for better or for worse.'

'When the time comes the Africans aren't going to distinguish between kind-hearted white liberals like us and the others. They'll simply cut the throats of everyone with a white skin.'

'Then at least my throat'll be cut on my own soil, in my own country. I'm not running away.'

'There's nothing white progressives can do any more. We aren't even allowed to do welfare work now. We aren't allowed any contact with the Africans at all. South Africa will be delivered by the Africans themselves without our help.'

'It's my country as well as theirs. I'm third generation. I could run away to England tomorrow if I wanted, but I'm sticking it out. South Africa is my country because I've always fought for racial equality. And if they stick an assegai into me on the day by mistake then there's no hard feelings.'

*　　*　　*　　*

I met an old school friend in the street. She was one of the big girls when I was new at school. I was very homesick, and she was good to me. Now she is a thin, anxious, greying woman. We exchanged small-talk for a time. Then she said:

'Good luck. I wish you all the luck there is. A lot of us hate what happens here. We aren't all bad, you know.'

'But I haven't said so,' I said.

'But you're always sorry for the natives. Well, I am, too. It's all awful. I know it is. But some of us white people have hard lives. Things aren't easy for some of us. My old man's failed in farming and he's got an office job. We don't do well. A lot of us don't do well. Some of the natives are earning nearly as much as we are. I know not many. But plenty of us are having bad times. And if you haven't got money in this country you're nothing. That's all that matters, money.'

'I'm sorry things haven't gone well for you,' I said.

'I'm not complaining, don't think that. Some people have it lucky and others don't. That's life, isn't it? But sometimes I think we're worse off than the natives. They don't seem to worry as much as we do. And they're such a cheerful lot—I envy them. I do envy them. And they're so poor. One of them's a friend of mine. Yes, a real friend. She was my nanny for my little girl. Now I go and see her. She's in Highfield—you know, the new township. It's pretty, isn't it? I told the Superintendent she is still working for me, so I can go and see her. She's always so cheerful and they live on £10 a month, five of them. It makes me feel ashamed, with my troubles. She says to me: "Now have a good cry, missus, and tell me what's wrong. We're both women, aren't we? We both have the same troubles." So I do. . . .'

She looked at me anxiously, afraid she had not made me understand something very important to her. 'You know, years ago, I'd never have believed it if someone had said I could feel about a native woman as if she were my real friend. But I do. So things are changing here. Don't you think they are changing?'

VII

ABOUT THIS TIME I began to feel a restlessness, the lack of something. What was it? Of course, a car—now in London I use buses and trains, and in moments of urgency a taxi, and never want a car. But in these American suburbs life is built around the motor-car. Without a car one is incomplete.

I therefore borrowed one and drove fast down to Bulawayo, passing Gatooma, Hartley and Gwelo.

In Gwelo I wanted to see the fine new steel-works; apparently there is only one other like it in the world. But they would not give me permission because of my political views. I do not know whether they imagined I would be able to deduce the secret processes of steel-making from a single walk around the works, and afterwards use these secrets for evil ends, or—but I don't know. I was sorry about this, because people tell me this is one of the most interesting places to see in Southern Rhodesia.

Instead I had a good look at the new secondary school for Africans which will be opened next year. It is built on a beautiful site on high ground outside Gwelo; a fine building, with accommodation for pupils and teachers every bit as good as that considered suitable for white pupils and teachers. I was told that they are now discouraging white visitors, because these go off and complain bitterly about the Government which is spoiling the natives.

Then I had a look at the housing in Gwelo itself.

All these towns, big and small, are on the same pattern, which is the same pattern as in South Africa. Flying over these cities one can see the shape of industrialization emerging: the white town rising tall and shapely in sky-scrapers, or spreading itself in gardened villas; and around them the native townships. From the air the townships look like a child's playing blocks arithmetically arranged; hundreds of identical small huts or houses. The older townships are a confusion of brick lines, shanties and shacks.

An African's experience of urban life is the same in any city of white Africa—Cape Town, Johannesburg, Durban, Salisbury, Bulawayo, the cities of the Copper Belt, the towns of East Africa. An African enters the white man's town with an assortment of 'passes' in his hand; must submit to the sometimes brutal, sometimes paternal, Location Superintendent, to the welfare officers and the police; he enters industrialisation through the only gate there is: the segregated township. The policy for the Reserves differs from country to country, but not for the towns.

Gwelo is a miniature of the bigger towns. There is a new township for the better-off Africans some miles out of town, consisting of hundreds of tiny, mass-produced houses. In the locations of the town itself I saw the worst conditions I have seen anywhere. In the brick lines, that is, small windowless brick rooms built side by side under a single roof, the doors open on to the dust between the rows. Inside, you see chairs and tables drawn up to the ceiling on ropes, to be let down as needed. On the walls, pictures of the Queen torn out of the magazines. These rooms are very clean and tidy, although a dozen or more people may be living in them.

In a courtyard in another part of the location, consisting of ten single rooms built around an unroofed, unfloored space, where the cooking and washing were done, about fifty people, men, women and children, were living. From the entrance to this court one could see, a hundred yards off across the dust, a straggling group of iron-dome shapes stuck here and there on the ground. That was where some of the municipal employees lived. A woman from the court said primly to me: 'Do not go there, madam. Those are very poor, rough people. They are no good.'

I began to walk off towards this camp, but was stopped quickly by my guide—for I had not got official permission to enter the location on this occasion. 'For God's sake,' he said, 'are you crazy? You can't just wander about here looking at things like that. If you stay in the car with me, it'll be all right: if any of the superintendents see you, they'll think you've got permission. But they don't let people in to see these conditions as a rule.'

So I did not see inside the iron kettles where the poor, rough, no-good people lived.

Then I drove on down to Bulawayo. There was nothing I enjoyed more, during the whole trip, than the driving very fast over those good, empty roads, between one little town and the next. Sometimes a ploughed field, sometimes the sharp green shimmer of late mealies, but mostly empty, rolling bush, with nothing, not a single human being, in sight. Sometimes I stopped the car and left it and went off into the bush and sat in the grass under a tree for the pleasure of being alone. I had not been alone in seven years. In London one can never be alone, not even with the doors locked and the telephone off the hook. Always there is the pressure of people. But here, it seemed, I was breathing free for the first time since I left home. No one knew where I was. All around me, acres and acres of empty country. It was like being a child again, when I spent all day alone by myself in the bush.

But, alas, I was being a journalist, and had responsibilities, so I had to move on again, down towards Bulawayo.

Bulawayo is not a pretty town, like Salisbury with its gardens and trees. Salisbury is the civil service town, rather smug and dull. Bulawayo is commercial and ugly, and much more lively and enterprising. It is typical of Bulawayo that the cooling towers of the power-station rise from the middle of the town, are not pushed off to one side as they are in Salisbury. One approaches Bulawayo through factories, watching how the cooling towers lift above the town; they are pale, squat, beautiful curved shapes, lightening and darkening as the heavy smoke sifts the sunlight over them.

In Bulawayo I interviewed a great many people, but they said nothing that had not already been said in Salisbury.

*   *   *   *

A visit to the Hope Fountain Mission, a few miles outside of Bulawayo. It is a London Missionary Society place, the oldest in the country, dating from Lobengula's time; and a house there is built on the site of one where the Rudd concession was signed.

It is run by a pleasant and humorous couple, Mr. and Mrs. Partridge. In their house I met some of the African teachers. We discussed Partnership, and how Mr. Todd was helping the missions with generous grants of money.

The teachers told stories about the colour bar with a gentle humour entirely unbitter.

The girls said that when they went into the shops to buy, the white assistant called them 'nanny.' 'Here, nanny!' or: 'Not that counter, nanny!' And the men said they were called 'boy.' 'Well, boy, what do you want?'

They are very poor. A matriculated teacher is paid £20 a month; a teacher with the Cambridge School Certificate, plus teacher training, gets £14 a month.

Many male teachers leave their work because they can earn more money in other jobs.

But for the women there is no alternative, unless they want to look after children at a few shillings a month, or to be trained again as nurses. A woman teacher, with a teacher-training certificate, gets about £8 a month.

Many of these teachers pay out of their small wages for the education of a younger brother and sister. For instance, a girl on the staff here pays £20 a year for her sister to be trained as a teacher.

Two things were particularly discussed. One, the uses and abuses of correspondence courses, which are immensely popular. It cost £12 cash, or 14 guineas in instalments, to take the junior certificate and £25 for matriculation. This is a great deal of money to find out of ordinary wages of £4, £5, £6 a month. Many begin the courses and find they cannot keep up the instalments. But in spite of these difficulties a great number of people manage to pass the examinations. Three Africans in Southern Rhodesia have got university degrees by correspondence course.

But while these courses help a number to get an education who could not otherwise do so, there are some unscrupulous firms, operating particularly from the Union, which batten on the ignorance of Africans about legal matters. For instance, there are many cases where people who had only filled in the form asking for a propaganda booklet have been sued by firms for the full cost of the course. Some, terrified, paid the money; others were rescued by worldly-wise friends.

The other thing discussed—and I was to hear it talked of many times—was the problem of the African who wants to take secondary education and can find no place in the schools. At immense cost and sacrifice an African will get his Standard VI certificate and then find there is nothing he can do but become an unskilled labourer.

'The argument is,' said Mr. Partridge, 'that a white child must have at least primary education even if he ends up by being a farm assistant or a ganger, and what is sauce for the goose is sauce for the gander. But the Africans do not see it in this way. For them, education is the path to a better life, or otherwise it is wasted.'

I heard this point put in various ways: for instance, about the kind of books that are popular in libraries. On the Copper Belt there is an attractive library attached to one of the mines. The official who showed me over it said that novels, plays or poetry were never taken off the shelves, while biographies, dictionaries, encyclopaedias and do-it-yourself books could not be supplied in big enough quantities.

'The African,' said this man with disapproval, 'is not interested in knowledge for its own sake, but only in knowledge that will pass an examination or get him a bigger wage.'

The novels in this library were mostly forgotten Victorian fiction; not a sign of that now considerable body of novels written in the last decade about modern Africa. I suppose it is not realistic to expect it, since all these novels are without exception a protest against the system. But while the authorities do not provide these novels in libraries—one official said he would not 'waste money in future on novels'—I noticed that all the Africans I met had read at least *Cry the Beloved Country*. So when what few African libraries there are cease to provide a home for rejects from the white libraries, fiction might become more popular.

The plays in this particular library were the complete works of Oscar Wilde, Noel Coward and J. M. Barrie. They had, said my guide, in the voice of one who says 'I told you so!' never been taken out.

Mr. Partridge, however, an intelligent and practical man, does not talk this sort of nonsense; and his mission is a friendly and hopeful place where white people and black people like each other.

And the country around it is beautiful; a tough, dry thorn-country, every tree full of doves cooing. It had rained, and the pale earth gleamed with silky brown puddles.

It reminded me of the big vlei on our farm, where I used to lie on an ant-heap with my rifle and pick off the doves as they settled on surrounding trees, and take them back to the house for pigeon pie.

That vlei was unlike the other big vlei at the back of our house, where my brother and I went shooting for guinea-fowl and for buck, because the road ran through it that went out to the gold mine in the Ayrshire hills, where big lorries were always passing; and because one of the main paths crossing it led from one Native Reserve to another; so it was too noisy a place for buck and guinea-fowl. But the doves and the pigeons did not seem to mind. There was a brief moment in every year when that dry, brown vlei blossomed with colour, for a variety of big white-and-pink striped lilies grew there at the moment of the first heavy rains.

The third vlei was the biggest of them all, three miles long, half a mile wide, full of thorn trees and grey rocks and heavy, long grass. I have never met anyone there, white or black; it was always empty, drugged with heat and loneliness.

The lilies grew there, too, for about a week in every wet season.

THE LILIES

This morning it was, on the pavement,
When that smell hit me again
And set the houses reeling.
People passed like rain:
(The way rain moves and advances over the hills)
And it was hot, hot and dank,
The smell like animals, strong, but sweet too.
What was it?
Something I had forgotten.
I tried to remember, standing there,
Sniffing the air on the pavement.
Somehow I thought of flowers.
Flowers! That bad smell!
I looked: down lanes, past houses—
There, behind a hoarding,
A rubbish-heap, soft and wet and rotten.

Then I remembered:
After the rain, on the farm,
The vlei that was dry and paler than a stone
Suddenly turned wet and green and warm.
The green was a clash of music.
Dry Africa became a swamp
And swamp-birds with long beaks
Went humming and flashing over the reeds
And cicadas shrilling like a train.

I took off my clothes and waded into the water.
Under my feet first grass, then mud,
Then all squelch and water to my waist.
A faint iridescence of decay,
The heat swimming over the creeks
Where the lilies grew that I wanted:
Great lilies, white, with pink streaks
That stood to their necks in the water.
Armfuls I gathered, working there all day.
With the green scum closing round my waist,
The little frogs about my legs,
And jelly-trails of frog-spawn round the stems.
Once I saw a snake, drowsing on a stone,
Letting his coils trail into the water.
I expect he was glad of rain too
After nine months of being dry as bark.

I don't know why I picked those lilies,
Piling them on the grass in heaps,
For after an hour they blackened, stank.
When I left at dark,
Red and sore and stupid from the heat,
Happy as if I'd built a town,
All over the grass were rank
Soft, decaying heaps of lilies
And the flies over them like black flies on meat . . .

* * * *

A telephone call from someone I didn't know. A South African voice. I met him in a café, a big man with the open, direct face and the blue, aggressive stare of a certain type of blond South African.

'Well,' I said, 'what did you want to see me for?'—he had insisted it was very important, he could not tell me over the telephone.

He sat opposite me, sideways, poking his head around to look at me with an insistent pressure of his full eyes. I had the impression that he might easily get up and walk off.

He was silent a moment, then he took a small pill-box out of his pocket, opened it, and picked out of it a white, fluffy chicken-feather smudged with tar. He pushed the feather at me over the table, and seemed to be waiting to see what I would do.

'What are you?' I asked. 'The Ku Klux Klan?'

Suddenly he got angry. He got angry as if he had been wanting an excuse to get angry. 'I don't like that kind of talk,' he said. 'I don't like it.' Chin sticking out at me, eyes blazing. All the same, he looked ill at ease, and as if the anger were mechanically regulated. The whole scene had something mechanically dramatic about it.

'For that matter, I don't like being given feathers with tar on them.'

'Oh, you don't?'—he was suddenly a small boy; it occurred to me that the things he was saying had the ritual quality of small boys' insults in a quarrel. Then, in a burst: 'I said I'd do it and I have. I have and that's all.'

With which he got up, hesitated, and went to the door. At the door, he swung sharp around, and marched back between the crowded café tables. Then he said in a half-angry, half-appealing way, a call to my better nature as it were: 'Hell, man, have some sense, man. You don't want to put all these ideas into these munts' heads do you? You've lived here, it's not that you don't know. What do you want to put ideas into their heads *for*?' He waited a minute, and then muttered, blue eyes wandering uneasily around: 'I don't get it, I don't get it.' Then he went out again, smartly marching as before, without looking back.

* * * *

An invitation by Bulawayo's courteous and liberal Dr. Ashton, to hear Dr. Holleman, an anthropologist attached to his department, lecture to a group of African welfare workers.

Dr. Holleman lived for some time in a Mashona village, and has written a book about these people. He is particularly interested in how industrialisation is affecting tribal patterns.

The room was in the Native Administration offices, and had about thirty African welfare workers in it, and three of the white officials.

Dr. Holleman spoke well and clearly, and not at all in the patronising way that is so common to white officials. He might have been delivering a lecture to a group of fellow-anthropologists.

'Now, gentlemen,' he said, and 'In other words, gentlemen,' and I could see how the listening Africans liked his politeness.

But it was very cerebral. 'The theme of my lecture, gentlemen, is the community. The African community. And the basis of community, which is the tribe.'

And with this he drew on the blackboard a circle—the tribe. 'And the unit of the tribe is the kinship group.'

And with that he divided his circle into neat portions—the kinship groups.

'And what gives the feeling of homogeneity in the village is the way these units are shaped.'

The Africans were listening very intently, and I was, too; for it was difficult for me to see the tribe as a circle and the kinship groups as segments of it.

Dr. Holleman was explaining how these units were broken into and scattered by the young men going into the towns to work.

'Gentlemen, nothing stays the same; everything changes; if you disturb one part of a cultural pattern, then every part of it changes. And so all your tribal patterns are changing, not only from the natural movement that is inevitable with time, but because of the single fact that the men are no longer part of the fabric of the tribe. You know that, of course, better than I do. But what I want to explain particularly today is how these changes have affected the lives of your women, and the role your women are playing—in the tribes, and also in the towns, when they follow their husbands into the towns.'

And now the lecturer broke off to explain how very wrong it is when people say—which so often they do— that African women are exploited and badly treated by their men. Newspaper men, officials, and all sorts of ignorant people, said Dr. Holleman, are always complaining about the poor tribal women. And nothing could be farther from the truth.

The tribal woman is a person of consequence, with property rights and authority. And even this question of lobola, which is interpreted through European eyes as payment for a woman, is in fact proof of an opposite truth: lobola is a complicated and dignified ritual, and above all it expresses the value of the woman, and is a guarantee of her good treatment in the new family.

In the tribe, said Dr. Holleman, the woman is weakest in her roles as mother and wife; strongest and most powerful as sister, paternal aunt, mother-in-law. As a sister, for instance, she will give her cattle to her brother, so that he may get himself a wife. As aunt to her brother's children, if he dies then it is she who is responsible for them, she who is in place of the father. As mother-in-law, the mother of her sons' wives, since the power of fertility passes from mother to daughter, she must be placated, respected, cherished.

And now this powerful woman, secure in her place in the fabric of the tribe, with all her responsibilities and duties well marked out for her, and understood by every-body—this woman comes into town, and she is nothing. She is nothing. She is only a wife, only a mother. All her other roles have gone. She sits at home, under the wing of her husband, and no wonder she is restless and bad-tempered.

(At this point there was a stir of agreement among the listening men.)

And her husband is restless and dissatisfied and bad-tempered.

'But the fabric of the tribe is broken, gentlemen, the fabric of the community is destroyed; and it is you who must rebuild it. It is your task, gentlemen, to create the new feeling of cohesion. I don't know how. By clubs, perhaps? Somehow you must find a way. Otherwise you cannot keep your feeling as a people.'

And now, said Dr. Holleman, he wanted to discuss the question of 'spares.' 'Spares' is the word among Africans for those women in the towns who did not marry, who lived with a man for a time before moving on to another. 'And how critical you men are,' said Dr. Holleman, 'of these women! How insulting! And whose fault is it that these women exist? Why, it is your fault, gentlemen. If they did not minister to your convenience, then they would not be with us in so great a number.'

And he went on to say that among the 'spares' were to be found the most independent and fearless of the women; and from them they, the welfare workers, should take the best for teaching the others. It was no use, he said, criti-cising these women and offering them nothing better. 'Give them responsibility! Give them trust! And set them to uplifting the level of the other, more passive women. It is for you to do this, for you to help them. . . .'

Dr. Holleman spoke on these lines for over an hour; and when he had finished, there were questions. A man whose voice was like a deep swarm of bees asked about some point of tribal law; and another spoke very crisply about the insolence of the 'spares.'

But what I was thinking about was how once I heard a violent feminist lecturing a group of English trade union-ists about how the British working-man treated his wife. 'Look,' she said, 'how you expect your wives not only to run after you day and night as if you were so many helpless babies; but half the time they have jobs as well, and children to bring up, and even so you don't lift a finger to help them. Why, your wives work twice as hard as you do; there is no more exploited creature in the world,' she concluded, 'than the British working-class wife.'

On the faces of these African welfare workers I saw exactly the same look of stubborn resistance as I saw then on the faces of those English trade unionists.

Later, I met a group of Superintendents for the Loca-tions and Townships of Bulawayo in another office, with Dr. Holleman. The difference between the old type of Native Department official and the new was clearly seen in the way they spoke of the Africans—one paternal, having no nonsense; one half-proud, half-apprehensive, the New Deal spirit.

We again discussed the women in the cities.

One official said how the men were dissatisfied with the women: always quarrelling, always visiting, always com-plaining. 'If only I had time to cook for myself I wouldn't bother with a wife.'

Another said husbands were continually coming to him asking for his support in matrimonial quarrels: 'I say to them, it's your job to keep your women in order, not mine.'

Because married accommodation is much better than single, men marry 'spares' so as to get a marriage certificate. But they do not regard them as true wives, and when they go back to their villages, abandon them.

So shortage of housing is perpetuating polygamy, or a form of polygamy.

Dr. Holleman, talking about 'spares,' suggested they were not true prostitutes. Immediate, and even shocked, disagreement from other officials: 'If they aren't prostitutes, what are they, then?'

'These women are a menace,' said one. 'All they care about is money and a good time. They'll leave their children with an old woman, or a relative, and go off after money.'

'And you can always tell the "spares" in a group of women; they are well dressed, and they don't carry their babies on their backs. And they look so damned insolent.'

I suggested that perhaps the 'spare' was a phenomenon of industrialising Africa; in Basil Davidson's book, *The African Awakening,* he described how the women of the cities in the Congo refuse marriage because they do so much better by themselves. And people familiar with the big cities of the Union say the same thing.

'There is no solution to this,' said an official, 'until we can house all the workers with their families. Until we can give the African a normal family life, we'll have prostitutes.'

'But supposing,' asked one, 'the African woman prefers not to marry even then?'

Here is a quotation from a letter by an African to the *African Weekly*; he begins by saying he has travelled widely in Northern Rhodesian towns, mines and villages, and says that 'prostitution is the gravest thing facing our community today.' He ends: 'The most dangerous side of this practice is its impact on family life. Some of the prostitutes I have met do not want to hear any word about marriage. To them marriage is the end of a profit-making career; it removes their freedom to go wherever they like. Now, knowing as we do that successful married life is the basis of any good society and the foundation of a God-fearing nation, we cannot be satisfied that they take such a poor view of married life. We cannot do without it, neither should our women be permitted to frown on it like that.'

It was generally concluded that adequate housing would solve this problem.

In short, the conversation ended on a familiar note: we all knew there is no hope of housing all the people who are coming into the towns on anything like a decent level; yet, if they are not housed properly, then the claims of Partnership will be proved false; it is intolerable that Partnership might fail; therefore better evade the issue. And so a sort of chivalry stops one, when with these earnest and sincere Partners, from pointing out these obvious facts; one begins to feel it would be in positive bad taste to say: 'Yes, but look at the economics of the thing.'

Report on Native Affairs, 1954: 'The presence of squatters in Municipal Areas and their peri-urban precincts is a persistent problem, the only satisfactory solution for which is the provision of adequate housing. Local authorities have been handicapped in this work by lack of finance, *and Government failure to obtain overseas the amount of capital required to launch a full programme to provide housing for Natives was a bitter disappointment to municipalities and other authorities.*'

Italics mine. To avoid taxing the big companies, and so that the privileged whites should not have to put their hands in their pockets, the Government goes hat in hand overseas, asking for money for native housing, education, and the Land Husbandry Act, as if the natives were a kind of responsibility for the international conscience.

'Do you want Partnership to succeed? Yes? Then give

us the money. And if you don't give us the money, this proves you don't understand our problems, and if Partnership fails it is your fault, not ours.'

A Government official from Northern Rhodesia said about Mr. Todd's trip to America to raise money: 'Well, these Americans are not such fools after all. They know quite well what's going on. Why should they fork out money, when they know that white farms are hundreds or thousands of acres big, and an African farm at best is a couple of hundred. They think: Why don't you give up some of your land to the Africans, and then you won't have to ask for charity.'

And when I saw Mr. Todd himself he exclaimed: 'It's a terrible thing! If I were trying to sell steel or Kariba or something with big profits, then I'd have no difficulty. But when I ask for money for something useful, like native housing, or agriculture, they won't give me the money.'

I was shown over Bulawayo's African housing projects.

The same as all the other cities: the majority of the Africans living crammed in the bad old lines and shacks and shanties, and then the new model townships outside the town.

Dr. Holleman was enthusiastic and hopeful about providing better beer-halls and entertainment places instead of the ugly prison-like beer-halls that now exist, which are mostly stretches of bare dust surrounded by wire, with a few wood benches in them—like chicken runs. He is a South African, and seemed to feel badly because the Union is under fire, when he says housing and welfare projects are on the same level as in the Federation, and sometimes much better.

'Everyone pats the Federation on the back, no one has a good word for the Nationalists, but the housing for natives is much better than here.'

There are one or two model townships in each city. An African is lucky if he can find a place in a house in one of these. In some, the houses can be bought. A model township looks like a thousand dolls' houses set out in neat rows. Sometimes they are very pretty, Highfield, in Salisbury, for instance; for someone with a marvellous sense of colour has designed the township as a whole, breaking up the regularity and uniformity of the place by painting the houses into individuality—not each house the same, but each one differently, porches, windows and doors emphasised by lime-green, yellow, magenta, ice-pink, blue-green, scarlet and cobalt, so that the township glitters on a slope against the bright blue sky.

The houses, considered as houses, are shocking.

The white people say: 'They are better than the huts they are used to.'

But while brick and breeze-block and board may be more hygienic than mud and thatch, what matters is the space. A family in an African village does not live in one hut, but in two or three big, airy huts, with as much space as there is in a medium-sized white house. Now, in these model townships, a family must live in two handkerchief-sized rooms. Some houses, a few, have indoor lavatories and showers; but most have the lavatories at the back of the house; so that each minuscule house has its minuscule lavatory, like a sentry-box, stuck mathematically behind it.

In these new townships the people live on every level, from a prim, proud suburbanity, in Victorian stuffiness, with shiny suites of furniture, antimacassars, heavy curtains, every surface covered with ornaments, through degrees where they may sleep on the floor wrapped in blankets but eat off a table; or sleep all in one big bed and eat squatting outside around a wood fire; or simply transfer their village habits straight into this urban setting, so that, looking through a doorway into the two minute rooms like large dog-kennels, at the rolled sleeping blankets, the cooking pots, the tin plates, a sack of grain or a sieve of ground-nuts, one imagines oneself standing in a village in the bush, looking into the doorway of a traditional hut. ·

The welfare officers busy themselves, and with the greatest faith and devotion, trying to make life palatable against odds. The women, they complain, are lazy, they don't take an interest in gardening as they do in their villages; the children don't get looked after properly; the people don't take hygiene seriously; the lavatories aren't kept clean. And: 'A family comes into town, you see the children losing their pot-bellies, the woman learns to keep house and cook and sew—then they go off back to the villages, to the old ways and the children die or get sick, and they forget everything they ever learned from us about hygiene and vitamins.'

Sewing classes, cooking classes, child-welfare classes are run intensively in all these model townships; some welfare officers talk as if a township is a kind of vast school for the people.

They look the same from city to city; because cheeseparing, mass-produced housing projects cannot produce much diversity of pattern; and often it is the same big firms which build them in several towns at once. They are unimaginably depressing and inhuman, and in five years they will be slums.

They are usually built a good way out from the white city, so that the people use bicycles to get to and from work, or walk the distance; sometimes there are bus services, but they are expensive.

In the old townships hostels are being built for single workers. I saw one in Bulawayo: a room has in it bunks in tiers; the men's possessions are in bundles on shelves, or in a sort of iron-cage affair which can be locked, beside each bunk. The rooms are big, bare, empty places, like a barracks. All the bicycles are kept in the sleeping-room for fear of theft.

Outside the old locations and the new townships are squatters' camps, for people who cannot get accommodation at all; and here houses are made of any material to hand—packing cases, beaten-out petrol and paraffin tins, bits of wood and sacking and cardboard. In Lusaka, for instance, which is a comparatively small town, there are twenty thousand people living in squatters' camps.

Bulawayo, it is estimated, has about a hundred thousand Africans living in it.

A group of Africans I interviewed said as follows:

The majority of men live in the single rooms. Many live sixteen to a room. The charge of £1 a month is paid by the employer. In such a room there will be one wood stove with two cooking spaces—the men line up to do their bit of cooking on it.

They get up at 5.30 and walk to work 5 or 6 miles, buying a piece of bread or sixpence worth of bones for soup on the way.

Buses cost 7d. a trip—that is, over a shilling a day, which cannot be afforded by people earning £3 or £4 a month. About 10 per cent have bicycles.

At midday there is an hour's break; they cook their soup on fires supplied by the employers, or eat the bread.

They walk back at five o'clock, cook their first good meal of the day at sundown.

At the native eating-houses meals can be bought: for 6d., maize porridge and two pieces of meat with soup liquor; for 1s., a proper meal with green vegetables and a sweet. But most use the eating-houses only on special occasions.

One man told me he was buying his house: £15 down, and the rest over thirty years. But the lease is only for forty years, so he is bitter because he will own his home for only ten years. 'It is because they are afraid the white people will want to spread over where our townships are, so they won't give us freehold unless we live miles away, and then we can't afford the transport.'

And: 'Here in Bulawayo the pass laws are administered leniently. It makes a great difference to us, not always worrying if we have forgotten one of our passes.'

This conversation concluded with: 'Our wages are geared to the old idea of us Africans—mealie-meal porridge and a loincloth. But we are trying to live decently. It is impossible on our wages to live on the European pattern, so we do as best we can, half-way between the two.'

* * * *

An evening at an adult night-school.

All classes are catered for up to Standard VI, with provision for leather-work and carpentry. The demand is such that the higher classes are all doubled—people have to be turned away.

Standing in the hall of this school, three young men were waiting to speak to the Superintendent, asking for a place in class. They went disconsolately away—no room until next term, possibly not till next year.

The Superintendent said: 'No class is in demand that does not show immediate results in the form of a certificate that might lead to higher wages; there is no interest in books that are not required for the syllabus or are related to an examination.'

In the first classroom we entered, the teacher was writing on the board: 'Increased poll-tax is good for Africans.'

Most of these young men—there are very few women—

work all day in the town and come here for two or three hours a night.

'But the terrible thing is,' said the Superintendent, 'that when they do get their certificates, after such a battle, what then? They seem to think the certificate will be a passport to a white-collar job or higher education. I don't know which is more heart-breaking—to have to turn them away when they come asking for a place in class or afterwards, when I have to say I can't find better work for them or a place in secondary school.'

After the night-school, a session in the milk-bar. Juke-box, Coca-Cola, the white boys and girls in jeans and crew-cuts, shouting and yelling and playing the fool. Our friend the teacher looks at them for some time and remarks: 'I loathe Americanisation. This place is getting more American by the day. And as for these white kids, they give me the creeps. Morons, most of them. And then I think of my poor Africans eating their hearts out for an education and they can't get it.'

This man says at length, and passionately, how he can't stand white-settler civilisation another minute. He is going to Britain. Yes, definitely, he is leaving, he can't stand it. What's the use of fighting this set-up? Ten years he's been in it now, first South Africa, but he left there thinking the Federation would be better, and now Partnership is the last straw—most of the whites think Partnership is just a bad joke, and so it is. All his energy is spent fighting over details, a few extra shillings here, a slight relaxation of a law there—never anything fundamental.

Then he tells how one of his African staff, a teacher, knows Shakespeare by heart, is a natural actor. 'What hope is there for him? Unless he leaves his own people and goes to Britain, he can't even see a play, let alone act in one. When the Reps. put on their last show, I begged them, I pleaded, to let some of my Africans come—they said *they* didn't mind, it was the audience they had to soft-soap. You'll never find anyone who minds—it's always the other fellow who's the villain. No, I'm getting out.'

Five minutes later he was back on his passion—African education.

I said, 'You know quite well you're not leaving, and if you did, you'd be back again in six months. You'd pine for Africa.'

'I'd pine for the Africans,' he said. 'They're a wonderful lot. But of course I wouldn't come back. What for? What good can a handful of us do?' And then he grinned and said: 'Of course you are quite right. I did leave once, and I came back again.'

Next evening, another night-school—this one a voluntary effort, the teachers giving one night a week of their time for the love of it.

In the Standard VI class I asked the first half-dozen pupils how they managed:

Up at five, with some bread to eat before leaving to walk five miles to the textile factory. They earned £1 2s. 6d. a week. Working hours, seven to five, with a half-hour break when they ate bread and drank tea. They went straight to evening classes from work, three hours every night. They lived in the brick lines, half a dozen to a room. It would take them three or four years to get the junior certificate.

I asked one what he would do then. 'I don't know,' he said.

'Do you want to be a teacher?'

'No, teachers don't get enough money.'

This class asked me to address them. I was in a dilemma. I could not speak my mind about the set-up without getting the people who ran the night-school into trouble.

But remembering how the Africans have to live under a

continual pressure of contempt and insult from the white people, how they are always being called backwards and ignorant and stupid, I said that the most exciting thing I had seen on my visit was how the Africans are fighting for an education; and how wonderful it was to see people who had to do hard physical labour all day working for hours every night, for the sake of knowledge. I said they were a richly endowed and talented people; and that, just as Africa is a wealthy continent with its wealth scarcely tapped, so, too, the African people are like a giant who does not yet know he is a giant.

Then they asked questions.

'In Britain, where there must also be many different tribes, do the tribes quarrel among themselves; or have they learned to get on well together; and is there a colour bar?'

I said that in Britain there was colour-prejudice among the ignorant and poorly-educated people, but there was no colour bar as it is known in Central Africa.

Whereupon I was asked how it was possible that the great white man could be poorly educated and ignorant?

I said that in Britain there were large numbers of poor and ignorant people, though not nearly as poor as the people in Africa, and these did all the hard work of the country, just as the Africans did here.

What did I think of Partnership?

I said I thought Prime Minister Todd and his men were quite sincere about Partnership. This was received in non-committal silence.

Why was it that when white people came out from Britain, first they were indignant about the colour bar and the treatment of the Africans, and then they very fast became just as rude and cruel as the old Rhodesians?

I said there were two reasons. One was that any white person who really fought against the colour bar was not popular among his own kind; and someone who had just emigrated from his own country to a new life here had great pressure put on him to conform. And besides, among any people, and no doubt that went for the Africans, too, there was never more than a minority who rebelled against a Government or a system.

This was received in silence; I think a dissenting one.

I said that the most important reason was that a number of the people who came out from Britain were not necessarily the best; and when they suddenly found themselves in the position of baases, able to push other people around, it went to their heads—I had been going to say that no doubt a certain number of Africans, if given the chance, would like to push other Africans around, a trend which was already very evident; but I was not allowed to get so far, for a stamping roar of approval went up, and what I was saying got drowned in the noise.

Then one of the teachers recited a piece from the American Declaration of Independence, and another came out and acted for us the old father in *Cry the Beloved Country,* mourning for his son:

> 'And now for all the people of Africa, the beloved country. Nkosi Sikelel' iAfrika, God save Africa. But he would not see that salvation. It lay afar off, because men were afraid of it. Because, to tell the truth, they were afraid of him and his wife and Msimangu and the young demonstrator. And what was there evil in their desires, in their hunger? That men should walk upright in the land where they were born, and be free to use the fruits of the earth, what was there evil in it? Yet men were afraid, with a fear that was deep, deep in the heart, a fear so deep that they hid their kindness, or brought it out with fierceness and anger, and hid it behind fierce and frown-

ing eyes. They were afraid because they were so few. And such fear could not be cast out, but by love.

'It was Msimangu who had said, Msimangu who had no hate for any man, I have one great fear in my heart, that one day when they turn to loving they will find we are turned to hating.

'Oh, the grave and the sombre words.'

We all listened in complete silence; and it was like being in church, too grave an occasion for applause.

And afterwards we, the white people, went to another juke-boxed, Coca-Cola'd milk bar, full of white youth who had just come out of the cinema, and the Africans went back to their brick rabbit-holes.

*　　*　　*　　*

Standing in the dust outside a long row of brick rooms, looking in: table and chairs raised to the ceiling on ropes, two narrow iron bedsteads crammed in, covering all the floor-space, and about a dozen people sitting on the beds. Four young men, who were legally living in the room; four young women, their 'spares'; a visiting preacher; four old wives, jolly and fat; and a sampling of small children. They were singing a syncopated hymn-tune to mouth-organs and banjos.

The supper of maize porridge was cooking on the fire outside—a handful of sticks in the dust, small flames, pale in the last sunshine around the big iron cooking pot.

The official said: 'These conditions are as bad as anything in Britain during the industrial revolution. But thank God we've got the sun; we've got this magnificent climate. Imagine this squalour under an English sky.'

And, from another official, who asked me to make a point of writing about tuberculosis—how it is on the rampage, a particularly virulent form of it; and how one of the reasons why it is spreading fast from the crammed cities to the Reserves is because there aren't enough hospital beds, so that the Africans when they are too ill to work are sent back to the villages: 'Do you know what's the mainstay of white supremacy? No, not the police. The sun. The only reason they get away with these dreadful conditions they make the natives live in is that the sunlight makes life tolerable.'

*   *   *   *

After I had left Bulawayo, I got a message telling me that the C.I.D. had been around interviewing the people I had seen, telling them I was a wicked and unscrupulous person, and they would get themselves into trouble if they consorted with such as me.

I know how these matters are conducted, because an African once described to me how, after he had been talking to a certain progressive churchman, the C.I.D. came around to his house.

'So you've been complaining to Father X?'

'Not complaining, no.'

'You've been telling him a pack of lies about your conditions?'

'No, I would not say I have been telling lies.'

'But you've been talking to Father X?'

'There is no law against it, so far as I know.'

'You'd better watch out. We've got our eyes on you. You needn't think we don't know what's going on.'

VIII

EVERYBODY TALKS about Kariba, with an odd mixture of resentment and pride: too big a project, they say, for two hundred thousand people—yes, of course it is an imaginative and bold step; but how can a handful of white people find £113,000,000?

This is the first big Federal project, a symbol of the success of Federation, a big dam on the Zambezi, 200 miles below the Victoria Falls. Before leaving Britain I had promised to find out as much as I could about the Africans who were working on it, and those who are being moved from the flood areas.

The Federal Hydro-Electric Board very kindly gave me permission to go up and see what was going on; and therefore, in our borrowed car, Mr. Paul Hogarth and I set off one afternoon; for he wanted to make drawings on the dam site.

The road up north is the one I had driven over a thousand times as a child; it was the road into the city, and I was afraid it might be changed. For the first 20 miles out of Salisbury it has become a fine, wide highway; but after that there are strips and corrugations and dust-drifts; and I was able to think myself back into those interminable journeys in and out of town; for my father hated driving fast, and in any case our cars were always very old and could not do more than about thirty miles an hour.

Strips are a Southern Rhodesian invention; instead of surfacing a whole road, a double line of strips of tarmac are laid, just wide enough for the wheels. They are efficient if kept in order; if not they become sharply-edged pitted ledges swirling with sand. It was pleasant to drive over the familiar route, watching the stations go by—Mount Hampden; Darwendale, with its chrome mountain —the one over which the sun rose through my window at home—and its soil glittering with fallen chrome fragments; and then on to Maryland and Trelawney, which are sandveld, the earth of a beautiful pale, crusty gold. And next there was Banket, which was the station we used. Impossible to give any idea how much the station meant to us farmers who lived so far from town. The little clutch of corrugated iron-roofed buildings, a couple of stores, the garage, the post office, the station-master's house—this was our town, and going to the station was always an event.

All the way from Salisbury I was telling myself that now I would be firm, and turn off from Banket up past the police station, and along that red-dust road between the trees that once was a railway track leading to a big gold-mine that has long since fallen into the status of a small-working operation. 'Yes,' I said, turning the car sharply over the glittering hot railway lines, 'now I must certainly go and see how the hill where the house used to be rises empty and bush-covered from the mealie-fields.' But I did not go.

We drove through Banket fast. There is a new hotel there, built just where at one time the mealie sacks used to be laid out waiting for the train to take them to Salisbury and the markets. The sacks were of new, strong, golden-brown stuff, with a double line of bright blue down them, smelling strongly of ink from the farmers' brand-marks. They were stacked up on each other 10 feet high, with dirt lanes between; so the children in for the afternoon from the farms used to play on them, jumping perilously from one barricade to another. The sacks were hot and smooth; and sitting on them the hard, small grains inside gave to one's weight like shifting sand. The smell was of sun-heated red dust, and ink, and jute and fresh, sweet mealies. The sacks were laid at either end of the rows in such a way that they made a bulging staircase; and if one sat on the top and let oneself go, one slid very fast and, bumping over the sacks, landed with a thud in the soft, warm dust.

But now there is a large, modern hotel. Because this is the main road north, along which cars come up all the way from the Cape, through to Northern Rhodesia, and so to Kenya, and ultimately, if they wish, to Egypt, there are hotels building all along it. This is the road from Cape to Cairo: but it is still a rough and primitive road; and thus, for me at least, enjoyable to drive over. Sinoia is twenty miles up the railway line from Banket; and that is no longer a station merely, but a small town. I remember sitting in the car waiting for my father when he had to drive there to get a spare part for the car, or for the farm machinery, or to take a labourer into the Native Hospital. It used to be just a station, a few buildings, the iron roofs glittering with heat, the earth rocking with heat-waves.

Sinoia is extremely hot; all my memories of it are of that truly withering heat. But on this evening we drove through it fast, past another fine new hotel, and along to Karoi. I had not before driven farther than Sinoia, for me it was the end of the stations; and beyond that there was the Zambezi escarpment.

The road became sharply worse, badly potholed and swirling with dust. The plan was to drive until the turn-off to the Kariba Gorge, and then find some hotel to stay the night. I was imagining the little hotels, lines of rooms built side by side under a low roof off a verandah, whose existence depended on the bar which was what Banket hotel used to be like. The children of the district would stand on the verandah and watch the Government officials and the commercial travellers and the insurance men, in their correct town clothes, standing at the bar drinking with the farmers in their khaki and their bush-shirts.

The road was twisting, swerving up and down; the air was full of reddish dust as the sun went down, so that as the car turned at a bend a blaze of red, glinting with particles of light, blinded us and made the car rock. That grass known as red-top, a soft, feathery, reddish-pink grass, was growing everywhere; and the sun swung over it, so that it was like soft flames springing up, or the sweep of a veld-fire with the wind behind it, when sun-thinned flames lap forward over unconsumed stems. The autumn green of the trees was gilded and burnished with the low sunlight. Once a small buck sprang across the road, and its coat was heated to a warm, shining, reddish-brown. The tree-trunks flashed up dark, showing red wakes of the rose-red grass behind; and the sun-heat slid fast up their solid heaviness, roughening the bark so that it held pockets of red glow.

Just before the sun sank, and a red blaze shot up the clear blue of the sky, the light was coming flickering through the tree-trunks and laying black bars over coloured dust; and, turning a corner, the glow was so intense it burned out the softness of small foliage up tall grass stems. The grass on a turn of the road was ten feet high, still stiff with sap; and each stem glittered a pale, clear red, like a forest of fine tinted wires; and the tree-trunks behind showed black and still against the flare of red, the roughness of bark swallowed in substance of shadow. Fine perpendicular grass stems; straight rising trunks; and, above, the flat-layered branches of the bushveld, black with glowing edges—a springing upwards of a myriad sharp lines, backed with soaring trunks; and, above, the blocking horizontal masses of the branches.

And then the big red sun dipped under, and there was an exquisite afterglow, warm and nostalgic and clear; and the air was sweet with hot dust and hot leaves and warm grasses.

Soon it was dark; the lights of cars showed miles away, dipping through the bush, or shining up in a wide, white dazzle over the farther side of ridges. And the road was very bad; and we hoped that soon an ugly little roadside bar-hotel would show itself; or at least, I did; for I wanted to sleep again beneath a corrugated-iron roof, and hear it sing and crackle as the night-chills fought in the metal with the day heat.

Then, where the map said we could expect Karoi, a big white hotel rose three-cornered on the road, shining with car lights and strung with little coloured bulbs.

So the car was left in a rank parked solid with cars and we went into a fine modern hotel, full of farmers in for an evening's relaxation, and travellers going north and south. The verandah was pleasant to sit and drink on, looking as it does on to a little court edged with flowers and decked with more coloured lights strung over white walls, which reminded me of a hotel I once stayed in in Spain, which had exactly this air of warm moon-lit laziness, and even more because of the women wearing bare-armed linen and cotton dresses, and moving with the indolence of hot weather.

The dinner was disagreeable because there was a middle-aged lady at the table from Kenya. She said she was leaving Kenya, where she had lived most of her life, because things were so bad there. Mau Mau? But no; the natives were under control again; it was the Indians, she said; the Indians all over the place; and Indians and natives coming into the bars now, and even to eat in some of the hotels. They had a bad type of Indian, she said, they were traders, and always speaking up for themselves. And now they were even asking for land; they were getting uppity. Who ever heard of Indians being farmers?

Perhaps in India, it was suggested, it could be said they were farmers. 'Then why don't they go back there? We don't want them.' But the Government was soft. It was soft with the Kaffirs and it was soft with the Indians. Look what it did with Mau Mau. Giving in to Britain as usual—our men knew how to deal with the natives, but the British troops had different ideas, and look at the fuss in Britain over nothing, the Kaffir never did understand anything but a good hiding. And she was going to live in Southern Rhodesia, which was the only civilized country left. South Africa was no good because of the Nationalists, and Northern Rhodesia was a Kaffir country, but Southern Rhodesia was still a British country, thank heavens for that at least.

After this, we followed the advice of the management, and decided to spend the evening in the drive-in cinema at the back of the hotel. Drive-in cinemas are now rapidly becoming a major feature of life in the southern half of the continent—naturally, since it saves one from being parted from one's car too early in the evening.

But I admit it seemed odd to find one in Karoi, which must be (if I remember it right) about 170 miles from Salisbury, and another 150 from the Zambezi; it is a little station stuck in the bush.

We took the car round to the back of the hotel, and there drove it up the ramp, anchoring the front wheels in a groove for the purpose, had the loudspeaker fixed on to the window, and looked at the big, white screen that glimmered soft in the moonlight against a blaze of enormous African stars. Then there was a newsreel, and then a British film whose name I forget, but the script was by Mr. Priestley, and the main part was played by Alec Guinness. The story was about a young clerk told he was soon to die; so he drew out all his savings and set himself to have a good time in a luxury hotel. I think I might have considered this a good film had I seen it in Leicester Square, but nothing could have seemed more incongruous and pitiful than this cosy little drama of provincial snobberies and homespun moralities played out in front of ranks of tobacco farmers in their big cars, with the African waiters hanging about in the shadows, watching the screen with one ear open for a summons from the verandah whence came the chink of ice in glasses; while behind the screen the Southern Cross moved sideways to make room for Orion, and the crickets chirped incessantly just off in the bush.

We were off along the road next morning while the moon still whitened it. The light changed fast and warmed; and the bush darkened and sprang up on either side of the road as the sun burst over the hills.

The turn-off to Kariba has a big notice that there is no accommodation for sightseers. After the pitted, rutted main road, the new dirt-surfaced road to Kariba was restful to drive on. It winds along through increasingly wild country down towards the Zambezi, for 60 miles or so; and the kloofs and hills and turning points along it have names like Puff-Adder Rise and Buffalo Nek.

From time to time the car was stopped at a tsetse fly post, and the wheels and body of the car were sprayed. When the car stopped for a couple of minutes, it was at once invaded by half a dozen innocent-looking flies, which we swatted at once, reminding ourselves that very few people die of sleeping sickness.

We reached the site at about nine in the morning, a turn off the road into a flat place between hills, which were covered all over with camps, tents and breeze-block huts shining white through thick trees, while land-rovers and bulldozers manoeuvred everywhere, over sun-dried mud-ruts. White men supervised groups of Africans doing this or that sort of work.

It all looked like a gold-rush film; another world from the comfortable conformities of little Salisbury; and I liked it very much. This was the atmosphere of the old days, the good old days that people remember so sentimentally; and I cannot help remembering them sentimentally too.

It took some time to track down the official who would be responsible for us—a young Frenchman from Mauritius who, after a few years here, was already completely Rhodesian and who went out of his way all day to be as helpful and as hospitable as he could be, in the Rhodesian tradition of fine hospitality.

First, he explained that all this scene of chaotic activity was temporary; for affairs were still in the stage of building access roads and permanent housing; and groups of people were being flown in daily from Greece and Italy; and the African labourers were being garnered in from wherever they could be found.

He took us in his land-rover over roads such as I have never even imagined; but they were not roads, merely those parts of a rough terrain that offered the least resistance to locomotion. I was filled with respect for land-rovers; this one climbed up tracks as steep as house-sides without any effort, and finally up a high mountain, so that Paul Hogarth could make drawings of the landscape.

On the top of this mountain we sat, therefore, for an hour or so, while baboons and monkeys swung through the trees and gibbered at us from the bushes; and we threw pebbles down a steep, narrow gully full of boulders, watching them bound off at angles or up into the trees, and we looked at a great expanse of landscape. It was an aeroplane view of the systems of the Zambezi and the Sanyati rivers, winding flat and brown through thick, green forest—a landscape that stretched off and away and around for nearly 100 miles, mountain and hill and plain, river and marsh and forest, with cloud-shadows moving over it like the stains on the bed of an ocean. At the side of the mountain we sat on was the Kariba Gorge, where the wide Zambezi narrows and runs fast and deep and browny-green, edged with white sandbanks.

All this wild and noble country will be under water in a few wet seasons. This will be the biggest man-made lake in the world, 200 miles long, with a shore line of over 800 miles.

I said it was sad to think of that wonderful country vanishing under water; but my guide said if it is cruel to break an egg, it is nice to eat the omelette. He was not thinking about the Africans who live in that valley; but I asked him if he had heard that there was any trouble about moving the Africans; and he said the Native Commissioners were handling it.

Later that day another engineer said with a sort of good-humoured amusement: 'They say that the natives of

the valley don't believe that the waters will come over
their villages. They think it's a trick to steal their land
from them. It's the Congressmen who work them up. But
they'll believe it soon enough when the water does start to
rise.'

Our Frenchman was more interested in the immediate
problems: very proud of the radio station on this mountain. No telephone lines were laid yet, so the radio linked
with Chirundu, and through Chirundu to the big centres
north and south. And all the supplies came through by
lorry from Karoi, 125 miles away, or by aeroplane. As we
sat on the mountain the planes were climbing and descend-
ing over the new air-strip, which in a couple of years will
have gone under the lake. People were flown in and out
for holiday week-ends; and all the officials and experts
came in by air.

Paul Hogarth having finished his drawings, we descended the mountain and went up to the mess on a hill for
lunch. The mess was an attractive little building, mosqui-
to-gauzed, full of refrigerators and amenities. The lunch
was the best sort of meal one can have in these parts,
quantities of admirable cold meats and salads: this is a
meat-eating country and rapid adjustment is needed after
life in England, on finding the table loaded with pounds of
meat at every meal, a steak covering a big plate, chops
coming in half-dozens, refrigerators crammed with sirloins
the size of boot-racks.

The people having lunch were mostly women and
children, who had already moved in after their men. The
children would have to be taught by correspondence
course for some months yet; and the women would have
to rely on each other for entertainment, with the men
working so hard; for it was made clear that the people
who came to work on Kariba were not clock-watchers and
chair-sitters. They were there because they wanted some-

thing worth while to do, and to get out of the city and to be free and unconfined by civilisation. Some of the men who had come first to the site, when there were only a handful working on it, had already left: with all these people being flown in, all these civilised amenities, and the women and the children, it was getting too tame for them.

Soon, everything would be tidied up and in order. There were two townships, one European and one African, being built up on twin hills, out of the reach of tsetse fly and mosquitoes; the roads would be good; schools would be built, and a fine hospital. It would be a centre, almost a city and was expected to stand for ten years, until the scheme was completed.

And at the end of ten years, what would happen to the two model townships on the twin hills? Why, then, if the industrialists had any sense, they would move their businesses up here, near to the source of power. Why shouldn't Kariba become a real city, like a Copper Belt town?

But later, when I recounted this conversation to a businessman from Johannesburg, he said, not without malice: 'Malvern and Welensky are mad—clean off their heads. They're spending every penny of the credit of the country on Kariba, and when it's finished they're going to have enough power to run a continent on, and no industries to run—or hardly any industries. Kariba's a project for a heavily industrialised country, and they aren't going to get the investment in industry because everyone knows the whole show might explode in race-war at any minute.'

And, from a politician in Northern Rhodesia: 'The reason why Lord Malvern's stuck out for his Kariba is because his fancy has been tickled by the fact that the lake will be the biggest man-made lake in the world. At last it's a monument big enough to retire on—like Rhodes and Rhodesia.'

But such carping remarks would not go down well at Kariba itself, which is infected, if any place is, by a pioneering, obstacle-crashing, rip-roaring atmosphere of achievement.

After lunch we descended to the verge of the Zambezi, where a hippopotamus stood shoulder-deep in the shallows, very enviably, for it was steamy and hot, 86 degrees in the shade. But apparently this is considered cool in these parts, for the temperature only a few weeks back was in the hundreds.

And then I returned to my proper business of looking at housing and collecting figures. I had read speeches by African politicians that the labourers at Kariba had been dying like flies and working in very bad conditions. I was shown the site where an African hut-camp had been, and was told things had been so bad there that the welfare people had insisted the whole place must be bulldozed down. So they must have been bad. But I do not believe that the Africans were dying like flies. Time and again, speaking to Africans, I hear the terrible: 'The Europeans want to kill us all off, they won't feel happy and safe until we are all dead.' But my personal belief is that no one African will be allowed unnecessarily to die as long as there is such a shortage of labour; they will be treated in such a way as to preserve health and working efficiency—no worse, and no better.

The temporary housing for Africans looked like that I have already described—adequate, inhuman, barrack-like. Showers one for fifty men, latrines one for twenty, three single men to a hut, twenty to a dormitory. The new township on the hill, which will hold eight thousand Africans, will be on the same lines.

I interviewed at random one worker, of whom Paul had

made a drawing. His name was Jeremiah; and he came from Portuguese East Africa, near Beira. He was a Shangaan, and had been three months working in Southern Rhodesia at £3 a month. In Portuguese territory he had been earning £5 a month. Why, then, had he come to Southern Rhodesia? He wanted to travel, he said. He had never been to school, was illiterate, did not know how old he was. He had a wife in his village at home, but no children.

My guide asked him: 'Which white men are kinder, those in Portuguese East Africa, or those in Southern Rhodesia?'—which was how my query, which nation he preferred working for, translated into kitchen Kaffir. To which he replied: 'All white men are nice.'

But he hated being questioned and wanted to get away.

I said: 'Well, we've got the facts, but we don't know what he feels.'

At which the official said: 'These types don't know what they feel. Only the educated ones do, and they're embittered.'

This official, when asked what he thought of Partnership, said: 'Huggins is a Kaffir-lover. He doesn't care about the white people, only the natives. I prefer the South African system.'

Again, much complaint about prostitutes. Most women here are not wives, but camp-followers: the welfare man's term for them. There are about three dozen; and they earn as much as £60 to £90 a month.

'We allow the prostitutes because if you have wives around there's so much trouble with the single men always fighting with the husbands. We see that the prostitutes don't live here; they live in neighbouring villages.'

The compound manager said: 'Everyone applying for married quarters here is going to have to produce a marriage certificate; we're not going to have these temporary wives here. And there isn't a Native Commissioner here to marry people quickly—the nearest Native Commissioner is in Miami. No, we aren't going to forbid wives, but we aren't going to encourage them either.'

I asked if convict labour was being used; he said he had never heard of convict labour—in the tones of a man well-used to unjust accusations. I pointed out that the new aerodrome near Salisbury is being built almost entirely by convict labour and that I had repeatedly heard rumours of convict labour being used on Kariba. But he heatedly denied it.

He was proud of the social amenities for his Africans— football and hockey, a cowboy film once a week, and regular lectures on hygiene. There is a choir which is popular, tribal dancing (which is not—'perhaps because there are so many different tribes here'), and a jazz-band. There would be primary schooling for all the African children, but no secondary schooling. All Africans are vaccinated on arrival and made to take quinine regularly. Domestic servants are examined regularly for venereal disease, but not the ordinary labourers.

The Africans working here, like those everywhere else, will be virtually the property of the company which employs them, housed, fed and regulated by the employers, under Government inspection.

Lastly we went to the site itself, where the dam is being built. As we approached, a crocodile drove straight upstream in the middle of the river, like a speedboat, away from the noise of the construction. Between high wooded banks, cables were slung over the water; a suspension bridge, half-finished, jutted across the stream; piles stood in the river-bed; and on the bank we stood on, a road was being built: gangs of Africans under European supervision.

I went down the deep tunnel which drove to water-level where the tunnel was under construction to take the main flow of the water when the dam itself was building; it was like going down a mine, damp and hot, with the electric lights shining dimly along earth roof, and the great cables unrolling downwards.

Then it was time to leave, for we wanted to get back to Salisbury that night.

Just past the turn-off on the main road, there is a little grass kiosk in the bush at the roadside, with a sign on it: 'Drink Coca-Cola.' Paul wanted to make a drawing of this evidence of the Coca-Cola revolution; so we stopped the car. He went off to draw, while a crowd of fascinated African children collected, and the Kaffir-fowls scratched about; and I sat in the car and drank Coca-Cola. Suddenly a big car came up along the road the way we had come very fast and stopped with a screaming of brakes, just behind our car. The man in it immediately got out; but he did not buy Coca-Cola. He stood for a moment, looking at the number-plate of our car; then remained standing on the road, looking suspiciously at Paul, who was sitting on his stool drawing, and suspiciously at me.

This went on for some minutes. I took another look at him and thought I knew his face. Then I understood it was not the face I recognized, but the expression on it. What was it? Of course! This was the look of those Afrikaner special branch police in the Jan Smuts airport, while they were shepherding me on to the plane like a pack of dogs herding one sheep.

But what could the C.I.D. be doing here?

Making sure that I did not, after my warning, take this route up into Northern Rhodesia? Making sure that I was not making seditious speeches to the group of black children, the chickens and the mongrel dogs and the salesman at the kiosk and his friends who were now gathering around from a nearby village to watch the process of drawing?

But there was no doubt it was the C.I.D. I think Governments should employ mercenaries for this sort of work; true believers are a bad policy; for there are countries where one can pick out the political police streets away by their look of disgusted and irritated hatred. This man walked up and down the road for half an hour, looking at Paul, looking at me, as if he would like to wring both our necks if only there was a law to permit it. When Paul had showed his drawing to the Africans, who liked it very much, and stacked his drawing things back in the boot of the car, and we had got into our car, the man got into his car. We drove off, but he remained sitting in his car looking after us, and did not follow us again, though we were driving slowly now, on purpose so that he should catch us up. So he must have turned back to whatever post he operated from.

IX

SINCE I MIGHT not get up North, and I wanted to write about the trends in Northern Rhodesia and Nyasaland, I made arrangements to meet representatives of the two Congresses. For to know what the Government, or white settlers' organisations, think about events it is only necessary to read the papers.

These arrangements were made carefully, since Congress representatives are not exactly liked by the Government; and for the same reason I shall not use the names of people or places.*

I wanted to find out two things. What was the attitude of National Congresses to the rapid industrial development going on in the Federation, and which must increase

*Two of the men I talked to have since been deported from Southern Rhodesia to Nyasaland.

the wealth of this backward and undeveloped area. Secondly, how did they now view Federation?

For, one evening in a pleasant house, a group of white progressives—a word which is rather more elastic in this part of the world than it is in Britain—had worked out an admirably logical thesis which went like this: That since it was unlikely the Africans would be given self-government in the next decade and it seemed they were not in a position to take it forcibly; since the most striking, the most basic fact about the Federal area is its poverty, and schemes like Kariba and other big projects will ultimately raise the standard of living of everybody; would it not be better if the African Congresses supported economic development, at the same time using their great strength to demand a steadily increasing share in control of government? For the phrases and slogans of Partnership offer a verbal basis to fight on: to put the flesh of reality on these words would be to create a real democracy.

In short, to make the architects of Partnership fulfil their promises.

This is a very brief summary of the conclusions come to after an argument that went on for some hours, with great heat, based on a wealth of knowledge and information and experience, between various sorts of Socialist, ranging from classic Marxist, through Fabian, to old-fashioned liberal.

There was nothing wrong with our methods of reasoning, which were, however, only possible because, being white, we had not been subjected every hour of our lives to the humiliations of the colour bar.

For when I met these Congressmen, in small, shabby, out-of-the-way rooms, in an atmosphere of secrecy and oppression, those very sane and sensible arguments seemed silly, or at least irrelevant.

I have known many Nationalists, but never any as bitter as these.

I hate nationalism; but I hate even more that soft-mindedness which deplores the colour bar and ideas of white supremacy, hopes they will soften and diminish, and behaves as if they have vanished already—that hypocrisy which acknowledges the ugliness of white-settler what-I-have-I-hold, and yet will not acknowledge the justice of the black nationalism which is its inevitable consequence.

Political emotion, that emotion which drives masses of people into action, is never reasoned and rational. The leaders of a movement may be thoughtful men; their followers are not.

The emotions of 'white civilisation' are not rational; nor are the emotions of nationalism.

Talking to these Nationalists—Nationalists for that matter from any part of 'white' Africa—I find that there are two nightmares or fantasies which haunt them.

One I have already mentioned: 'The whites want to kill us all off, they won't be happy till we are all dead.'

Yet manifestly a dead African is a bad African—that is, unless he rebels; since a dead African is not able to do the dirty work of the country.

The other is: 'They are going to bring in hundreds of thousands of white people from Europe and swamp us, and take our land.'

Ever since I can remember, the white settlers have been agitating for mass white immigration, so as to strengthen them against the Africans. This heart-cry is perennial; it is never absent from sundowner talk or newspaper column. But there never has been mass white immigration. Nor can there be. Having reached, since the war, a figure of twenty thousand a year, the Government has had to peg the figure there, because the existing facilities are so overstrained they can't feed more people: not only the black men's towns, but the white, are short of schools and hospitals, let alone housing. And that figure of twenty thousand is itself a defeat, for at last the Government has given up the dream of 'sound Nordic stock'—meaning Britishers, Germans and other Northern Europeans, the arguments in favour of which are the same as those used by Hitler and Goebbels—to import quantities of Italians and Greeks, peoples who, to the average white settler, seem not far removed from the Africans. These people are already undermining 'white supremacy' since they are a cheerful and happy-go-lucky lot, who do not take easily to the neurotic rigidities of white settlerdom.

And a great many of the recent immigrants promptly left again. According to figures recently published, fifty thousand white people have left the Federation in the last five years. Why? Because accommodation is hard to find; because everything is overcrowded; because it is a boring and provincial life; because if you are not prepared to talk about the colour bar there is nothing else to talk about; and because the place is as insecure and explosive as South Africa, which is also losing its white citizens in large numbers.

In short, these two powerful fantasies, of being killed off by the whites, and of mass white immigration, are absolute nonsense, economic and political nonsense. Yet they are all-powerful and likely to remain so.

The arguments of the Congress people are very simple, the same whether one listens to a Nyasaland man or a Northern Rhodesian. We were free men, we Africans of Northern Rhodesia and Nyasaland. We made voluntary treaties with your Queen Victoria, and became British-protected persons. We opposed Federation with Southern Rhodesia; yet your Government forced it on us. We have been tricked and betrayed by the British Government;

and now we are in the same position as our brothers in Southern Rhodesia, who were physically conquered by force of arms. Yes, now we know that the whites of the Federation will force on us *apartheid,* the South African system. Why, we already have *apartheid,* although they call it Partnership. It creeps north from Southern Rhodesia already; already they begin to enforce pass laws here, and to take away more and more of our land. No, we shall have nothing to do with any Federal Government project. No, we do not understand this argument you use, that economic development will benefit the Africans—when has development benefited us? On the contrary, it is the whites who gain, who always gain, and everything that is good is taken away from us. No; when you speak like that, you speak as a white person; you are against us. The simplest child in the village knows that Federation made a dupe of him. But he will not understand what you call tactics. Tactics are immoral. For an African, a thing is good or it is bad. Federation is bad, and we will have nothing to do with it. We will fight to get Nyasaland out of the Federation if we can. And besides, even if it were true that we would earn more money if factories and industries came to the Federation, we would have lost our freedom, we would be slaves. No. We know only one thing, that the white people want our land. They will take our land, as they have in Southern Rhodesia. How can we support Kariba when thousands of our people are being moved off their good, rich, fertile land, where they have lived for generations, to bad distant soil, which has never been theirs and which does not know them and their ancestors? No, no. We will not listen. Now we know only one thing—we are black men. You are white. Therefore you are our enemy. No, no, no.

This is the voice of the Congresses.

The men who lead the Congresses are intelligent politicians who understand the modern world. The whites see them as raving seditionaries. Behind these men are a massed, embittered population. This is the same situation as in Kenya before the outbreak: the national movement was suppressed, because it demanded a share in government. Behind it was Mau Mau.

Behind the Congresses in Northern Rhodesia and Nyasaland is Mau Mau, perhaps half a step behind.

The motion behind Mau Mau was a very natural desire for revenge for humiliation, for being made slaves in their own country.

In arguing with Africans who support Mau Mau—for at the bottom of every African heart is a profound natural sympathy with Mau Mau—I have been saying: 'I have every sympathy with Mau Mau; it is the fault of the white idiots in Kenya that this bitter war began. But I think it was a mistake to fight knowing that you could not win, that you were bound to be destroyed, your people made captive, your leaders hanged, everyone humiliated and discouraged.'

To which the reply is: 'You destroyed our national organisation, you took from us every hope of sharing in the government of our country—so what did you expect us to do? We fought with what means we could. We showed at least that we were not cowards and slaves. And the fact that we could fight at all put heart into Africans all over Africa.'

That *we* comes from Africans who are not Kenyans, as well as those who are, from Africans who identify themselves as completely with the black side in Kenya as that white South African announcer identified himself instinctively and completely with the Kenyan white settlers.

The voice of the national Congresses is the most powerful factor in Central Africa now: it will determine what happens there; it is the bitter, desperate, proud, angry voice of a people betrayed to the gods of money and expediency.

*   *   *   *

I re-read the preface to *John Bull's Other Island*. Here is Bernard Shaw on the 'Curse of Nationalism':

It is hardly possible for an Englishman to understand all that this implies. A conquered nation is like a man with cancer: he can think of nothing else, and is forced to place himself, to the exclusion of all better company, in the hands of quacks who profess to treat or cure cancer. ... English rule is such an intolerable abomination that no other subject can reach the people. Nationalism stands between Ireland and the rest of the world ... a healthy nation is as unconscious of its nationality as a healthy man of his bones. But if you break a nation's nationality it will think of nothing else but getting it set again. It will listen to no reformer, to no philosopher, to no preacher, until the demand of the Nationalist is granted. It will attend to no business, however vital, except the business of unification and liberation. ... There is indeed no greater curse to a nation than a nationalist movement which is only the agonising symptom of a suppressed natural function. Conquered nations lose their place in the world's march because they can do nothing to strive to get rid of their nationalist movements by recovering their national liberty....

*   *   *   *

I intended to try to get up north, even though I was told I would be forbidden. So I waited a week, delaying my plans, to see that statesman who, I had been told, intended to prevent me. I interviewed him as a journalist and did not ask his permission to go north, which I could

not do, in any case, since I had promised my informant
not to say a word of what he had told me. But I said that
I was going to Northern Rhodesia and Nyasaland, and
waited for him to forbid me. He said nothing, rather
grimly, admittedly, but he said not a word. So I made
plans to go to Northern Rhodesia.

*   *   *   *

An interview with Lord Malvern, Prime Minister of the
Federation. He used to be my mother's doctor, when he
still practised as one; and I had often heard him speak at
meetings when I was a child. He is an old man now,
sitting behind a big desk under a portrait of Cecil John
Rhodes in a long room where you walk towards him,
seeing him black and rather hunched against the strong
light from the windows behind.

Most of this interview, like all the other interviews, was
off the record; for he complained that people were such
fools they always misunderstood him. It is no secret, I
think, that Lord Malvern or Dr. Huggins has never had
much respect for other people's intelligence; and this tend-
ency has been strengthened because he has always been
the most quick-minded, lively, sharp-tongued of the politicians in a country that is naturally short of able politicians. Now he gives the impression of being tired, no less
asperous and impatient, a brooding and rather lonely
figure.

He said he thought Federation was successful, though
suffering from growing pains. When I suggested that perhaps the opposition and political feeling it had created
among the Africans might ultimately wreck it, he said
impatiently that I must not get the impression that the
Congresses had any influence; they were just a few noisy
agitators.

He said he understood I had Left Wing views. I said

yes, strong Left Wing views, to which he replied that he believed in making haste slowly and the middle way.

He understood I wrote; what did I write about? This is a question which always annoys a writer; but I said that for the purposes of this discussion I wrote against the colour bar. To which he said: 'Well, that's all right. Of course you know there's hardly any colour bar left in Southern Rhodesia.'

I asked him if he did not think, since he had got the public to swallow an interracial university, something that would have seemed impossible ten years ago, he could have pushed it through another stage and made it truly interracial and non-segregated. He said, no; it was touch and go as it was; and if those fools in England didn't shut up, they'd defeat his purpose, scare off the whites and make a black university. 'As it is they won't send their daughters —not at the beginning.'

I said I knew one or two families who were sending their daughters, but he said impatiently: 'I know these people. It's no good rushing them. All this business of principle, of right and wrong—how can there be right and wrong in politics? You do what you can as you can.'

I said: 'All you people seem much more scared of white public opinion than you are of African opinion.'

He said, very quickly: 'No.'

'You're the first who hasn't put it like that, just as plainly.'

'There is no such thing as African public opinion. They're not educated enough to have an opinion. We have to steer a middle road and hope the two extremes won't start shouting. The thing is to make a beginning. After all, nothing's static. In ten years' time, when people have got used to the idea of a multi-racial university, we can go a step farther. I have no colour feeling myself—I wasn't brought up in this country. But you have to recognise it exists.'

And then we got on to the Colonial Office, and kindred matters, and I agreed not to quote him.

X

As I MIGHT not be allowed to returned to Salisbury, I spent a sentimental morning driving around it, looking at the innumerable places I have lived in. Most, so fast are things changing, no longer exist. Most are not to be regretted. The house I would have been pleased to see go was still there. In it, for over a year, I was very unhappy. I have since learned to distinguish between unhappiness which is simply temperamental, and has to be suffered through, like an attack of flu; and the unhappiness caused by circumstances. At that time I could not distinguish between them. I was dumbly, hopelessly unhappy; I could not believe I would ever have a hopeful thought or feeling again. It was therefore salutary to go and look at the small brick house, in its garden, warm in the sunlight, with children playing on the verandah. It was hard to identify it as the same place, indeed. A year is a long time to waste in being unhappy; a year is a good part of one's life.

IN TIME OF DRYNESS

There is no dryness like this drought.
Thin flesh burns, skin cracks, lips strain.
A dull drum tom-toms in the brain,
Low thudding rising to a shout:

There have been years that no rain knew,
And skulls lay bleaching in the dust
That rose and clung like thickening rust
On everything that lived and grew.

Small skulls that are so pitiful,
I flesh your bones with anger, and
Inhabited you walk the sand
And watch the skies to see them fill.

Seven long years a drought can wait.
I think how with each year you cried—
You knew that hell before you died—
That rescue now would be too late.

The thick grey rocks compress you round.
The thick sky presses down like steel.
You have forgotten how to feel
Except as parched plants in parched ground.

Day after numbing day you grieve
For auguries of rain, and yet
You know that grieving you forget
How truly living people live.

Despair has taught you to rely
On memories of waterfalls
That broke from barren rocky walls,
Of bright drops squeezed from leaves half-dry.

Outside that house I walked up and down a few minutes, doing penance on behalf of the selective memory: after all, just because I don't like to remember that year, and disapprove entirely of my state of mind at that time, it doesn't mean to say it didn't exist. . . .

*   *   *   *

I am canvassed by innumerable people to support Capricorn.

Capricorn is not a political party, but a kind of ginger group. It deplores racial prejudice and makes all sorts of intelligent suggestions about breaking down the colour bar. It is admirable in a country like this that black and white people, even if only a few of them, should be able to sit around the same table at a committee meeting. It is admirable that white audiences should listen, at times, to black speakers. It is good that people should talk about harmony and understanding.

But then, so do the Partners—who have no intention of letting the African have any real share in the government of the country. Here is Lord Malvern, quoted in the *Rhodesia Herald* for May 19, 1956: 'We want to indicate to the Africans that provision is made for them to have a place in the sun as things go along. But we have not the slightest intention of letting them control things until they have proved themselves and perhaps not even then. That will depend on my grandchildren.'

Lord Malvern's recipe, and Sir Roy Welensky's, for keeping the Africans in their place is the weighted vote. A minority of privileged Africans will be allowed to vote, in key with the general policy of creating a malleable middle class.

With this, Capricorn agrees. As a result of Capricorn, one finds all sorts of people sitting about and earnestly discussing the real nature of democracy. Obviously it cannot mean what it has come to mean in Europe; it does not mean 'no taxation without representation' or 'one head one vote.' Not at all; only the civilised may vote. And the definitions of civilisation all depend, directly or indirectly, on property qualifications. Therefore I cannot possibly support it. Not that I don't believe that many of its supporters are quite sincere in saying that they hope, some time in the future, that the franchise will be extended to everybody. But a sop thrown out to keep hungry people quiet never becomes a satisfying meal: it becomes a minimum right; it hardens and becomes a bulwark against just those forces which are not satisfied with the sop.

The Africans in Central Africa are hungry for the vote. Democracy may be tarnished in Europe; here we may be as cynical as we please about Parliament and the vote. But in Africa the vote has become the symbol of equality in the system the white man has imposed upon the black man. It has become a symbol of human dignity.

People concerned with human dignity, people who care that others may respect themselves—such people must support democracy, must support the principle of the universal franchise in Central Africa. When the African there asks for the vote, he is asking for more than it has ever meant in Europe. There no person has been refused the rights of citizenship because of the colour of his skin.

A WHITE TRADE-UNION LEADER came to see me, to put the white trade-union case. What he was saying in effect was: 'For God's sake! The white trade unionists are human, aren't they? What do you expect?'

All the time he was talking I was remembering the Whartons, who used to live opposite to us in the Mansions.

The Mansions had been built by a young architect who wanted to astonish the city with modern design. (That was fifteen years ago—now the city has fine modern buildings.) They were flats, shaped rather like a magnet standing on the closed end, with the open ends bent inwards.

We had a flat on the top, on one side, and the Whartons had the flat on the other. Between the flats was a gulf, crossed by a small iron stairway shaped like a rounded bridge.

We first got into acquaintance with the Whartons because they sacked their servant, Dickson, and he came to us. The Whartons never kept a servant longer than a month. Dickson was a gay and amiable person, who spent all his money on clothes. At any reference to the Whartons, or at the sound of the raised voices, the quarrelling, that came continuously from over the gulf, he would roll up his eyes, grimace, shrug deeply, and then laugh.

Sometimes Alice Wharton would yell across to him to bring in that cloth or keep an eye on her baby while he swept out our rooms, but he went on working as if he had not heard her. Alice Wharton shared the attitude that any black man in sight was available for doing odd jobs for her. Once she came across to complain that he was cheeky, just as if he had not stopped working for her weeks before. Alice Wharton's servants were always cheeky. One could hear her, or Bob Wharton, shouting to their servant. Their voices held that tense exasperation, that note of nagging despair, that means an obsession. In places like the Residence and the Mansion one heard that note often. Paternalism, that fine feudal kindness with one's servants, does not occur below a certain income level.

Bob Wharton came from England with his wife and two children in the hungry 'thirties. He was a bricklayer and a Socialist, interested in his trade union, and on his bookshelves were Keir Hardie, Morris, Shaw, the old stalwarts of British Socialism.

At first things went well with him. He rented a small house, the two children went to school, his head was well above water. He became an official of the trade union, and was well liked by his mates. And then there was a third child, a spastic; and it was too bad to be cured. Both parents adored this child; and soon, with hospitals and doctors and the illnesses that he kept having, their heads were no longer above water. They were in debt.

There was no sense in having a fourth child, but one was born, and Mrs. Wharton, who was now a tired and harassed woman in her late thirties, swore that she would never, never have another child. She would no longer sleep with her husband, and went into the bed beside Robbie, the sick boy, as if she were married to him. And the marriage, which had been a good one, was full of bitterness. As for the two elder children, they were tender with the sick brother, but there was a terrible resentment in them. Deep down they felt as if they had done wrong in being born healthy and strong, for their mother's love went on the sick child, and she was only brisk and irritable with them. Bob Wharton began to drink, not heavily but enough to make a difference to the monthly bills. One night when he came home quite drunk he made a scene with his wife, and after the scene they broke down and wept together, and from this moment of warmth there began another child. But now Alice Wharton was determined. She used a knitting needle on herself, and killed the child, and nearly killed herself, but she could never have children again, and that, as she told me often, was the one bright thing in her life, the one weight off her shoulders. She used to say it loudly, and the elder children heard it, and they used to look at each other helplessly, trying to share the awful guilt of being born at all, and being such a burden to their parents.

After Alice Wharton came out of hospital, they could not pay the hospital bills, or the doctor. Bob Wharton was too proud to ask for the relief hospitals give to poor people. They sold what furniture they had, or nearly all of it, and they moved to the Mansions, which was cheaper, being only two small rooms, and they sold their little motor-car.

At this time, things were like this: Bob Wharton held his job steadily, and worked all the overtime he could get. He was not afraid for his job, for he was strong, not fifty yet, a tall man, rather thin, bent a little at the shoulders, with a way of poking his head forward, chin up, to look into your face with anxious, serious eyes, as if he might find a reason there why he had come to such a permanent morass of worry and unhappiness. He was still an official of his union, and this was what he was most proud of in his life.

Alice Wharton went out to work for a time, not as a cleaner or a charwoman, as she probably would have done in Britain, because here there were black people to do such work: she found a job as saleswoman in one of the stores. But if she worked, she had to pay for someone to look after the sick child, who was inert all day, sitting where he was put. They would not let her take the child with her to the store: it might put customers off. So, finding that it cost more to pay for the child in a nursery than she earned, she stayed at home and earned a little extra making dresses for friends.

The baby was healthy, and no trouble to her. The two elder children were at school; and when they came home it was usually to go straight off to friends' houses, where they were not shouted and nagged at. Alice Wharton used to come crying across the iron bridge to me, saying she did not mean to shout and nag at the two children, but she could not help it, something got into her and she could not help it.

So the family all day was Alice Wharton, making dresses and underclothes on her sewing machine, and the sick boy, lying beside her in a wheeled chair, never speaking, never moving, his big, loose head swaying on the top of a long, skeleton neck, looking vaguely around him with large painfully bright blue eyes, and the baby, who rolled and staggered around the two rooms, and terrified the mother by trying to climb out over the edge of the small porch where it met the iron bridge that came over to us.

In the evenings the family was also Bob Wharton, doing his trade-union books at another table, and the two elder children, trying to find some space to do their homework in.

Alice used to complain all the time to Bob that he was mad to waste his time on the union; hadn't he got enough to do, didn't he care about his family; if he wanted to spend his evenings working, then he might just as well get work that was paid for. But Bob would not give up his union. It was the one thing that held him in his idea of himself, and connected him with Britain, where he had had such hopes for the future.

He used to work under the lamp, while Alice nagged and grumbled, a tired woman, chained every moment of her life to the sick boy, until he would fling down his things and bang out to the bar around the corner, or shout at the servant, and then the whole flat would ring with quarrelling and complaints, and the two elder children shrank away to their beds.

Things were bad. But they might get better. Why not?

They could at least not get worse, provided there was work. For Bob Wharton, with the memory of the 'thirties and unemployment behind him, there was always the terror of finding himself out of work.

And there was only one thing that could put him out of work, and that was if the blacks were allowed to do skilled work.

Of an evening he would come over to us, and say, 'We don't mind if the employers pay the blacks the same as us. That's fair, isn't it? Well, isn't it fair?' But he was always uneasy, always guilty about it. Here he was, a trade unionist with experience of trade unionism in Britain; and he was standing shoulder to shoulder with his white mates, keeping the black men out of skilled work. He knew it, and he was tormented by it. He would sit on our little porch, keeping an eye over on the windows beyond the gulf, where his wife sat sewing beside the sick child, her face rigid with hostility and bitterness, and he talked and talked endlessly about the native problem. 'After all, they aren't on our level, are they? It's not so bad as it is for us, being hard up: we're civilised, aren't we; they aren't civilised yet, are they? . . .'

That winter, the spastic child got pneumonia and went to hospital where he nearly died. Both parents were sick with worry, and good friends again because of it. Mrs. Wharton visited the hospital three times a day, taking the baby with her.

When the spastic child came out, the bills were over £50, and now they really could not meet them. There was no money and Bob Wharton had to accept charity from a fund that existed for such needs, and to do it changed him in his own eyes from an independent man to a beggar.

But this was not the worst. During those weeks when the child was nearly dying, he neglected his trade-union work, and when it came to re-election, one of his mates got up at the meeting, and said that Brother Wharton was having too much personal trouble; he should be released from trade-union activities for the time being. And so Bob Wharton was no longer an official. He felt as if he had been condemned by his society.

He grew morose, and began to drink badly. Mrs. Wharton nagged at him, and he shouted back; and they would sit together, frightened because they were hating each other. And things would be all right for a little while.

Then the eldest child, a girl, got ill for the first time in her life; and it was terrible, for there was no person in that family with the right to be ill but the spastic child.

The bills were there again, the doctor's bills and the hospital bills. And when the girl came out, they said she must go for a holiday, so she went to the seaside on charity.

But Alice Wharton was saying to Bob that they could have paid for that holiday on what he spent on brandy.

They quarrelled and bickered, and Dickson, our servant, would stand on his broom, listening, and say with a small shake of his head: 'That child it should die. That sick boy, it is no good for them.'

Which is how everybody in the Mansions felt, but no one dared to say it.

Bob used to come over the iron bridge to our porch and sit and talk, not about the native problem now, but about his own.

There were two solutions to his difficulties, as he saw them. First, since all their debts and troubles came from illness, they should go back to Britain. There was no unemployment in Britain now, and above all, there was the health service. Of course, one paid for the health service indirectly, but one could go to a hospital and have a doctor and not have to face these heavy bills afterwards. But to pay the fares back to Britain would cost over £300. He had not got it.

The second solution was this: Bob had worked out that during his ten years in this country he had spent enough on rent to have bought a house by this time. If he had had the capital to buy a house in the beginning, or to put down a payment on one, he would be out of the woods now.

Capital. Capital was what he needed. It was not fair that capitalists had capital and the working man had not.

It was extraordinary to hear Bob, a Socialist all his life, say these words, as if he had never heard them before, as if this was the first time he really understood them.

He would sit on our porch, railing against the capitalists like a man with a fresh vision.

And it was at this point that Mr. McCarran-Longman came into our lives. Bob met him in the bar, and brought him up the long, winding stairs to meet Alice. She said to us that Bob was very taken with him. She said it drily, meaning us to understand that *she* was neither taken, nor taken in. And yet there was an uncertainty in her manner. Some time later Bob brought Mr. McCarran-Longman to see us, with the manner of presenting something without prejudice for our judgement. And yet he was feverishly anxious to believe in Mr. McCarran-Longman.

He was a man of 45 or so, heavily built, an open good-fellow's face. He was well dressed, very neat about the wrists and collar. He used to talk, without interest, of the weather and so on, until he was asked a direct question about himself, and then his polite eyes took fire and he shifted himself in his chair, to a talking position, and began.

It was a question of several people grouping together to buy a large piece of ground, and building houses on it instead of buying houses already built by a company. It would be cheaper this way. Why should one put money into the pockets of the capitalists? About ten people would be the right number. He knew of a good piece of ground, in the path of the town's growth, but one needed to raise at least £10,000. It was after the ground was bought that Mr. McCarran-Longman's special talents would come into play. For he had thought of a wonderful invention. One took a large tank, which should be square, more like a swimming bath than a fish-pool, and one filled it with water. Then one shook into the water some chemicals, like shaking salt into soup. Then one stirred the mixture with a large stick or spoon, and behold, it would foam into a myriad bubbles, like the baths of Hollywood film stars.

This would set solid in about twenty-four hours, and one should cut it into suitable bricks or pieces with a very large sharp instrument. The resulting walls, or roofs, or portions of house would be rain-proof, dirt-proof, sound-proof, wear-proof—proof against any risk one might tentatively mention, only delicately, however, to Mr. McCarcan-Longman, who grew tense and uneasy when one made such suggestions.

Water, he said, would cost nothing, particularly if we were prepared to wait for a receptacle to fill with rain-water. And the chemicals were dirt-cheap. He would tell us the ingredients if it were not that he had applied for a patent. It wasn't that he didn't trust us, but it was a legal matter. The problem really wasn't the consistency of the bricks the houses would be built of, but the tanks to put the water and chemicals into.

He said he had considered having made several dozen shapes or forms, some ordinary brick-size, and some wall- or roof-shape, into which one could pour the water and then the chemical, so as not to have to cut the stuff with a knife or saw afterwards. But if you considered the thing practically, he said, perhaps fifty or a hundred receptacles, lying side by side in some barn or shed, or even in the open air, with water in them, and then shaking chemical in, it would be a tricky thing, and unless one was very careful, the stuff of the walls, roofs, etc., would come out a different consistency each time. Much better to have a large, square tank, big enough to give the stuff a thorough-going stir, and be done with it. So, in addition to the £10,000 needed for the ground for the building stands, and for the lawyers, one would need about £500 to buy or have made a really large square or perhaps oblong tank.

Having got the roofs and walls and floors ready—and the beauty of the thing would be that we could make our houses exactly to our own fancy, even colouring the foam mixture bright original colours, then one would need only to stick them together with a sort of glue. Mr. McCarran-Longman was working on the glue now. It was quite good enough as it was, but scientists are never satisfied with less than the best. Another two weeks would see him through. He had the test-tubes on his washstand in the hotel; but the proprietor was getting unpleasant, and the sooner we all bought our bit of ground the better, so that he could build a little shed to do the research in.

So far, Mr. McCarran-Longman had only found Bob Wharton and two other families interested, all people desperate to have homes of their own; but none of them had any capital at all.

I was fascinated by the thing, but it was a dilettante's interest. Having spent so much of my life moving from one place to the next, I had a natural inclination to schemes of this kind.

And besides, whereas it might be said that Mr. McCarran-Longman was obviously a spiv, that is not altogether true.

Each country has its own type of rogue. Britain, for instance, has the spiv, and one has only to write the word to see him standing there. It was about this time that I got a letter from a friend in Britain saying: 'We have a new word. Spiv. I bet you don't guess what it is.'

I guessed it must be either a sort of meat-mixture, like Spam, or a detergent, but as soon as I heard about spivs, I asked my husband if he thought Mr. McCarran-Longman was a spiv.

He said: 'No. Because a spiv is someone who consciously deludes his victims. But this man believes in every word he says.'

'Conscious or unconscious,' I said, 'I think a great many people are going to be very unhappy because of this man.'

'But,' said he, 'you will not be unhappier, because by now you have learned to take my advice. And you are being very bad for him, because you listen when he talks. You must not. And I shall tell Bob he must not. Yes.'

With this, he went across the iron bridge and knocked on Bob's door, and seeing that the living-room was so full of people, children and illness and the noise from the radio that one could not think in it, he invited Bob over for a drink.

For several hours he explained to Bob why he should not put any trust in Mr. McCarran-Longman.

Bob listened, rather suspicious, as if he thought that he was being done out of something. It was this that made us worried for the first time about Bob, because he was not a suspicious person.

Then he said: 'Why shouldn't a man make bricks this way? Look what scientists do. They can do anything. So why shouldn't McCarran-Longman have invented something important?'

Then, his ears closed against everything that we said, he remarked finally that in any case nothing could be done until the ground was bought. After that evening he did not come near us for some days; he only nodded, rather stiff, from over the bridge.

We heard that he and another family and Mr. McCarran-Longman had raised between them £500, borrowing it between them here and there. They were going to the big firms, who lend big sums of money, asking for £10,-000 on the £500. All these firms wanted was some security. And there was not the vestige of security in the lives of the Whartons, the Strickmans, or, for that matter, Mr. McCarran-Longman.

Weeks went by, and we hardly saw the Whartons. The elder daughter came back from her holiday, 14 years old now, and her horizons widened by the sea, and badly wanting some space to spread her soul in; and as a relief she took to dropping over to see me of an evening, and she talked steadily about her father, who was crackers, she said, and her mother, who couldn't manage her servant, and the baby—she couldn't do her homework because the baby's things were everywhere. Not once did she mention that sick boy who sat in the middle of the family draining the life out of them. Her mother, she said, was learning shorthand in the evenings at the Polytechnic, between eight and ten, so she must stay in with the children. When we asked about Mr. McCarran-Longman, she said: 'He's gone to see some friends in Portuguese East who will lend him the money for the project.' When she called it a project we could see that she believed in it, even though she had called her father crazy. She brought out the word delicately, with a respect for it.

And then nothing happened. Nothing. Mr. McCarran-Longman did not come. But it was nothing sudden. It was not a question of saying: 'If Mr. McCarran-Longman does not come back by the end of the month it means we have been made fools of.' For he had gone off, telling them reasonably that since none of them could raise enough money for the project, he would have to tap resources elsewhere, and that would naturally take some time. He even wrote a letter from Beira, saying he had great hopes of a certain man he had met.

And then the silence set in, and Bob Wharton did not even nod over the gulf, and Mrs. Wharton pretended not to see her neighbours: her face was stiff, proud, angry.

Twice we were awakened early after midnight, hearing Bob Wharton, drunk, coming up the narrow stairway, arguing with someone he could not see. And then one morning he was found lying at the foot of the stairs, dead, where he had fallen down in the dark.

And now the Wharton family fell to pieces. The sick

boy had to go to an institution at last; and the elder girl, the one who came to see us, was a salesgirl at the stores, though she had set her heart on going to university, and she lived in an institution that provided cheap accommodation for girls without proper homes. And Mrs. Wharton moved into one room with the baby and the second child, the boy of twelve. She earned their living doing shorthand and typing.

Much later Mr. McCarran-Longman did come back. And he had done very well for himself. He had sold a patent for a child's toy. One took a whole lot of fancy little shapes, fishes, dolls, flowers, birds, and poured water into them, and into the water one sprinkled chemical; and the stuff set solid and could be turned out. He made quite a lot of money out of it in the end. And so he was proved finally not to be a spiv, but a man of enterprise.

XII

A NYASALAND CONGRESSMAN came to see me, very bitter about Federation.

We got on to the subject of the regiment of his people serving in the war in Malaya. He said: 'This is a terrible thing. They make us into slaves, and then they take our young men for their war in Malaya. They say we are fighting Communist terrorists. I don't know anything about Communism. I don't care about it. But they call *us* agitators and terrorists. We know that the people want only to have their own country back. Why should we fight them?'

I said: 'Why do the young men go to fight?'

He said: 'There are no industries in our country. If our young men want to earn money they must go to other countries. Ours is a very poor country. Our average income is £3 10s. a year. That is, for us Africans. And the recruiters come around to the villages, and the young men are excited at the idea of the uniform, and the pay is very high: it can be £15 a month. And it is a way of travelling and seeing another country. And they are made a great fuss of, with bands playing, and speeches on the wireless.'

I asked him: 'When they come home, what do they say?'

'They don't like it. They say: "What are we doing fighting those people for the white man? They are people with dark skins like our own." '

I said: 'You are a person involved in politics. Perhaps the young men who said that to you weren't ordinary people, but political people, friends of yours?'

He said: 'No, no, that is not true. They were ordinary young men, village boys. They had had time to think. When they come back they have all sorts of attentions paid them; they are asked to make speeches over the air, they are great heroes. But then they are back in the villages, and they start thinking.'

A great many Nyasaland Africans work in Southern Rhodesia. Dickson, the man who worked for me, came from Nyasaland.

I have often wondered what happened to him. He left us very suddenly at the time of the big strike in 1947.

This was the first strike in Southern Rhodesia. It began in Bulawayo and spread fast to all the towns. It was well organized and well disciplined. The most remarkable feature of this strike was this: that because, as always happens on these occasions, the white people got very angry, and armed themselves, so that bands of self-appointed custodians of order were roaming the streets armed to the teeth, looking for Africans to beat up and punish, the Government ordered all the Africans in the cities to get back into their locations and stay there. Troops and police saw that they stayed there. It was as if, in a big strike in Britain, the Government kept the strikers forcibly in their homes and prevented them from working. Because the Government's first fear was that the white defence committees and guardians of white civilisation would start racial battles in the streets. It is safe to say that probably most of the Africans in the country knew nothing about strikes, had possibly never heard the word before. Many were reluctant to leave work; they did not understand what was happening. But because they were forcibly locked into their townships for several days, with nothing to do but listen to the speeches of the strike leaders, they were all given a useful political education.

Dickson Mujani, our servant, was one of those who did not want to leave his work.

But he went, and he was away for five days. Then the strike was over, and the Africans coming back to work said that the Government spokesmen had promised them all a minimum wage of £4 a month. At that time the average was £1 a month.

But Dickson did not return. A week passed. Then, late one evening, long after the hour when Africans are legally forbidden the streets, Dickson came creeping up the narrow iron staircase that came to the back door of our flat. He looked ill and frightened. His polished black skin had a harsh, greyish look, and his eyes darted this way and that with a roll of frightened white eyeball.

He had under his arm a parcel of dirty, tattered paper. First we made him eat. Then we tried to find out what had happened. But it was difficult; he was at first too frightened to tell us. He kept begging us to take the papers, because 'they' would kill him if they knew he had the papers. Who were *they*? When we had got the story more or less straight, we put him to sleep on a bed in the kitchen. He did not want to sleep. He said he must get away quickly before 'they' got him. We said there was nothing to fear, and in the morning we would take his story to the proper authorities and get justice done, if possible. But in the morning he had gone, vanished. And we never saw him again.

The story he had told us was not about himself but about his father. This was the story:

Long ago, he had forgotten how long, Samson Mujani came from Nyasaland south to find work. He was a young man then, with a wife and child in his village. In the big city he found work on the railways, at the station. He swept the platform, and ran errands for the white bosses, and was a messenger boy. He earned a few shillings a month, and he lived in the location. It was still called the location then. At first it was all frightening and difficult, after the peaceful green village he had known. He did not understand the money, he did not understand at all the customs of the white men, and he was puzzled and unhappy because of their rudeness and rough ways. After a while, he learned how to live, keeping quiet, dodging trouble and the police, keeping a smiling face always for his masters. The green village he had come from seemed a long way off, another world. He thought often of his wife and child, but the women in this town were not as he would wish his own wife to be, so he did not send for her. He took up with one of the women of the town and lived with her in a shack made of iron and brick on the borders of the location where the ground dipped towards the river. She bore him a child, and then another. It was at the birth of the second child that she died. It was then he sent a message to his wife, and after many months she came south, walking with some relatives who looked after her. She brought their own child, and so there was a family of three children in the little shack.

The years went past, and the town grew so that now instead of trains once or twice a week, they came every day, and then several times a day. Samson was a well-known figure on the station. White people who used the trains a great deal grew to know him, and used to give him bits of money, and call him by his name. His own people knew him, too, and when they found it hard to understand the business of buying tickets for a train, and the times of the trains, he would be called in to interpret. By now he was earning about 20s. a month, and it was hard to live with all the children, five of them now, so his wife went to work as a nanny at one of the white houses.

She was a good woman, strict with her children, and with her own behaviour in this city.

And now the elder children were growing up, and Samson thought hardly at all of the green village in the mountains. It was as if he had lived all his life here. But once, feeling tired and sometimes dizzy, and sometimes with pains in him, he went home with his wife, and the younger children, this time on the big lorries that go to and fro over the long distance. He found the village hard now; he had grown away from it. He loved it, and he didn't love it. His wife would have stayed, but he fretted, and returned to the big city. His wife came with him. But he was growing to be an old man. He did not know how old he was, but it was harder to do the work, carrying messages around the offices on a bicycle, and the sweeping, and sometimes the moving of the luggage. And then there was a change in the way of work, for the union of the white men who worked on the railway was always very careful of what work the black men did. There was a reorganisation, and work like Samson's, which was neither one thing nor another, must be named and ordered. It was at this time that he changed from sweeping and running messages on the platforms, to becoming an assistant of one of the white men who tended the big engines. He might oil certain parts of the engine while the man watched him, or he might take tools and do small repairs under inspection. This was easier work for him, now that his back was stiffening. Also he had better hours. He was a real railway worker. And then the war came, and again it was as if the town had been fed with new life. It began to spread in all directions, and the trains were in and out all day, carrying troops wearing different coloured uniforms. That easy-going pace of the life along the platforms that he remembered was gone. Often he did not know the faces of the white men who drove and tended the trains. And only the older men in the offices of the station remembered him as a young man, the youth from Nyasaland.

In the location, too, things were changing. Instead of huts and shacks of all kinds, there were houses being built for the Africans, and it was called the township. The Superintendent of the township, who liked those he looked after to be willing and cheerful and obedient, liked Samson, and he was given one of the good houses for men with families. It had two rooms in it, and a kitchen. They all lived in it, the mother and father, and the oldest son, Dickson, who had been born in Nyasaland and had come down with his mother, and the four younger children, all of whom were working in the houses of the white city.

But the new house cost more money than the old one, the rent was higher, and because of the war, the prices of food and clothing were rising all the time, and although everyone in the family was working, it was hard to live, harder than it had ever been.

Around him on the railway, his people were talking whenever they met of the difficulty of living. Often they would send a spokesman to the management about their wages. But the management now was not in the station buildings, it was as if whenever they spoke to a white boss, he said he was not the real boss, but there was another over him ... they could never get at this real boss to speak to him face to face, as had been possible—so Samson told them— in the old days.

When the strike began, although there had been so much discontent for so long, it was a surprising and troubling thing even for those who had spoken most of it. To begin with, a strike was not legal. And to one like Samson, who had spent all his life avoiding trouble, learning the taboos that hedged his life so as to respect them, to do something illegal was frightening. But there came that evening when all about him walked off from their work, saying it was a strike, and of course he went with them.

There were no blacklegs in that strike.

And the white men, that is the white men who worked on the railways as workers, wished them good luck as they went; because although they were not on strike themselves, in their capacity as workers they were sympathetic.

That first day on strike Samson stayed at home— by himself—since everyone in the family was out at work in the city, and knew very little about what was to happen. And then, on the second day, he was not alone, for all the houseboys and cooks and messengers of the city struck, too: it was spreading. The last to come home was his wife; she stayed at home on the third day. There was little food in the location, or township, because the authorities, who were now very angry, were not bringing food in. All the Africans were in the townships of the city, and there was no food. And around the townships were cordons of police to prevent white men getting in, or Africans from getting out.

But the family stayed in their little house, and kept themselves out of trouble.

It was on the third day that a man came to Samson and said: 'May the committee of the strike come to your house tonight to discuss matters?'

'But why my house?' asked Samson, deeply troubled. And then he said yes, that they would be welcome.

As the time came near he sent his sons and daughters to a neighbour's house, and his wife went into the second room, leaving the front room free for the men who wished to talk.

When they came, they said that they moved from this house to that for their discussions, because even their talk was illegal, and they did not wish to remain always in one place, in case the police came to arrest them. Samson was old and he was respected, and his house was a good and respected house.

He received them politely and asked them to sit down, and the wife brought tea for them from the kitchen.

There were seven men, and Samson sat, saying little, while they talked. The matters which they discussed were difficult for him. Regulations and laws and prohibitions and white papers and blue papers and the reports of committees—these were what these men discussed. But at the end of all their talk was one fact only: the strike was not legal. Yet it existed. There were no Africans at work that day, none, in any place in the city, not for cooking, or for cleaning, or for digging gardens, or for looking after children, or for taking messages, or for driving cars or lorries. So what they had to say to the Government was only: 'Look, here is this strike. Here is this thing. And now what will you do?'

They talked for a long time, and again the wife made tea and brought it in, and the lights were going out in the houses around them.

Samson would have liked to say that it was getting late, and it would be wiser for them to go now; but he was proud they had chosen him, and so he said nothing.

Then there was a knock on the door, and through the small window they could see the shape of a policeman against the sky, and then another policeman. Four of the men in the room got up, and without a word ran out of the house by the back door into the night. For they were citizens of other countries, that is to say, they came from Nyasaland or from Northern Rhodesia, and even though they might have worked in this country all their lives, like Samson, they could be deported within a day.

When the two policemen came in there were only three men and Samson. But it could be seen that there had been more in the room. They asked to see the papers of the three men, and from these papers it could be seen that they were from this country. The three men wished Samson good night, like friends saying good night after a visit, and went out.

Then the two policemen went into the kitchen and

saw Mrs. Mujani sitting by her stove knitting a jersey for her daughter. She looked up and went on knitting, though it could be seen that her hands were trembling, and her knees were held together to keep them still. They left her, and went back into the other room, and Samson was straightening the chairs, like a host after his guests were gone. They stood for a moment, watching him, with their sticks in their hands, and then one saw a bundle of papers lying on the table, and he jumped forward for it.

'And what are these papers?' he shouted at Samson, unrolling them.

'I do not know,' said Samson. And then, thinking he might get his friends into trouble, he said: 'I found them lying on the ground.'

The two policemen, both tall, strong, fine fellows, spread the papers on the table, and looked at them, and then one turned to Samson and said, 'Do you not know these papers are forbidden?'

'No,' said Samson. 'I know nothing.'

And now the two policemen came towards Samson, threatening. And the old man shrank back a little and then stood his ground. A timid man he had always been, a gentle man, a man who avoided trouble, and yet here he stood, in his own house with two big policemen standing over him. And his wife was crying in the next room. He could hear her.

'Where did you get these papers?' asked one of the policemen, and he hit Samson with his open hand across his head. Samson fell sideways a few steps, recovered, and said:

'I know nothing.'

And then the other policeman, grinning, moved across and hit Samson with his open hand on the other side of the head, so he staggered back to the first.

Now the wife was in the open door, wailing aloud.

The first policeman said: 'We will put you in prison, my fine fellow, you damn fool, you Kaffir.'

'What are you doing in my house?' asked Samson, breathing hard. 'This is my house.'

'Your house—you say that to the police?'

And he hit Samson again, with his closed fist, on the side of the head, and as Samson reeled across the room the other policeman hit him with his closed fist.

And now there was a silence, for instead of staggering back, to be hit again, Samson stood, his face screwed up, eyes shut, then his mouth dropped and his head fell sideways, and he slumped to the ground.

The wife wailed again.

The two policemen looked at each other, hurriedly bent over Samson who was lying on the ground motionless, and then ran out of the house into the night.

When Dickson came in from his friends', he found his mother sitting beside his father, swaying from side to side, moaning. His father was dead.

When the other sons and daughters came in, they talked over what to do.

Some said to go to the Superintendent. But the mother was frightened.

One said that policemen were not allowed to kill a man by hitting him, but another that the policemen would lie and there would be trouble.

At last one ran for the nurse at the hospital, and

men came with a stretcher and carried Samson away.
They said he had fallen down dead suddenly.

He was an old man, and none had eaten for two
days.

On the next day the mother sat wailing in her
kitchen, and the sons and daughters were with the
crowds around the hall and the playing ground, listening to the talk about the strike, and to the men
who were standing on boxes explaining about the
strike. It was here that Dickson saw a policeman
looking close at him. And the policeman came up to
him through the crowd and stood by him and said:
'Where's your situpa?' Dickson produced his papers,
and the policeman said: 'You'd better go home, you
go to Nyasaland, before they catch you. I know you
have those papers in your house.' Dickson looked at
him, and then around for help, but the people about
him had melted away to give distance to the policeman. He said nothing. Then the policeman went
away, swinging his stick, and Dickson slowly went
home.

'What is this about the papers?' he asked his
mother.

She raised her voice and wept. He said: 'Mother,
mother, it was those papers that killed him.'

She had put them in the back of the cupboard in
the kitchen, and Dickson took them out and looked
at them, and understood nothing. But he put them
under his coat, and was going to find the men who
had been there the night before, to ask why these
papers had killed his father, when he saw the policeman again, walking slowly past his house, looking at
him, and then he turned and walked slowly back,
looking at him all the time.

And now for the first time he listened to the

wailing of the old woman, who was saying that she was alone, she was alone, and she wanted to go home. She meant to Nyasaland. In Nyasaland the police did not come into people's houses and hit them, there the police did not walk with sticks in their hands. She spoke as if she had come from there a week ago, instead of so many years. But Dickson listened, and he stood by the window and looked out and saw the policeman go past again, looking at him, fierce and threatening.

The papers were hot and uncomfortable under his coat. When at last the policeman went away, he left his mother and hastened to the house of one of the men who were directing the strike, but he was not there, and he did not like to leave these dangerous papers. He went to another house and another, but no one would tell him where the men were. So at last he returned to his own home, and all that night the mother and the children discussed what it was they should do. One of the daughters and one of the sons said they would stay in this city. Why go back home? There was nothing there, only the old people in the villages, and no work, and nothing to buy with money—no money even.

But Dickson and his youngest brother, who was only twelve years, and one sister said they would go with the mother.

But first they must get money from the people who employed them, and then there was the question of the papers.

On the next day the strike was finished. The mother and the youngest son, who worked as piccanin, or odd-job man in a house at the other end of the town, and the daughter, who was a nanny, went to tell their employers they must leave quickly, they must go home, their mother had died, or their father, or their child—anything, so as to leave quickly.

But Dickson, who had the papers under his coat and who seemed to see that policeman everywhere, waited until night came. When the dusk had fallen, he was hurrying out of the gate of the township, when he did indeed see the policeman, who fell into step beside him, and said, 'Where are you going?'

And Dickson said quickly, in a low voice: 'We are going to Nyasaland, we are going home. . . .'

And then the policeman swerved off and away, on his own business, and Dickson came quickly through the streets to the Mansions, and up the narrow staircase and to the kitchen.

In the morning, when we went to look for him, and could not find him, we examined the bundle of wet and torn papers. In it were copies of the *World Federation of Trade Unions Journal* from Britain, which is banned, and other journals from down south. There was a copy of the Industrial Conciliation Act. There were also two pamphlets, very worn, as if innumerable hands had held them, one called *Peoples of Soviet Asia Awake!* and the other *Fight the Devil Drink.*

XIII

GOING TO Northern Rhodesia means visiting the Copper Belt, which is the backbone of the country; so that unless one is careful one sees the place as a string of little mining towns. But the country is a vast, scarcely developed, hardly populated area with a tiny metal spine. From the point of view of the Africans, the Copper Belt and Lusaka are places to earn money in. Their life is based on the tribe and village much more than in Southern Rhodesia. For one thing, only about 5 per cent of the land has been alienated from them. For another, there has been no deliberate attempt to smash the tribal system, as is being done in Southern Rhodesia. Outside the towns, the Chief is the focal point of authority and respect, the symbol of the old feeling, where land is owned in common, everybody knows his or her place in the community and rights and duties are not in dispute because they have been established for generations.

The paradox of Northern Rhodesia and Nyasaland is this: the Africans are avid for advancement, to acquire skills, to become educated, to find a place in the modern world. But because of Federation, because of their fear of the Southern Rhodesian and South African systems, which they see as identical, because they see every move the white settlers make as a trick to take their land from them, they are resisting what they most desire and need. They fall back on the Chiefs and on tribalism because that is something of their own, a protection against the destruction of their dignity as people.

What they are saying, in effect, is this: 'If the price of entering the modern world, civilisation as it is defined in Europe, of becoming industrialised, is to lose what small vestiges of liberty we still retain, then we prefer to remain what you call backwards.'

The symbol of this choice is the Colonial Office.

'As long we can keep Colonial Office control here, it will save us from being handed over body and soul to the white settlers.'

And so, in Southern Rhodesia, officials argue bitterly: 'We are advancing the Africans much faster than the Colonial Office because under our administration they are going to have no choice but to enter industrialism, to leave tribalism behind.' And they really feel aggrieved about it because they cannot see the Africans as a people, as a people with its own soul.

This is one of the cases, I think, where liberty has become more important to a people than more money, better living conditions.

The Copper Belt is owned by two big companies, Anglo-American and the Rhodesian Selection Trust. The ramifications of the finance are involved; but, broadly speaking, Anglo-American is South African, that is, British capital; and the Rhodesian Selection Trust is American. That, at least, is how they are spoken of by the citizens of Northern Rhodesia, and a great deal of interesting gossip goes on about the rivalries between the two, their different methods of handling labour, and how Anglo-American is conservative by temperament, while the Selection Trust is more flexible and go-ahead. But after two weeks in Northern Rhodesia I had formed an image in my mind of these two copper giants facing each other with an angry scowl, left hands secretly linked, while they shadow-boxed with their right.

The rate of exploitation in Northern Rhodesia is higher than in any other Colonial territory.

The annual profits from the copper mines have reached £50,000,000, of which more than half leaves the country for external shareholders. The annual wage bill for the Africans is less than £5,000,000.

I was going to Kitwe-Nkana, under the aegis of Anglo-American. With their representative in Salisbury, a most courteous and helpful man, I had had the by now familiar interview, during which I had been able to agree, with every sincerity, that the industrialists were against the industrial colour bar and for African advancement, and that the white trade unions were in comparison reactionary.

I therefore took the plane north to Ndola.

Ndola is a small-scale Bulawayo or Salisbury, and I had no wish to stay there; but I wanted to find the friend of a friend who lived there, a man who spends his time investigating African conditions of living, and who could give me the sort of information I wanted. For in a town in Southern Rhodesia twenty-four hours with a couple of anthropologists investigating urban Africans had taught me more than interviews with several dozen officials. (Incidentally this couple had asked permission to do a survey on the effects of the colour bar on the lives of the white people; this caused great offence—they were instructed to stick to the Africans.)

But I could not find the man I wanted. The address given me by the bank turned out to be an empty house, and I pursued various false scents without result. The time was not wasted, because my African taxi-driver, having heard I was a journalist from Britain, talked without inhibition or a moment's pause about what he thought about Federation, Partnership, white supremacy and so on. Nothing new; but I had, after all, chosen his taxi at random. Again I was struck by the comparative independence of the northern people; no Southern Rhodesian African would ever express himself to a stranger with such confidence.

There being no train, plain, or coach to Kitwe-Nkana, I went by taxi, harangued all the way by my driver. An expensive business; 50 miles so far as I can remember.

Kitwe-Nkana has one hotel, at which I found a bed with difficulty. Everything is so overcrowded in all these cities that one had to book weeks in advance.

I tried to get through to my hosts at the mining offices, but it turned out to be Labour Day and an official holiday. Therefore I went in search of Mr. Katilungu, President of the African Mineworkers' Union. The taxi-man knew at once who he was and where I might find him. 'At this time of the day he will be at his house.'

This taxi-driver was a Southern Rhodesian, come up to the Copper Belt in search of higher wages. But he did not like Northern Rhodesia, in spite of the wages. 'They do not enjoy themselves here as well as we do,' he said. But I think he was simply homesick.

He asked me spontaneously, 'Why are these trade

unions? What is the good of them? Why do you want to see Mr. Katilungu?'

I explained the purpose of a trade union.

'Yes, I know that is what is said. But our wages are still very low, and already trade unions have been here many years.'

And then, after listening politely to what I said: 'Congress is good, yes. Congress makes white men frightened. But white men do not mind trade unions.'

Mr. Katilungu has a little house in one of the townships. It was filled with people—a friend of his, a visiting Chief from the Northern Province, was there with his entourage of young men.

So there was a three-cornered interview.

The Senior Chief, a very dignified old man, expected and got homage from Mr. Katilungu, and everything that was said was translated for his benefit.

Discussion about the trade union centred, of course, around the industrial colour bar, and about the attempts by the Companies to form a stooge union, the Salaried Staffs Association.

Federation: 'Even the whites don't like it,' said Mr. Katilungu. 'All the Copper Belt money goes to Southern Rhodesia. Everything has gone up in price since Federation.'

And the Senior Chief joined in here to say: 'They promised us complete social, economic and political equality. They have broken their promise.'

Capricorn: 'They were campaigning here for Federation, trying to get us to support it. Now they want us to forget that campaign, and to believe they are for racial equality.'

During the discussion children were drifting in and out of the room, perching on the arms of chairs, standing by the knees of their elders. A tiny child came and climbed on my knee, sat staring with solemn interest into my white face. This touched me very much, though I told myself it was nothing but sentimentality that it should.

It was the Senior Chief who particularly interested me. The moment I began to ask questions about what was happening out in the country, he said: 'I am glad the foreign journalist is interested in the people in the villages as well as the people in the towns.' I think he was a little resentful because I had been asking questions mainly of Mr. Katilungu.

I asked about the position of the Chiefs. He emphasised that the Chiefs were superior to the District Commissioners, that only they had the right to distribute land, and that because of their strength and authority the Northern Rhodesian Government had not been able to destroy the people's cattle as had been done in the south.

As soon as he finished talking, one of his young men said in English: 'Yes, but a Chief the Government doesn't like is deposed. And the District Commissioners put what they call troublemakers into prison. We young men are always going to prison. And don't forget to write in your articles that it is the District Commissioner who tries a man, as well as sending him for trial. The District Commissioner can do as he likes.'

I don't think the Senior Chief understood these remarks. He said something in his own language, which sounded to me like a demand for them to be translated; but Mr. Katilungu went on quickly, talking about something else.

That afternoon, in that small, hot room, I was seeing the clash between the two different kinds of African leadership: the traditional and hereditary, and the new leadership of the towns. It seemed to me that the great courtesy and deference shown by Mr. Katilungu towards the old man was the willing deference of a man who knows himself to be stronger and can afford to give way, all the more so because with a part of himself he wished to pay homage to the old ways.

As for the young men, save for that one who spoke about troublemakers, they sat and said nothing, leaving their elders to speak for them.

At the hotel I found my room already shared by a young woman called Eileen. She was a fat, phlegmatic, freckled girl who sighed at every second breath, while she told me the story of her life, which she did at once.

It seemed that Eileen was thirty years old, and she lived with her Mom in Salisbury. Mom did not allow her to smoke or to drink, although she allowed her married sister to smoke and drink because she was married. Eileen was a typist, earning £65 a month; although she could earn far more if she wanted to move to another firm which was offering her £80. But she was used to her boss, and preferred being respected to earning more money. But last year she had got restless and went to Johannesburg, where she at once secured a job out of 120 applicants. But she got homesick at the end of the first week and went back to Salisbury. Then she got restless again and applied for a job on the Copper Belt at £80 a month, and got it; but Mom said: 'You are a nice girl, Eileen, and you'll never be happy with those rough types on the Copper Belt.' So she had thrown up that job before even starting.

Almost at once, restlessness had set in again; and she had come up here with five other girls just to see.

'And besides,' said Eileen, 'some of these men here earn more than £200 a month. You don't catch me working after I am married.'

While she was telling me all this, she was dressing, and I lay on the bed and listened.

The indolence of heat emphasised her characteristic lassitude, and it took her over an hour to dress. Finally she stood before the looking-glass, in a tight dress with pink flowers all over it, pink beads, pink sash. A little girl's dress. And the fat, timid face was that of a fifteen-year-old. She went out saying she must get a breath of fresh air; and ten minutes later I saw her on the verandah with a glass of whisky, half-full, a cigarette, and a young copper miner. There is a shortage of women on the Copper Belt.

This hotel may aim to offer other amenities, but it is a drinking hotel above all. I imagined that Southern Rhodesia was talented for drinking; but I had seen nothing till I went to the Copper Belt.

Around the corner from the hotel is a bar. Outside the bar are rows of cars. At sundown, the families come driving in; the men leave wives and children in the cars and go into the bar. From time to time they come out with a drink for the wife and a lemonade for the children, and then go back into the bar. And so they all spend the evening, until the bar closes.

As for me, I went back into the bedroom and studied the newspapers.

At that time the African National Congress had imposed a boycott on shops that had used unfair trade practices.

At that particular moment, in the early part of May, the boycott had been called off on the Copper Belt, but was still in effect in Broken Hill. The newspapers were full of it.

The boycott movement is more than an effort to force equal dealings in shops between black and white. It is also a trial of strength for Congress. Here is a news item from that time:

'A warning to the Government that the African National Congress has already a Government within the Congress that will one day rule Northern Rhodesia was given at a meeting here today. The Congress warned the Government that they wanted no interference on boycotts. Resolutions passed at the meeting included: (1) A protest against the District Commissioner and the District Officer asking for identification certificates in the compound area and fining those without them. (2) The boycott would end when the person who was imprisoned for nine months on charges arising from the boycott was released. (3) The reasons for the boycott were the imposition of Federation, equal representation when the Northern Rhodesian constitution is changed, shop prices are too high in comparison with African wages, and Indians have monopolised African trade so that Africans could not start their own businesses.'

And: 'When the Indians in Broken Hill say that Congressmen have threatened customers there is no truth in it. The African National Congress believes in non-co-operation, but without violence. If there have been threats, they have not been by Congressmen. We are not barbarians. To end the boycott is simple: prices must be reduced, and colour discrimination completely abolished by the Government. We are not worried about the Colonial Secretary's refusal to see Mr. Nkumbula . . . and we shall never see him. All the African beer-halls must be abolished; we want to enter the European bars. The anti-boycott movement will never end the boycott simply by calling us foolish. . . .'

From the *Northern News* of April 30th: 'Alex Masala, chairman of the Broken Hill Branch of the African National Congress, was jailed for 9 months here on Friday by Mr. Colin Cunningham on a charge of unlawful assembly. . . .'

From *Northern News* of June 12th: 'In the Livingstone Magistrates' Court today, Amon Lungu, vice-secretary of the Libuyu Branch of the African Congress, was sentenced to 2 years' imprisonment with hard labour on counts arising from speeches he had made at a meeting of Africans at Maramba Market on June 2nd. Lungu was guilty of threatening damage to property for having said: "If you people feel as I do in my heart we should go down and break down the police camp." '

Northern News, June 12th: 'Two Africans were today sentenced by Mr. W. H. Hannah in the Magistrates' Court here to 9 months' imprisonment with hard labour on charges arising out of the boycott of European-owned stores in the African township. The Africans ... both mine employees, were convicted of the theft of a threepenny candle and resisting arrest. On the first count they were sentenced to 6 months' imprisonment each, and on the second count, 3 months each.'

June 16th: '. . . At Kitwe, a 25-year-old African, Nondo Mbuwa, was sentenced to six months' hard labour for stealing 1s. 6d. worth of meat from another African when trying to enforce the shops boycott.'

June 1st: 'A plea for greater consideration for Africans who have proved themselves was made by Mr. John Roberts at a public meeting here. He said: "There is quite a fair percentage of Africans who have stabilised themselves and who are well known to the provincial administration and the Government. They should no longer be required to carry the multifarious papers and passes which are at present required. They deserve exemption." '

May 26th: 'Fort Jameson. The Governor, Sir Arthur Benson, warned Paramount and Senior Chiefs at an indaba here yesterday to ignore people who urged them to resist the activities of Government departments. "They are your enemies who want to take away your power," he told them.'

June 5th: 'Mufulira. Between twenty and thirty cars were stoned by a crowd of Africans near Mufulira yester-

day evening following an accident involving an African
and a car driven by a European. The stoning occurred
after the car overturned and struck the African. There was
no trouble immediately, but later a crowd of Africans
threw stones at passing cars and at a lorry which was
carrying an African football team.'

African Weekly, May 23rd: 'Sir, none of the people in
the Federation knows the harsh and cruel manner in
which Africans from the Federation, particularly Northern
Rhodesia and Nyasaland, are repatriated from the Union.
They are all arrested, even on the streets, bundled into a
lorry with little ventilation, and driven to Bulawayo, at
times even without the knowledge of their wives in a
South African location. This is not the right way to treat
people, the more so when it is realised that the South
Africans who come to the Federation are not sent back in
that manner. I appeal to African Federal M.P.s to bring
this matter up in Parliament with a view to effecting an
improvement in repatriation methods.'

Northern News, May 27th: 'About thirty African wom-
en today tried to enter the delicatessen at Kitwe in what
seemed to be a demand for service equal to that given to
Europeans, but were refused entry. . . .'

June 16th: 'Mufulira. A warning that if car stonings
continued the Legislature might have to consider increasing sentences was given in the Magistrates' Court here
today by Mr. A. R. W. Porter when he sentenced seven
Africans to 18 months' imprisonment with hard labour for
riotous assembly. The charges followed a stoning incident
about three miles from Mufulira. . . . Seven Africans
pleaded guilty; two others pleaded not guilty. Mr. J. H.
Daniels, prosecuting, said that after a report of a collision
between an African cyclist and a car near Mufulira, police
found a crowd of about twenty Africans had gathered. By
the time an ambulance took away the injured cyclist the

crowd had grown to fifty. An African was arrested because he was making the crowd aggressive. When he was put into the police truck, stones and sand were thrown at the police and the vehicle. . . .'

June 20th: 'Kitwe. For threatening violence during the boycott Masonda Bwalya, a 45-year-old contractor's policeman, was sentenced to 3 months' hard labour by Mr. W. H. Hannah in the Kitwe Magistrates' Court today. . . .'

June 18th: 'Lusaka. "I can see nothing that will stop us from achieving Dominion status in the near future," Sir Roy Welensky said today. . . .' (Sir Roy is Deputy Prime Minister of the Federation, in the line of succession from Lord Malvern.*) ' "There are small people with small minds in all countries, but I must admit I find it difficult to follow their thinking when I look at the assets, both human and mineral, that this vast Federation possesses. I just cannot understand people who doubt that we will succeed in building a great State here. I do not believe that the people of the Federation will be misled by the doubting Thomases who lack the courage to grasp the great opportunity that destiny is offering us to provide an example of how people of different races and culture can combine to work for the common good of their land. . . ." Speaking of his travels in America, Sir Roy said that having seen the problem of colour in other lands he could say that in the Federation there was less racial tension.'

June 19th: 'At 4 A.M. today three members of the African Congress were arrested at their homes here, and later appeared at the Magistrates' Court. They were charged under Section 358, sub-section 4, of the Penal Code with unlawfully conspiring together to injure Euro-

*Sir Roy has now become Prime Minister of the Federation, Lord Malvern having retired.

pean traders in their trade by counselling, exhorting or inducing Africans in Mufulira to withold their custom from stores. . . .'

June 11th: Headline: *50,000 leave the Federation in five years*. 'Nearly 50,000 Europeans have left the Federation in the past five years, a fifth of the country's present white population. This is more than half the total number of immigrants in the same period. . . .'

After having read this sort of news for an hour or so, I went to dinner in the hotel dining-room, where a young man with the typically aggressive-suspicious face came up to where I was sitting in a corner, carrying in his hand a full glass of whisky which he held tipped towards me, saying: 'You're that Kaffir-lover. Well, you know what I'm going to do with this?' The whisky being on the verge of landing in my face, I said hastily: 'Well, I think you'd better drink it.' For a moment his hand trembled, then he set down his glass, stood looking at it, and sat himself down beside it. 'Listen,' said he, poking his chin forward and up, and narrowing his eyes in a glare. 'Do you know what I'd like to do with people like you? Do you know?' After he had told me, we discussed for about half an hour whether or not we would allow our female relations to marry black men, while he kept remarking in the voice of a betrayed child: 'But the Government's doing everything for the blacks and nothing for us.'

Eventually I said I had some work to do, and left him brooding over his fifth whisky in the corner of the dining-room.

Lights were out in the bedroom. Eileen from her bed said that she thought her Mom was right, the Copper Belt was too tough for her.

I suggested that perhaps what it needed were some nice, refined girls to raise its tone and standard, but she said very seriously, 'But I'd have to live in this hotel, because there isn't anywhere to live and you'd have to have a lot of girls to refine this hotel.' Besides, she said, she was used to living at home with Mom making her clothes for her. She was used to being respected, she said. I took this opportunity to ask her what she thought about Federation. 'What's that?' she asked. So I asked her if she thought relations between black and white were getting better or worse. 'The munts are getting awfully cheeky,' she said.

With this, we went to sleep, and were awakened in the morning by an African putting tea down beside our beds, or rather, slamming down the tray between us, and striding out again with a crash of the door. Eileen got out of bed, went to the door in her night-dress, half-shut it, leaned the upper portion of herself through the space, and yelled: 'Here, boy, clean the bath.'

But he did not reappear.

'I am not used,' said Eileen, 'to cleaning the bath for myself: if my Mom knew, she wouldn't like it. But the munts up here they do as they like: it's because of the Parliament.'

'Which Parliament?'

'That Parliament in London. They have no respect, because those people in London always stand up for them.'

*   *   *   *

A couple of days spent interviewing various types of mine official. They were all concerned to make me accept three facts. First, that since I was a Southern Rhodesian, I could never expect to understand Northern Rhodesian problems. I must admit I had not expected this. At last, getting a bit exasperated, I asked one man: 'Supposing that at the end of a week here I professed myself a partisan of Federation and of making haste slowly. Would you then say I had been here long enough to understand your problems?' To which he replied, with perfect seriousness, as it were encouraging me onwards in a comradely way towards unanimity with common sense: 'Quite a lot of our immigrants get the right idea straight away.'

The second point was that housing for African workers was better than anywhere else in the Federation. Which is quite true. The conclusion a lot of people draw from this fact is that what Central Africa needs is more big companies, so rich that they can afford to spend a few hundred thousand extra every year on building roads in the locations and supplying electric light.

The third point of extreme importance—that is, judged by the amount of time given to it—was the Salaried Staffs Association. The African Mineworkers' Union, being powerful, well organized, and in fact the most influential body in Northern Rhodesia, the mine management naturally spend a great deal of time trying to weaken it in various ways.

What, one asks, is there new to say about the fact that big capitalist companies create stooge unions when they can? One would have thought, nothing.

Yet one suave, plump gentleman after another earnestly persuaded me that the Salaried Staffs Association was in the best interests of the African people as a whole, that the Mineworkers' Union was generally a rough, crude and ungentlemanly organisation, and that the Africans' low level of intelligence was proved by the fact that they did not understand the Salaried Staffs Association was entirely for their own good.

As hour succeeded hour, and one plump gentleman succeeded another in solemn exhortation, I began to ask myself: Was it that they imagined visiting journalists were so innocent as not to understand these ancient and time-honoured tactics? Was it that they imagined *I* was?—but obviously I was not prepared to admit this. Or perhaps—and I believe I am right—the colour bar caused them to see these commonplaces of industrial struggle as new and original?

In order to pass the time, I worked out an imaginary scene, thus:

PLACE—The bedroom of the mine manager.

TIME—About three in the morning.

The manager, a rather fat pink-and-white gentleman, in pink-striped pyjamas, is lying awake; his wife placidly asleep beside him in the twin bed.

HE (*suddenly shooting up in bed*): Darling, wake up! I have an idea!

SHE (*sleepily*): Would you like one of my sleeping tablets, darling?

HE: Darling, I said I had an idea. Listen. . . .

SHE: Oh very well. What is it, darling?

HE: You know that damned outfit of that scoundrel Katilungu?

SHE: Since you never talk about anything else, darling. . . .

HE: But listen. I've thought of a way to break it.

SHE: No! How, darling?

HE: What do you think of this? I'm going to take all the better-paid workers and tell them they are too good to associate with that rough lot of Katilungu's, and I shall form another union. And when Katilungu tells me that his union is representative of all the workers, I shall be able to say it isn't. All I have to do is to flatter a few of the types who think they're better than the others. What do you think?

SHE: Darling, you're wonderful. (*She turns over and goes to sleep.*)

HE (*to himself in the dark*): And I only earn £5,000 a year!

The reason why I think this dialogue is not so far-fetched is because when I interviewed a certain high official in Southern Rhodesia, he said to me: 'Do you know how I got my Trade Union Bill through? I sat in the House afternoon after afternoon, and I looked at the faces of all those who were my opponents either to the left or to the right, and suddenly I had an idea. What do you think?'

'I really can't!'

'I thought: I'll put all my opponents on to the Select Committee, so they'll have to take the responsibility. Good, eh?'

And he radiated an innocent delight at his own shrewdness.

*　　*　　*　　*

A Colonial good-time evening: sundowners in the hotel, while the long yawn of the hours ahead deepens. The idea of food recedes under a tide of alcohol. We move to one bachelor flat, then, collecting people as we go, to another and then another. Eartha Kitt's records, talk about the South of France where people will go, or dream of going, on the next leave. Talk about the colour bar. More talk about the colour bar. The musicals now running in London. The colour bar.

The young woman journalist, aged twenty-three, who by eleven in the evening has drunk more than a bottle of whisky, without apparent ill-effects, suddenly becomes very confidential about her own private view of the colour bar, which, it seems, is not the official one, but unfortunately is so thick-tongued one cannot understand what she is saying. She goes home, dignified by an immense private sorrow which is incommunicable, supported on either side by a young man.

Whereupon the survivors tell how old so and so has just broken the record between here and Salisbury, at the cost of a cracked axle, so as to fit in a week-end party; and how somebody else took a horse into the ballroom at the big official dance in L.

Never have I been anywhere where the feeling of boredom, of boredom crystallized into activity and alcohol for salvation's sake, is so strong as in the little mining towns of Northern Rhodesia. Never, that is, since my adolescence in Salisbury, which, from the dusty distances of the Copper Belt, seems like an oasis of civilisation.

Back in the hotel, Eileen is still awake, mournful in the dark behind a cigarette. She has not told me the whole truth, she says. She came up to the Copper Belt really not for the money, but because last year she had been going out with a man, but he suddenly dropped her and came north to copper. So she had come, too, not to get him back, but simply to confront him, and say to him: 'But why, Johnnie? Just tell me why?' That evening, luckily, she was sitting on the hotel verandah with her new friend, when who should come and sit at the next table with a group of men but Johnnie? 'I nodded to him and said, "Is that you Johnnie? Well, I didn't know you were up here." And after dinner he came up to me and said: "How about a drive?" And I said, "Thank you, but I'm tired this evening. Another time, Johnnie." So I hope tomorrow my new one will ask me so that I can say I am engaged. Not that I want him back, don't think that, but when he says, "Why are you always tired or engaged?" I just want to say to him, "Johnnie, it stands to reason I am tired for a man who took me out for a year and then went away not even saying me why. . . ." And then he will say to me, "Hell, man, give me a chance." And I will say to him, "Johnnie, you had your chance, and you threw it away. Now let us be friends." '

A silence. I put out the lights and get into bed.

Eileen lights another cigarette. 'If my Mom knew I was smoking,' she says, with the most dignified melancholy in her heavy voice, 'if she knew, she would say the Copper Belt is ruining me.'

'You should leave it,' I say.

'Yes,' she says, 'but first I must tell Johnnie I am too good for him.'

*　　*　　*　　*

A visit to a scheme for recovering young hooligans from a future of crime. The mines do not employ children under 18. Gangs of boys who could not get into school were roaming the townships making mischief. The company supplied a piece of land, and employed an enthusiastic man who teaches these boys agriculture and carpentry and arranges extra classes for them.

Admirable. As usual one feels it would be churlish to say, well, if there were enough schools there would be no need for all this philanthropy.

There is nothing more moving, or more exasperating in the Federation than these devoted, enthusiastic people who sweat their lives out on pittances and idealism to save the Africans from the worst effects of a savage exploitation. Just as the motives behind Federation have perverted all the good things one believes most in, have made suspect the phrases of goodwill, so that one can scarcely talk about interracialism, or equality, or advance, since these words have been poisoned by dishonesty; so, too, the honest idealism of people who are sickened by the condition of the Africans and who spend their lives trying to help them is made cheap by the cynicism that makes use of these emotions. Let's have the figures again: Profits annually: £50,000,000. More than half to overseas share-holders. And a £5,000,000 African wage bill. Yet not one of these mine officials talks as if the copper mines were anything else but a philanthropic device for improving the lot of the Africans.

On the Rhokana mine one of the show-pieces is a building where an enthusiastic man teaches the Africans to make bricks, literally, out of straw. It seems that the management some time back had the idea of providing a place where the employees could learn carpentry. But the man they chose to run it had ideas more far-reaching than this. He said that the Africans must make use of their ingenuity to provide for themselves out of what materials lie to hand. Thus, any man or woman who comes to the building asking if he can make a bed, or a cupboard, is taught not only how to do this, but how to use bits of packing case, wood thrown away by the mine, or discarded furniture from the white man's house. In that building ingenuity has become a passion. Sandals are fashioned of tyres; baskets and brooms and brushes out of wild grasses; jugs and plates from copper waste; furniture from almost anything one can think of; clothes out of trade rejects; and tools out of scraps of waste mine machinery.

It is one of the most interesting places on the Copper Belt. Its manager devotes his life to it.

And why should the African workers on this fabulously rich mine have to spend their time learning to make the necessities for their living out of the waste from white civilisation?

But one asks this question afterwards, not at the time, because of one's deep respect for the man whose motives are goodness of heart and compassion for suffering.

*   *   *   *

In the newspaper it says that the Rhodesian Selection

Trust is making a gift of £3,000,000 for African development. Everyone, it seems, is deeply moved by this generosity.

*   *   *   *

An interview with a Welfare Officer at which I am told that all the children are now going to school. I am naturally very impressed by this. Afterwards discover from the figures of the Minister of Education that either this welfare official is badly misinformed or that he is deliberately lying. Forty-six per cent of the African children in towns get some sort of an education; 58 per cent in the rural areas.

*   *   *   *

A trip down one of the mineshafts. I have been down gold-mines before, but since I know nothing about the techniques of mining, I regarded this rather as a joy-ride than a contribution to information. Besides, it was the mineshaft the Queen Mother was taken down, presumably the one reserved for visitors.

My guide said that an American journalist he had taken down wrote an article about the enslaved workers who were chained to their jobs underground. 'So ignorant he didn't even know a safety-chain when he saw one.' I said I would make a point of not falling into the same error.

Whereupon he said: 'I spend half my time taking journalists around, and none of you ever has a good word to say for us. So I suppose you won't either.'

'Well, not many,' I said.

'Oh well,' he said, with a sort of stolid intention to endure the whips and arrows of unfair criticism, 'we all do our best, you know; we all do our best.'

*   *   *   *

An evening with a man not employed by the company. He told me that because of the enormously high price of copper, still unnaturally high although it has recently dropped a little, the copper bonus raises European wages to more than twice what is normal. Shop-keepers raise their prices to suit; but Government employees and independent men are left behind and comparatively badly off. A mine employee (white) pays £3 a month rent, and can earn as much as £200 a month. He says: 'Most people have nothing to spend their money on but drink or saving for the next holiday or buying new cars.'

It seems there is considerable ill will between the mine people and the others.

*   *   *   *

A trade-union official spent most of his time during our interview slanging my friend Simon Zukas, whom he referred to as a stateless Lithuanian agitator. Simon has lived in Northern Rhodesia nearly all his life, but due to the intricacies of the citizenship laws is not technically a citizen. Therefore he was deported, after helping to organise the Congress. I was not surprised that every time I mentioned his name, which I did as often as possible to see the reaction, people became abusive, but I must say I was surprised at the level of the abuse. Nothing short of hanging, it seems, is good enough for Simon. Incidentally the man who called him stateless was an immigrant into Rhodesia of three years' standing, and became positively hysterical at Simon's inability to understand local problems.

Whenever I mentioned Simon, people were at great pains to say how badly Congress had treated him; so insistent were they that I became suspicious, scenting another version of 'Africans are so ungrateful.' Having been told a dozen times that Congress had been so mean as only to raise £4 for Simon's defence, when he was deported for helping them, I made a point of seeking out the man who had been treasurer at that time.

I found him very bitter over this rumour. 'Congress raised £1,000 for Simon, and spent £661 of that sum in ways that seemed useful, mostly on appeal expenses. It was a complicated trial, and it wasn't easy all the time to see what was the right thing to do. For one thing Simon was being held at Livingstone, which is a long way from Lusaka. Mr. Nkumbula was there anyway for the trial. What did people expect us to do? Send the entire Committee to Livingstone? No, these rumours were deliberately spread around so that other white men who might help us would think we treated Simon badly.'

I spoke to several Congress people about this business, and they all spoke angrily about this malicious attempt to smear them over their treatment of Simon.

'People are always ready to believe bad things of us Africans. Even progressive people believe that business of us raising £4 for Simon. The rumour started because the Luansha branch of the General Workers' Union raised £4. The Press seized on that figure and did not mention the real figure at all.'

* * * *

Time was running out fast. I telephoned from Kitwe for information as to when I could catch a plane across to Nyasaland. I was informed that no planes went from Northern Rhodesia to Nyasaland and I must go back to Salisbury and then up to Nyasaland. Therefore I left Kitwe sooner than I wanted to and went to Lusaka. No sooner had I descended in Lusaka airport than I found a plane had just left for Nyasaland. No, they simply could not understand how I had been given such a nonsensical piece of information. Planes went regularly from Lusaka

across to Blantyre. But now I would have to go to Salisbury to reach Nyasaland since it would be several days
before the next plane left Lusaka.

*   *   *   *

An interview with Mr. Nkumbula and Mr. Kaundu,
President and Secretary of Congress. Their views on Federation, Partnership and so on can be taken as read, for
what is remarkable about this vast area covered by Federation is the unanimity of African opinion all over it. I was
particularly concerned to find out the state of affairs in the
Kariba Valley, and what was happening to the people
being moved.

Mr. Nkumbula had just returned from a trip to that
point which is the nearest to the area he is allowed to go.
He had come back at six that morning after travelling all
night, and was aroused from his bed again at nine to see
me. He was extremely tired, and very bitter over the
treatment of Congress.

He told me that the villagers of the valley were angry
and miserable; that Chiefs supporting Congress were being
threatened or deposed; that young men talking Congress
language were suffering all kinds of ill-treatment from the
District Commissioners.

These people are being moved from rich, well-watered
land to high, poor, undeveloped land, and their resentment is both on this count and because their attachment to
their soil is religious and ritualistic. They are not prepared
to believe that schemes like Kariba will benefit them at
all, either immediately or in the future.

*   *   *   *

Interview with an opponent of Sir Roy Welensky. He
says: 'Roy is a typical white trade unionist. Now he makes
himself sound like an old-fashioned liberal in public, but
the leopard hasn't changed his spots. Consider what he's

doing with the railways, now he's minister. Our railways must be the most inefficient in the world. Why? Shortage of labour. In the meantime hundreds of Africans hang about, quite able to do the work, but unable to because of the colour bar. Welensky brings in unskilled Italians and Greeks on the grounds that "they will learn quicker" than the Africans. Why? Do you have to ask? Read his speech to his white trade-union electors at Broken Hill, which is his constituency. When he's talking to his constituents he is all in favour of the industrial colour bar and white supremacy. He loathes the Africans. He doesn't dare to say so now, of course. But he does. The only place he can afford to say it is in the pub with his trade-union buddies.'

I asked what sort of Prime Minister Roy Welensky would make.

'What difference does it make? Garfield Todd is a decent type who really likes the Africans as people. But he has to toe the white line or he'd lose his job. Roy Welensky will do the same thing from conviction—that's the only difference. Whether Garfield Todd or Welensky becomes Federal Prime Minister, they'll have to do exactly the same thing in the end.'

*   *   *   *

The numbers of the police have been multiplied by seven since Federation. When asked why, the Administration said: 'The white population has doubled.'

*   *   *   *

An interview with an African M.P. who told me, half-humorous, half-sad, about a long struggle he had just finished in his local council to get the Africans to accept a Government grant to improve their land. He said: 'We need that money badly. We need to learn better farming methods. As an example of this, in our area there are a lot of Southern Rhodesians farming, and in a couple of seasons they outstrip our people and leave them behind because they've learned modern husbandry in Southern Rhodesia. But our people say: "If we accept the Government money and improve our land, the white people will take it from us." So they prefer to remain poor. This Federation was a terrible thing, a terrible thing. And simply because I tried to persuade them to accept this money, they said I was a Government stooge. But I am not a Government stooge. All I want is the best for my people.'

*   *   *   *

I wanted to visit the radio station in Lusaka, which people say is enterprising and efficient. It is listened to by Africans all over the Federation. It broadcasts in various African languages and has programmes of traditional music. But I rang up Central African Airways, was told an aeroplane was leaving early on Monday morning from Salisbury for Nyasaland, and so I could not stay. I took a plane to Southern Rhodesia, leaving Northern Rhodesia, without much regret, behind me.

Having arrived at Salisbury, I was told I had been misinformed about the plane to Nyasaland. There was no plane until Tuesday. My plane to London left on Thursday. Since all the planes are heavily booked I could not afford to miss it. I worked out a rather precarious plan to rush up to Nyasaland for one day, try and see Chief Gomani, who is in considerable trouble with the Government, and then rush back again, taking a chance on getting into a plane at Blantyre. But in the end I decided not to.

It was a big disappointment to me, giving up Nyasaland. I have never been there. Everyone who has speaks of it as the most beautiful country. The Africans I have known from Nyasaland are a fine lot: alert, independent, subtle, proud. And the white people (there are only six thousand of them) are less colour-ridden than anywhere in the Federation.

But it is not like Northern Rhodesia, which has its Copper Belt towns strung out close together, easy to reach. Nyasaland is a long, narrow, mountainous, lake-divided country, with bad roads and widely-scattered towns. Useless to go there for a couple of days.

Being in a paranoiac state of mind just then, I was convinced that all the wrong information that had been given me about the places was deliberate, part of a plot to prevent me from going there. But now, having recovered, I don't think so. It was due to the natural inefficiency of the place.

And so I left, to return to London, where people ask: 'Well, what is the future of the Federation?'

I don't know.

There are two vital questions to which no one knows the answer. One is, will there be a slump in America? If so, and the price of copper is seriously affected, the very precarious financial structure of Federation can crumble into chaos.

The second is, will the Labour Party get back into power in Britain? If it does, and its Left Wing is strong enough to force a more liberal policy, it is possible African bitterness may be softened. I have heard it suggested that the white settlers, afraid of the Labour Party getting back, may stage some sort of *coup d'état,* taking complete independence by force or trickery. I don't think so. I hope not. I hope they have more sense, for I am convinced that if they do the whole place will go up in flames like Kenya.

But the real question, the big imponderable, is this: Just how much are the Africans prepared to take?

It has been said that the epitaph of the white man in Africa will be: He allowed his intelligence and his conscience to become blunted by colour prejudice, and did not realize it until too late.

I am certain only of one thing: that if the Federation does not advance very fast, and with real sincerity of motive, towards complete racial partnership, it must retreat rapidly towards what is happening in the Union of South Africa. There is very little difference even now.

I don't feel very optimistic. I don't see how the next decade can be anything else than stormy, bitter and unprofitable.

LONDON,
August 26, 1956

*   *   *   *

While I was writing the above, I had a letter from the Immigration Officer of the High Commissioner's Office in London, saying that he wished to see me.

Being familiar with the devious ways of Partnership I wrote asking that he should put what he had to say in writing. But he wrote back saying no, the information he had to give would be better conveyed verbally; it concerned his Government's decision about my future visits to the Federation.

I know of various people who have been allowed into the Federation on condition they took no part in politics, and I decided that I was likely to be such a case; also, I understood very well that the Federation was trying to prevent me from returning without having to suffer the moral inconvenience of putting it plainly.

I therefore arranged for a solicitor to go with me.

On arrival at Rhodesia House, and having given in

my name and that of my solicitor, I was requested to go first and by myself. But I ignored this and took my solicitor up with me.

The official began by saying that he had been asked to tell me that if I wished to make any further trips to the Federation, I should first please make an application to him.

At which I pointed out that as a British citizen I had a right to enter as I liked, unless special provisions had been made against it. To which he returned: was I planning any further trips shortly? I said that that probably depended on what he had to tell me.

And now he exclaimed, with that engaging naïveté which makes contact with Partnership so rewarding: 'You've forced my hand! Actually even if you did make application, you would not be allowed in.'

I asked if I had been declared a Prohibited Immigrant.

He said that I had, by Declaration in Council of the Governor-General.

Against which, of course, there is no appeal, as he pointed out, very shocked at the idea that one might question the orders of a Governor-General.

(But for the honour of the Federation I must say here that this deep and supine respect for high officialdom is confined to small officialdom. The best characteristic of the white citizens is their lack of respect for traditional authority.)

I suggested, trying of course to annoy the man, that the position was, in fact, exactly similar to that in the Union of South Africa, which also refuses to give reasons when it deports or prohibits a person. But he did not seem ashamed at the comparison.

On the date of this interview, the position in the Federation is as follows:

A State of Emergency has been in existence in Northern Rhodesia for nearly three weeks. The African Mineworkers' Union ran a series of small protest strikes, very well organised and disciplined, against the creation of the African Salaried Staffs Association, the stooge union. But the companies refused to negotiate. Then bitterness broke out in a different form: the miners decided to go to work without their identity bracelets and their leg-guards, as a protest against colour discrimination: the Africans feel this as a humiliation, as the white miners do not have to wear them. As *The Times* put it: 'White miners do not have to crawl about on their hands and knees underground.'

The miners were not allowed to go down without their identity bracelets and leg-guards.

The companies called this a strike; so did the Press in the Federation, and many of the newspapers here.

But to the miners, and to anyone concerned with the principles of trade unionism, it was a lock-out.

But these details of conflict do not matter: it was bitterness and frustration on one side, and the desire to weaken the union on the other.

For two weeks there was a deadlock. Then a State of Emergency was declared. Troops and police were flown in from Southern Rhodesia: for the purposes of preserving white supremacy Federation is truly a Federation—but trade unionism is kept strictly territorial, and union officials are not allowed to move from territory to territory. Meetings of more than five people were banned. Press censorship was imposed. Planes hovered above the compounds to spot any gathering of miners in order to direct ground troops to break them up.

Tanks were paraded, and tear gas used against crowds of protesting women. The women had their babies on their backs, as is customary.

Because of the Press censorship, exact details are not yet known, but here is an item from the *Rhodesia Herald* of September 14th. 'When a mobile unit of the Northern Rhodesian Police, the specially trained riot-breakers, went into action against demonstrating mobs in the Ndola location last night, they used rifles, sten guns and tear gas shells, fired from riot guns, to break them up. . . .'

And the inevitable note of virtue: 'Tear gas shells are considered throughout the world to be the most humane method of mob control. . . .'

More effective, perhaps, than the tanks and the humane tear gas shells, was the fact that the entire leadership and local administration of the African Mineworkers' Union were put into prison, seventy in all, where they still are, on this date.

Three days ago, in Southern Rhodesia, a State of Emergency was declared, and the troops and police called out, because the railway workers threatened to go on strike.

The strike, it seems, has not been much of a success, but since practically no news has come out of Central Africa for the last week, it is difficult to know what is in fact happening.

One may be quite certain that whatever methods the Government is using are entirely humane and decent, and in the best interests of the Africans themselves—though they cannot be expected to be intelligent enough to see it.

One may be quite certain that in the Federation,

Government officials, even when calling out troops armed with sten guns and riot guns—described by the *Rhodesia Herald* thus: 'The riot gun is 28 inches long, with a barrel of 12 inches, and a bore of 1½ inches. It weighs 7 lbs., has a rubber recoil pad on the butt, and may be fired from the shoulder or hip as circumstances require'—these Government officials, using troops at the mere threat of a strike, and protected by the most comprehensive and high-handed legislation against dissidence yet seen anywhere in the world outside the Union of South Africa or Nazi Germany, are still talking fervently about Partnership, British fair play and Advancement.

Personally, like the Africans, I prefer the straightforwardness and lack of hypocrisy of Mr. Strydom.

September 26, 1956

*   *   *   *

NOTE I.—Fifty-six officials of the African Mineworkers' Union having been kept in prison for several weeks, the Chief Justice of Northern Rhodesia ruled that their arrest and detention had been illegal. Whereupon the Legislative Council of Northern Rhodesia—the white settlers' Parliament—passed a law banning fifty-three of them from returning to the Copper Belt. Thus the effective leadership of this union has been removed. This law had to be approved and signed by a British-appointed Governor, one of whose tasks it is to watch over African interests.

The most effective and the biggest African trade union in Central Africa has therefore been deliberately crippled —for the time being at least—by the white administration acting hand in hand with the mining interests and backed up by a British-appointed Governor.

When, in the Union of South Africa, Strydom and his gang smash opposition organisations, they at least attempt to draw a cloak of legality over the performance. But to the honour of South Africa there is still a liberal voice which has not yet let itself be silenced. In Central Africa there are no white people prepared to protest openly against the contempt for democracy and decency shown by their Government; although I know there are some who are ashamed of what is being done, even if they don't say so. There is no white opposition; only black opposition—and the Africans have no effective vote.

NOTE II.—A few days ago I had a letter from a relative in Southern Rhodesia saying she had met and talked with Lord Malvern at a party. He said: 'We prohibited this woman for her own good; and in any case, what she doesn't realize is that she was made a prohibited immigrant years ago, and we only let her in this time by accident.'

This cheers me up: the existence of this sort of Alice-in-Wonderland inefficiency seems to me the one way in which Central Africa is superior to the Union.

NOTE III.—In this book I have made various statements about the possibility of Communism becoming democratic. Since writing it, the Soviet intervention in Hungary has occurred. It is hard to make adequate political assessments on notes added hastily to galley proofs as a book goes to press. But it seems to me that during the last three years the great words liberty, freedom and truth have again become banners for men to fight under—in all the countries of the world. It seems to me wrong that so many people should be saddened and discouraged by this sudden violent crisis we are all living through: it is a crisis in the battle of truth against lies, of honesty against corruption, of respect for the goodness of people against cynicism.

January 6, 1957

ELEVEN YEARS LATER

ALWAYS SALUTARY to read over something written years ago. Particularly something written in emotion—that was 1956, a climactic year for everybody. I was far too heated by the end of that trip; but being chased around by the C.I.D. and then forbidden entry to the country you were bred in, does arouse emotions the reasonable mind finds an impediment. Hundreds of people are now Prohibited Immigrants into the southern part of Africa: anyone who has been critical, is critical, or even might be critical. Of course: dictatorships can't stand critics. And the attitude of mind which says 'of course'; 'if you do this that will follow' is much more useful to judgement than indignation. The trouble is, to understand a place like Rhodesia, like the Republic, it is no good looking coolly from outside. You have to experience the paranoia, the adolescent sentimentality, the neurosis. Experience—then a retreat into a cool look from outside. Most politicians and journalists do their judging from outside only. And most of the people on the spot are lost in a violent emotionalism.

Federation has dissolved: it was unworkable, as certain people foresaw. But it would not have been agreed to by this country (the Labour Party) if the politicians concerned had understood the force of the Northern Rhodesian and Nyasaland Africans' feeling of betrayal. They had made an agreement with Queen Victoria, as free men, that they would continue as free men. Admittedly the administrations of the Colonial Office were not exactly what had been envisaged by them when their spokesmen treated with the Great White Queen, but to force them into Federation against their will was the final confirmation of cynical betrayal and the breaking of a solemn promise. No modern politician thinks in terms of promises, betrayals—in terms of honour. Federation outraged a sense of honour not admitted as anything but a quaint—and, at best, touching—anachronism. But it was this force which broke up Federation. The nationalist movements of Northern Rhodesia and Nyasaland (now Zambia and Malawi) were fed, fuelled, powered by this feeling of having been betrayed, sold out.

No one can remember now what 'Partnership' was. It was the product of a sense of panic in Rhodesia because of what was happening in the Republic, which coldly and honestly told the world what its regime was—a machine to maintain white supremacy. Rhodesia's regime was similar, but that country has never been able to see the truth about its own nature. The Rhodesians at that time liked to think of themselves as 'British,' meaning good, kind, decent, civilised, and not 'Afrikaans,' which meant crude, backwards, bad. But they are quite prepared to consider the Afrikaaners as brothers now that the heat is on, just as the British in South Africa voted for the Afrikaaners when their position as whites was threatened.

One could afford to be amused by 'Partnership' now as then, if it were not that so many people were taken in by it, and if the way of thinking that made it possible to be taken in by it were not as strong as ever in this country. When I came out of Rhodesia on this trip I tried to sell articles to newspapers about the unreality of Federation and of Partnership. But only the *Statesman* and *Tribune* were interested—all the others, including pillars of liberalism now full of moral indignation about the regimes in the Republic and Rhodesia, were enthusiastically selling Federation and Partnership. One was wrong-headed, if not worse, to cast doubt on these concepts. I am still angry about this. But the anger goes back much further than the 'fifties. When I first became interested in politics, in 1939, I was introduced, by the Left, to a knowledge of the monstrous nature of the regime in South Africa. That was under Smuts, the great statesman who laid the basis of 'baaskaap,' so well and firmly that it has served ever since. And Rhodesia was never anything but the modern version of a slave state.

Who was saying so, apart from a handful of Communists, cranks and Socialists? No one. Why not? I'll tell you, it was because no one was interested except those who wanted to maintain the status quo.

This raises that most extraordinary and paradoxical fact which nearly caused me to call this piece 'The Irrational in Politics.'

There have been two powerful emotions simmering in Rhodesia ever since 1924—a white emotion and an African emotion. In 1924, Southern Rhodesia was given self-government: she became a 'self-governing colony,' but with two entrenched clauses in the Constitution. One clause was to do with defence, and of no interest in this context. The other was that the white people of Rhodesia were being given self-government on condition that no legislation discriminated unfavourably between white and black.

The whites having achieved control, they proceeded forthwith to set up a state in every respect identical to the Union of South Africa. It was a political commonplace among those prepared to look at facts rather than submit to self-deluding phrases that any law passed in Rhodesia would have come off the Statute Book of South Africa,

modified to local conditions and given another name. The
basis of white domination in Southern Rhodesia was the
Land Apportionment Act, which took away land from the
Africans and gave it to the Europeans, and laid down
where and under what conditions Africans were to live in
'white' areas. The Land Apportionment Act is not so
much a piece of legislation as an octopus. There is no
single document you can refer to. It has been growing,
spreading, burgeoning for forty years; and if you made a
trip to the Government Stationery Office in Salisbury to
buy this Act, you'd need a cart to carry it away. The most
nastily repressive bits of law are likely to read something
like: 'Subclause (f) of Clause A2(g) of paragraph 6 of the
Land Apportionment Act as amended by clause 7 of the
Amendment of 1945 will read "not" on line 5 instead of
"will be." ' You think I'm joking? Not at all. A temple
full of lawyers would be needed to make sense of that
Act—and no accident either, I assure you.

There was no law passed in Southern Rhodesia that did
not, directly or indirectly, discriminate between white and
black, thereby making 'self-government' invalid by definition. And meanwhile, was Whitehall protesting? Not at
all. Never. Not at any point a cheep out of our British
Parliament. It is possible that some governor exerted influence in the time-honoured way by saying to some prime
minister: 'I say, old chap, don't you think that. ...' Possible, but the results were not shown in legislation.

Meanwhile, and this is the point, the whites simmered
perpetually about interference from Whitehall preventing
them from civilising the blacks as only they, the local
whites, understood they should be civilised. I was brought
up on this extraordinary emotion. Year after year, season
after season, decade after decade, those white farmers sat
round on their verandahs, talking bitterly about interference from Whitehall. The only tangible bit of interference

was that a white farmer was not allowed to flog an erring labourer or servant himself (he did, of course) but should take him into the police-station to be flogged or imprisoned by a white policeman. That was all. But still the whites talked about 'the old country,' stood to attention when 'the King' was played and complained about the politicians in Whitehall. Regardless of party. It was not so long ago that I had a letter from a white man in Rhodesia which contained the words: 'If you think that Reds like you and McLeod are going to ride rough-shod over our rights. . . .'

Meanwhile the Acts of Parliament were passed, the Land Apportionment Act proliferated and in every way Southern Rhodesia became like the Union of South Africa, which place the whites of Southern Rhodesia despised because it wasn't British. To understand the background of this particular bit of emotionalism, it is necessary to remember that Rhodesia came into existence as a flight away from South Africa, as a British colony, conquered by and for the British.

And the Africans? Well, the Africans were sitting around complaining that they had been betrayed and sold out, and why wasn't Whitehall protecting them as promised. So there were the whites, on their town and farm verandahs, complaining about interference from Fabians and Reds, and the blacks complaining that there wasn't any.

When I became involved in African politics—not much of them before the nationalist movements developed—one sat hour after hour in smoky little rooms listening to black men who possess, until it turns sour, an innocent faith in honour and decency which is truly appalling, because of the bitter harvest it must grow, while they said: 'when our friends and brothers in England learn how we are being treated they will see justice done.'

Ridiculous. Absurd. Painful—because, of course, no one in Britain cared a damn.

No one. It was in the 'fifties that I was attending, in the basement of the House of Commons, a meeting of one of those ginger-group organisations dedicated to aiding the colonies. When Southern Rhodesia was reached on a long agenda which included at least two dozen embattled colonies and ex-possessions, the chairman noted certain unsatisfactory conditions—and went on. On an enquiry why, it transpired that these people, members of that tiny minority in Britain who cared at all about Britain's responsibilities abroad, did not know about that entrenched clause in the Constitution of 1924, and that at any time since 1924 what was going on in Southern Rhodesia could have been challenged legally and effectively, from Britain.

It was not until the 'fifties that any section of British opinion took an interest in Rhodesia, let alone any action. And by that time action could not have been effective.

There is a right time to do things. If an action is not taken at the right time, it doesn't work. That is why this U.D.I. business seemed so unreal. It was unreal.

From the Rhodesian side, it was nothing more than a confirmation of something already existing. For Britain suddenly to take moral stands on issues that she had ignored totally for decades was unreal, absurd. She had allowed Federation—against the wishes of the Africans; blessed Partnership; imprisoned and harried the Africans now governing Zambia. Why, suddenly, in the 'sixties, be shocked and outraged by a society she had always condoned? Why the language of moral indignation about legislation she had had the right to veto but had never protested about—or, for that matter, had noticed. Whose responsibility was the slave state in Rhodesia? Why, Britain's—no one else's.

U.D.I. was final crystallisation of the 'we won't have interference from Britain' attitude. All through my childhood I heard them joking: 'What are they going to do then—send gunboats on to the Zambezi?' Quite so. At last, at long last—and how very satisfying to these naughty children—a real interference, a real threat, even though a muted one, from those Fabians and Reds in Britain. How satisfying—even if so late. It was during the U.D.I. crisis I got a letter from a friend saying: 'We are not prepared to be pushed around by Britain.' The point is, he was speaking out of a 40-year-old myth.

I tell you, if Wilson had landed troops in Rhodesia, the entire white population would have picked up its rifles and revolvers and taken to the hills—delighted. Absolutely thrilled. I think Wilson was right not to land troops. I would be surprised if he took the decision for the right reasons, but I've a feeling that that nation of nose-thumbing schoolboys would have had the time of their lives. 'I will pick up my rifle and defend my rights to the last drop of my blood.' Quote from a very typical white citizen. How they do all long to have an excuse to pick up their rifles: at long last their paranoia justified, and their sentimental heroics given a cause—and all in a mood of roaring adolescent enjoyment.

During the crisis the stickers on the cars read: 'Good Old Smithie!' 'Up with Smithie!' 'And the Same to you Wilson!' When they holiday in the Union, Rhodesian cars read: 'Thanks to our Pals—from Rhodesia!' 'Thanks to the Nats!' And so on. Whitehall—when it has been in a responsible mood—has always made the mistake of treating these children seriously. And in the meantime they control a country half the size of Spain and in a key position for the entire continent.

As for sanctions, they were bound to be ineffective, since white Rhodesia could count on aid, open and hidden, from the Republic and from the Portuguese territories. If sanctions prove uncomfortable enough to force concessions, then we can expect some face-saving formula to be agreed to by Britain which will give the appearance of an agreement by the whites to advance the Africans. The whites will hold their power; the Africans will stay exactly as they are. Meanwhile, in the background, that handful of dedicated heroes, black and white, will continue to work, trying to improve conditions, trying to let in a little agitators. For how long? For a very long time, I believe. What is to change things?

I think that, in politics, people do not consider geography enough. The realities tend to be rooted in geography. Rhodesia is now one with the Republic in everything but name, and the southern part of the African continent is isolated. On either side, thousands of leagues of sea; just below, the Antarctic. Embedded between the two white-dominated countries, Bechuanaland (now Botswana), a bitterly poor country concerned only not to let itself be swallowed up by its very powerful neighbours. Then, north, across the Zambezi, Zambia, with problems enough of her own and certainly in no position, as romantics seem to expect, to fight a liberating war. And Malawi, which has turned out to be a black dictatorship, with all its opposition in exile, is fighting some solitary battle for its own interests. Africa, now that the white men have left most of it, has become like any other continent in the world, a mass of nations, each one of which has its own interests, its own form of nationalism. And every one of these countries is very poor. It is not likely that these nations, even if they were able to agree among themselves to do it, could launch a successful war to 'liberate their brothers down South' as some people seem to believe they will. Brotherhood and entrenched national interests, as recent history has abundantly shown, don't march together. The Republic and Rhodesia—and they would be aided by the Portuguese colonies—have highly equipped modern armies, highly efficient secret police and sections of their black populations corrupted into spies and informers. And besides—look at the map.

And, more importantly, consider world priorities. As I write, there is danger of a war between Egypt and Israel; and the war in Vietnam is at crisis point. The world is so precarious that nasty slums like Southern Africa, slummy explosive continents like South America, must get on with it, they aren't a danger to world peace, they don't threaten our very existence. Southern Africa will go on exactly as it is now, as it has been for decades. What is to change it? The much-too-lately aroused moral idealism of small sections of Britain and America? If the big mining interests that own most of the wealth of the sub-continent put pressure on—but big companies don't behave like this. And *if* they did—in *Going Home* I said that the whites would prefer to dwindle into a poor isolation rather than give up their idea of themselves. I think I was right. They would. This particular complex of manias is more powerful than long-term self-interest. It always has been. I can see, unless international influences (a really effective United Nations?), now unlikely to do so, exert pressure, the whole of the Southern continent becoming more cut off, bigoted, ignorant, backwards; the whites deliberately closing their minds and forcibly keeping the minds of the Africans dark—with more and more prisons, whips, jailors, hangings, and forcible exiles.

The man Vorster is bringing a new sophistication to *apartheid*. For instance, 'white' liquor is now available to Africans until recently forbidden it. Outside the bottle shops, Africans queue for the status-symbol. Alcohol has always been used on the farms—tots of brandy have been part of wages for brutalised farm workers for decades. But now alcohol has moved into the cities, enlisted by the Nationalists. And the hard edge of white supremacy has been taken off for a few privileged Africans, in small limited areas. In some of the big stores a black man or woman may be served with courtesy, called Sir and Madam. Certain Africans are highly paid to spy, inform, infiltrate. In the African townships you keep your mouth shut, no one knows who may be in the pay of the Government. The opposition has been destroyed. You can visit the lush swimming-bathed, lawned and gardened suburbs of the white cities and forget that anything exists outside them. When the journalists are asked why they keep quiet about what they know of the oppression, of the tortures in the prisons, the savagery of the machinery of *apartheid* they reply they would lose their jobs, and anyway, no one would believe it. They mean: the whites who pay us don't want to believe it. Where have we heard all this before? Yes, it has become an easy cliché to say that oppressive states are Nazi. But this state is Nazi. Behind Vorster are Nazis from Germany, some who have been there, biding their time for years; some recently arrived; and the techniques now being applied in the Republic were developed under Hitler.

It is just possible that if Rhodesia could develop an efficient African movement, the Republic would benefit by its example. But the Rhodesian movement is divided, and on personal grounds, and is not likely to be of much use. But, detention camps and prisons are great educators, and perhaps now in some bush prison a leadership is developing itself—a Kaunda, a Kapepwe. If this happens, we can expect the usual campaign of denigration from all the whites, some of the bought blacks and most of the British Press.

I went to Zambia for the Independence Celebrations. When I had been there previously, the Nationalist leaders,

Kaunda and the rest, were reviled by the whites; and the Africans were rioting, stoning white cars, challenging the colour bar everywhere, going to prison. The atmosphere was very ugly. It went quite without saying no white would be prepared to stay in a country run by these unscrupulous black agitators. But the Celebrations were attended by a great many white people who had forgotten their own attitudes of less than ten years before. They were admirers of Kaunda and his cabinet to a man. It cannot be said that the majority of the whites in Zambia are happy in their position—most are there only because of the money they can earn. But they *are* there, working and behaving more or less decently. That's something. The really unpleasant people were the old Colonial Office officials who, having administered for years a policy which must ensure that when the Africans got self-government they would have no more than a couple of dozen educated men to run a country with, sat around, gloating openly or furtively over the inefficiencies of the new regime. They are people unable by nature to connect their own attitudes with the results of them. There were a great many like this, and not all from the old Colonial Office. And a lot of them are still there.

But—nothing succeeds like success. Consider Kenya. What could be more extraordinary than the way that evil, black-magicking demagogue Kenyatta has been transmogrified into the respected Daddy of Kenya? Old-hand whites go around saying: 'What is going to happen to this country when The Old Man goes, I can't think.' They were raving to tar and feather him not so long ago. It is not that one wishes people to have integrity of memory, for the sake of it, but it would be nice if, as this country or that heats up and political temperatures rise, people would remember how often we have been there before.

I remember, thinking of Kenyatta, a man called Montague Slater, now dead, who wrote a book called *The Trial of Jomo Kenyatta.* Montague was a quiet, doggedly humorous man, a Communist, and the difficulties of writing that book at all in the suspicious violent atmosphere of Britain during and just after the Mau Mau Rebellion he described to his friends—humorously and doggedly. That trial, the farcical brutality of it, is how "British Justice" has been experienced by many Africans, and how they think of it. But we forget nasty lapses like that trial when we have returned to our senses again. I sometimes wonder how Montague Slater would now regard the metamorphosis of the villain Kenyatta into a trusted statesman. Humorously I suppose. We owe more than we ever admit to these quiet and patient fighters in the background, who change atmospheres and attitudes in small but important ways.

When I wrote *Going Home,* I was a Communist—that is, I was holding a party card. I am not one now. The trouble is, being an 'ex-Communist' is just as much of a false position as being a Communist. But I've long since understood that what it was like being a Communist in a certain time and place can be understood by no one who was not. Which is why I am so glad I was one, had the experience. And I'm grateful to the Communists for what they taught me: particularly about power, the realities of political power. It is no accident that the only group of people who knew that Federation was dangerous nonsense, that Partnership was a bad joke, were Socialists of various kinds.

With the opposition in South Africa defeated, and filth being piled on its memory by very efficient propagandists, I want to pay tribute to the Communists and Socialists there who fought so well and bravely. (No I am not saying that all the people who fought the nationalists were Communists and Socialists.) But when the historians come to write the story of the fight against the nationalists, the Communists will come out very well. They can be faulted on mistaken judgements about the Soviet Union, and on their analysis of the 'class struggle' in Africa, but not on common sense about the colour struggle, nor on courage, nor on humanity. When I became political and Communist, it was because they were the only people I had ever met who fought the colour bar in their lives. Very few other people did—not the Labour Party except for a few individuals—not the 'liberals,' the word means something different there than it does here—and not the members of the churches. No one. But when you joined the Communists you met, for the first time, people of other races, and on equal terms. It was for this reason the Communist party had influence: not because of its theories.

There are no Communists now in South Africa. When the fighting lawyer Bram Fischer was sentenced for life he said he was a Communist. That was brave of him, because it made it so much easier for him to be blackened, denigrated, forgotten. He is now in Pretoria jail, the ugliest prison in a country full of them. It is where they keep people who are sentenced to death. He could easily have denied that he was a Communist. He knew quite well what it would mean, not only there, but here, saying 'Yes, I am a Communist.' But he said it. It was the end of an epoch, the sentencing and silencing of Bram Fischer. He was, and is, the most extraordinarily brave man. And the time will come when South Africa will be proud to have bred him.

I can write something now that I couldn't when I wrote *Going Home*. I was on that trip just after the Twentieth Congress. Water under bridges, it seems, because last week I said to a young man interested in politics, 'The Twentieth Congress,' and he said: 'What's that?' Well, it was the Congress of the Russian Communist Party when Khrushchev stood up in the Kremlin and said that Stalin was not all what he had been cracked up to be. Now this may have been a revelation in Russia, but it wasn't in certain Communist circles here, who had for some time been fighting to get the leadership of the Communist party to tell the truth and divorce itself from Russia. The Twentieth Congress came as a relief for many Western Communists. What sent so many Communists out of the Western Communist parties was not Hungary, but Hungary, coming so soon after the Twentieth Congress. To put it oversimply: if the Russian troops had gone into Hungary as they did before the Twentieth Congress, it would have been shocking but no more than could have been expected. That they crushed the Hungarian uprising in the brutal and cynical way they did after the Twentieth Congress, meant that Congress was more of a safety-valve than a promise of change.

I see that I said in *Going Home* that within a decade the Communist countries would have become more democratic than the Western countries. This has turned out to be untrue. But the Communist countries, save for China, have all become much more democratic, so much so as to make obsolete all the patterns of thinking of ten years ago.

But to return to '56. I was in the position of someone coming from 'the centre'—which is the romantic way people living in outposts see people who live in London. I would be in a position to deny the horrid truths of the Twentieth Congress—which were nothing, said the local Communists, but revolting lies and inventions. They were able to feel like this because they were isolated in Rhodesia. Who were the local Communists? They weren't Communists at all. There has never been a Communist party in Rhodesia. They were a couple of dozen people scattered about the country who were inspired in the long, thankless, draining battle against colour bars and white supremacy by the glories of the Russian revolution. It is always a mistake to discount such people and their influence for good. If you are living in a country which is stifling, backward and provincial, and you are a lively idealistic person, you need something to buoy you up. For many people, in many parts of the world, this idealistic flame was Russia. Your local conditions may be primitive —but somewhere is good, the truth, progress. Your neighbours think you are mad and treacherous Kaffir lovers— but in other parts of the world you have friends, even if you don't know their names. No one should laugh at this, or think it childish who has not lived in a backwater full of neurotic and bigoted racists.

Well, the Twentieth Congress was a blow to such people, and the tragedy was that in any place I went, they were the core of sensible opposition to Partnership and associated foolishness. I spent my days during that extraordinary trip being escorted around manifestations of Partnership by Garfield Todd's publicity men and shadowed by the C.I.D., as described, and my nights talking to groups of people whose hearts had been broken and who wanted to believe that I was a corrupted person for believing one word that Khrushchev said. They could not bear to believe him—yet. It was all very painful.

There were a good many other interesting aspects of this trip I still can't write about, because people would get into trouble. That is why I shan't lightly again go on a trip as a political journalist. Most of the really interesting things you discover you have to keep quiet about. Some journalists enjoy precisely this aspect of their work—being in the know. I find it more frustrating than enjoyable. And besides, it's a responsibility, remembering to keep your mouth shut, because people's jobs, lives, are at stake.

The financing of this trip was tricky. I had to go home, for emotional reasons. I needed to see how Rhodesia struck me after living in a civilised country. I needed to feel and smell the place. But I had no money. I was very hard up. I did not have the money for the fare—£250. The *News Chronicle* said they would send me, but they changed their minds. Meanwhile I had made arrangements to leave. But I was determined to go somehow. What to do? I had no idea. The way I saw it was one of the newspapers ought to send me, because I was equipped to write sense about Federation and Partnership, while the professional journalists were all writing such nonsense. They did not see it my way. With my departure date a month off, on an impulse, I got onto a bus to Fleet Street, walked into *Tass* and proposed to a charming but surprised young man behind a desk that *Tass* should pay for my fare home. Every civilised country in the world, said I, paid journalists to visit countries and report on what they found there, and why should not Russia do the same? This, of course, sounds very naïve. But I do not feel this is the place to discuss the usefulness of naïveté. Besides, a good many Communists at that time conceived it to be their duty to influence the Soviet Union towards modern ways. Journalism, then as now, in Russia was old-fashioned, and one of the thoughts in my mind was that I might be adding my mite towards dragging Russia kicking and screaming into the twentieth century.

Tass was noncommittal, but he put me into his car and drove me to the Soviet Embassy, where we saw the cultural attaché, a very urbane man, to whom I put my proposition. I was not even asking for expenses, I said, I wanted my fare paid, in return for which I would write articles for any newspaper in the Soviet Union he cared to name. The point was, I said, hammering at it, the Russians were not to behave in their usual indolent fashion: it was not the slightest use the money for the fare arriving in six months' or a year's time: the Russian time sense was not to operate in my case, because I needed the money to board the plane. Would they let me know, inside a fortnight, if they would pay the fare and what newspaper I would write for? We parted on this basis. The weeks went by. Suddenly, just before departure date, rather less than the fare arrived from the Narodny Bank, but no word about what newspaper I was hired by. Later, after returning from the trip, I found out that the money represented payment for some short story of mine published in the Soviet Union, which I had not been told about. They seldom do tell you. What happens is that a friend who has been on a jaunt to Moscow rings up and says, 'Did you know that your work X is on sale on the bookstall in Moscow?' No, you hadn't known. The Russians behave inexcusably, pirating what they fancy. They pay money into an account in Moscow and if you go there you can spend it. But one isn't always able to go to Russia—hasn't the time or the inclination. If you nag, are unpleasant, make a fuss, you can get money paid here. I once got a large sum after a long, nagging campaign for payment for some stories. But the point is, it is a favour, a kindness, not a right. This isn't excusable. It is not excusable for a large, rich, modern country to behave in such a way. The Russians, like most countries, often behave out of emotions appropriate to a previous epoch. For decades they traded on: 'We are a poor, struggling, Socialist country surrounded by capitalist enemies. You are a friend, therefore don't criticise us.' This was legitimate once, but isn't now. And—I think unconsciously—they trade on their charm. Few people visit Russia without being slaves ever

after to the Russians, if not to their regime. Their warmth
of heart, their kindness, their sympathy, their generosity
are impossible to forget.

But—the fare. I had it, or almost. When I came back I
wrote a lot of articles and posted them off to Moscow.
Now comes the really unforgivable naïveté. It never
occurred to me, since the conditions I was describing were
so black a case against "imperialism" they could not be
worse, that there was any need at all for them to gild their
lily. But then I got a letter from a friend in Moscow
saying why had I written this and that? But I hadn't
written this and that. It appeared that the articles had
been edited, cut and bits put in. This is why it is not
advisable to write for the Russian press until it modernises
itself: until the rights of an individual journalist, an individual point of view, can be guaranteed.

The individual—democracy, liberty—I am concerned
now with these more than with anything. One has to
choose one's battleground, limited for every one of us.
The individual is threatened, now more than ever, by the
increasing poverty of the world which spends money on
armaments rather than development; by the mass hunger
that is approaching so fast; by the wars being fought—and
every time a war is fought anywhere the individuals concerned cease to matter until it is over.

The price of liberty is, more than ever, eternal vigilance, which is why I think the most valuable citizens any
country can possess are the troublemakers, the public
nuisances, the fighters of small, apparently unimportant
battles. No government, no political party anywhere cares
a damn about the individual. That is not their business. So
I believe in the ginger-groups, the temporarily associated
minorities, the Don Quixotes, the takers-of-stands-on-
principle, the do-gooders and the defenders of lost causes.

Luckily, there are plenty of them. So—to the barricades, citizens! if we don't fight every inch of the way, we'll find ourselves with our numbers tattooed on our wrists yet.

London, May, 1967.

Like JORDI/LISA AND DAVID—the deeply moving account of a small boy's successful struggle for identity. . . .

DIBS
IN SEARCH OF SELF

by Virginia M. Axline

Virginia M. Axline, author of *Play Therapy*, is the acknowledged authority on play therapy in the treatment of disturbed children. In *Dibs* she makes the reader a partner in an extraordinarily affecting—because true—situation: the emergence of intelligence and emotion in a five-year-old boy so withdrawn that even his own parents have judged him mentally defective. But Dibs, as it turned out, was a brilliant child, and in this transcript of his treatment, much of it taken from actual tapes, there emerges the personality of a child whom the reader will leave with an enormous sense of affection and admiration. In his spirit and courage, Dibs is as wonderful a child as the young Helen Keller, and his final mastery of emotional communication parallels her physical triumph. *(224 pages, $.75)*

To order by mail, write to: Dept. CS, Ballantine Books, 101 Fifth Avenue, New York, N.Y. 10003